The Joy of Religious Pluralism

The Joy of Religious Pluralism

A Personal Journey

Peter C. Phan

ORBIS BOOKS
Maryknoll, New York 10545

ORBIS BOOKS
Maryknoll, New York 10545

Fathers and Brothers
MARYKNOLL™

Founded in 1970, Orbis Books endeavors to publish works that enlighten the mind, nourish the spirit, and challenge the conscience. The publishing arm of the Maryknoll Fathers and Brothers, Orbis seeks to explore the global dimensions of the Christian faith and mission, to invite dialogue with diverse cultures and religious traditions, and to serve the cause of reconciliation and peace. The books published reflect the views of their authors and do not represent the official position of the Maryknoll Society. To learn more about Maryknoll and Orbis Books, please visit our website at www.maryknollsociety.org.

Library of Congress Cataloging-in-Publication Data

Names: Phan, Peter C., 1943– author.
Title: The joy of religious pluralism : a personal journey / Peter C. Phan.
Description: Maryknoll, NY : Orbis Books, 2017. | Includes index.
Identifiers: LCCN 2016030370 | ISBN 9781626982253 (pbk.)
Subjects: LCSH: Phan, Peter C., 1943– Being religious interreligiously. |
    Christianity and other religions. | Asia—Religion. | Catholic Church—
    Missions—Asia. | Religious pluralism—Catholic Church. | Jesus Christ—
    Person and offices. | Catholic Church. Congregatio pro Doctrina Fidei. |
    Catholic Church. United States Conference of Catholic Bishops.
    Committee on Doctrine.
Classification: LCC BR127.A77 P483 2017 | DDC 261.2—dc23 LC record available at
https://lccn.loc.gov/2016030370

For my mother, again

Contents

Preface . . . . *ix*

Chapter 1: How It All Began:
History of Two Investigations of an Obscure Book. 1

Chapter 2: Different Ways of Doing Theology:
Why Do the Episcopal Magisterium and the Theological
Magisterium Often Disagree? 21

Chapter 3: Divine Spirit:
Is He/She/It Present Always and Everywhere in
Human History? 51

Chapter 4: Jesus Christ, the Unique and Universal Savior:
Possibility of an Interreligious Christology? 75

Chapter 5: Holy Pagans in Other Holy Religions:
The Salvific Significance of Non-Christian Religions? 99

Chapter 6: Church and Mission:
Walking Together with Other Religions toward the
Kingdom of God?. 129

Epilogue: The Joy of Religious Pluralism. 165

Appendix: Correspondence Regarding Being Religious Interreligiously 173

Index. 227

Preface

When my then-eighty-three-year-old mother, who is a twice-a-day churchgoer, told me in 2006 that her friends had confided to her that I was being "investigated by the Vatican" and that she was so worried and ashamed that she had not been able to sleep for weeks, I knew that my worst fears about the investigation of my book by the Congregation for the Doctrine of the Faith (CDF) were being realized. I had kept the investigation hidden from my family for over a year so as not to alarm them. For simple and pious Vietnamese Catholics like my mother, *the Vatican* is only a little less than God Almighty and omniscient, and for them, being an object of its investigation must mean that I had done very evil things. Only after I had explained to her that I was not being charged with any crime was she somewhat relieved. There was of course no point in explaining to her the theological opinions for which I was investigated because she would not have understood them, and in all likelihood, couldn't have cared less.

My mother's eventual regaining of her peace of mind of course did not assuage my anger at *the Vatican*. In my letter to Cardinal William Levada, Prefect of the CDF, dated April 4, 2006, I had warned him that the investigation would cause much pain to my family and that its unjust procedure—prohibiting the reprinting of my book before I had the opportunity to defend myself—would shake their trust in the church. I asked him to reconsider the whole process. I never received a reply, not even an acknowledgment of receipt of my letter. Presumably, *the Vatican* is too busy to be bothered with such social courtesy. I knew that, fortunately, the investigation could not do me much harm professionally, and I refused to let it destroy me physically and psychologically, though of course I would be lying were I to say that it had not caused me a few sleepless nights.

Temperamentally, I am too much of a fatalist to be shocked by personal tragedies. Bad things just happen (as a bumper sticker stoically declares: S*** Happens), and you have to take them in stride. My favorite philosophy of life is: "It could have been worse." I have always viewed scholarly criticism—even the proverbial *odium theologicum*—as an occupational hazard and have not been terribly bothered by it. Also, compared to my past ordeals— being forced to leave Vietnam with little more than half an hour to gather all my earthly possessions and with literally nothing but a shirt on my back, and having to start all over again as a refugee in a foreign land—my "troubles" with the CDF were little more than skin-deep scratches. I was well aware that my fifteen minutes in the glare of ecclesiastical spotlight would soon pass, a tiny blip in the *churchy* news cycle. Indeed, I was bemused that the CDF had decided to draw attention to an obscure and dense little book that was destined to gather dust on library shelves, to which the people whose spiritual welfare the CDF professed to be concerned about would not even give a first look. It was with complete sincerity that I wrote to Cardinal Levada that I am but a very small fish in the theological pond, a tiny minnow as it were, deserving neither fame nor fortune that might come my way from ecclesiastical censure.

I have decided to write this short book to recount the investigations of my *Being Religious Interreligiously* by the CDF and the Committee on Doctrine of the United States Conference of Catholic Bishops, and to explain my views on matters in which I have been judged *confused* and *confusing*. This is not an autobiography—my life so far has been so boring that such a book would be the best cure for insomnia.

But why write it now? In fact, it was started some eight years ago, and I had completed a substantial part of it, but then for various reasons, left the project aside. With the election of Jorge Bergoglio as Bishop of Rome in 2013, a new way of being church—a new Pentecost, it has been said—began. Everywhere I traveled, Catholics, Christians of other churches, believers of other religions, and even nonbelievers kept telling me that with Pope Francis a new era has been inaugurated in the church. For theologians, there seems to be the freedom to think and write without having to look over their shoulders. One of the Asian theologians who had been censured by the CDF under the previous regime recently told me that Pope

Francis met him shortly after his official "dialogue" with Cardinal Gerhard Müller, the current Prefect of the CDF, on his writings. To his immense delight, the pope thanked my friend for his theological contributions and encouraged him to continue his work. The CDF's power as the doctrinal watchdog, it seems, has been severely curtailed under Pope Francis.

I, for one, am also persuaded that a wind is blowing in the Catholic Church as a force for good. But I have lived long enough to know that because of the very power structure of the church, what one pope has done can be undone by another with a stroke of the pen. It is not far-fetched to believe that the pope's opponents, some in high positions and not hiding their displeasure, for whom Francis's church reforms are not a breath of fresh air, as Pope John XXIII had allegedly said of the council he convoked, but a destructive hurricane, are biding their time and are hoping (and praying?) for a quick and triumphant restoration of the former regime with Francis's passing. In light of this possibility, I thought that it may be useful to return to the unfinished project. I hope that this book will be of some guidance to my fellow theologians, especially lay, should their writings come under the scrutinizing eyes of church authorities.

I would like to express my deepest thanks to all the members of my family for their unconditional love and support after learning about the investigations. I burst out laughing when one of them wrote, in the idiom that only her generation could understand, "Older Brother, you rock!" I was also amazed by their theological astuteness. One of my younger brothers wrote a lengthy and sophisticated exposition and defense of my ideas to our family. This thoughtful response instilled in me a greater trust in the *sensus fidelium*. It made me suspicious of the official claim that controversial theological books must be censured because they may confuse the "simple faithful."

I also thank my colleagues and friends, too many to list here, and total strangers from all over the world, who wrote to me to show their support. To the very few who sent me critical e-mails, my sincere thanks too, for they showed that we should care deeply about matters of faith and the well-being of the church, though of course I do not share their theological views.

One person deserving my most sincere gratitude is Dr. William Burrows, former managing editor at Orbis Books, to whom the book that got me into trouble had been dedicated, though he is of course in no way responsible for my theological views. A gentleman of generosity of spirit and a theologian of deep learning, he has shown me constant support and offered me wise counsels and editorial guidance. Above all, without overtly trying to, he always gave me reasons for the Christian hope (1 Peter 3:15), and more specifically, for being a Roman Catholic, and in this sense he is a missionary at heart. My deep thanks go also to Robert Ellsberg, the current editor in chief and publisher of Orbis Books, for his persistent and gentle nudge that I finish this and other books before taking up other business. Than he there is no more patient publisher!

Throughout the investigations I sometimes wished I had written all my books and articles in Vietnamese; this would certainly have spared me all my troubles with the Vatican. I have also thought of composing all my correspondences to church authorities in my mother tongue: why should I write in the language of the powerful and make it easy for them? But I did not wish to be accused of obfuscation and prevarication. However, if I could not write this apologia in Vietnamese, at least some Vietnamese should benefit from its royalties. All the proceeds of this book will be donated to charities in Vietnam.

A word about the style of the book. Since it is addressed to a general readership, I will limit the citation of sources to a bare minimum, and as far as possible, will avoid technical language. Academic conventions dictate that scholarly writings be buttressed with a battery of notes and bibliographic references—to forestall charges of plagiarism and, truth be told, to display the breadth and depth of one's learning. In my younger days, I confess, I did a fair bit of that. Now that mortality's intimations are growing more insistent, and time becoming a scarcer and more precious commodity, I will permit myself the luxury of doing without such scholarly apparatus. This should not to be construed as ungratefulness on my part to all the authors whose works have taught me immensely but that will unfortunately not be cited in this volume. However, readers who are interested in knowing my scholarly sources and reading a fuller exposition of the arguments I make in this short book are kindly referred to my previous publications.

CHAPTER 1

How It All Began

History of Two Investigations of an Obscure Book

I must confess a very bad habit. I usually ignore correspondence from church offices, the way I do advertising materials, since invariably they deal with matters that do not affect me. I am apt to do this especially after returning from a long trip when piles of mail accumulate on my desk. On September 19, 2005, I received a large envelope from the chancery of the Catholic Diocese of Dallas and, as was my custom, discarded it without opening it. Later, its unusually large bulk caught my eyes, and I thought it might contain something important; out of curiosity, I fished it out of the round file and opened it.

What I saw made my heart skip a few beats, my blood pressure rise, my hands shake. My eyes were transfixed by the large letters stamped on the various enclosed Roman documents: CONGREGAZIONE PER LA DOTTRINA DELLA FEDE (Congregation for the Doctrine of the Faith [CDF]). The envelope was dated August 30, 2005, and had arrived at my office at Georgetown University during my absence. It contained a letter, addressed to me, by Charles Grahmann, the bishop of the Diocese of Dallas. The bishop requested that I comply with the CDF's directives within the time frame set by it.

The CDF

Enclosed in the packet was a letter from the CDF dated July 20, 2005, and signed by Archbishop Angelo Amato, S.D.B., secretary of the CDF, addressed to Bishop Grahmann and transmitted to him by the Office of the Apostolic Nunciature in Washington, DC. Enclosed also was a seven-page legal-size document entitled "Some observations on the book by Rev.

Peter C. Phan *Being Religious Interreligiously: Asian Perspectives on Interfaith Dialogue* (Orbis Books: New York, 2004)." The document presents nineteen "observations" on my book under six headings and states that my book "is notably confused on a number of points of Catholic doctrine and also contains serious ambiguities. Taken as a whole, it is in open contrast with almost all the teachings of the Declaration *Dominus Iesus*."

Because of these alleged "serious ambiguities and doctrinal problems," the CDF requested that Grahmann instruct me to do four things: (1) correct the problematic points by means of an article; (2) submit it to the CDF within six months; (3) have it published in an appropriate journal; and (4) instruct my publisher (Orbis Books) not to reprint my book.

Because the CDF's letter was dated July 20, 2005, the deadline of "within the next six months" stipulated by the congregation for my "correction" of the "serious ambiguities" allegedly present in *Being Religious Interreligiously* (*BRI*) by means of an article would be sometime in December 2005. Since I only received Grahmann's letter on September 19, I would have had little more than three months to write the required article. This would be an impossible task for me. Given my teaching responsibilities and other duties connected with my job as the Ignacio Ellacuría Chair of Catholic Social Thought at Georgetown University, not to mention the pressing business at the beginning of a new academic year, I saw no way to respond to the CDF's nineteen "observations" adequately within the imposed time frame. Consequently, I wrote to Bishop Grahmann asking for an extension to March 20, 2006. I presume that Grahmann forwarded my request to the CDF, but I have never received word either from him or from the CDF whether my request for an extension was granted.

When, and how, and under whose authority was the investigation of *BRI* initiated?[1] I had of course not been informed by the CDF of its decision to investigate my book. As to its time, a friend of mine, who is well versed in these matters since he himself had been censured by the CDF, told me to check the protocol of the CDF's letter. From the protocol number 537/2004-21114, it may be inferred that the investigation of *BRI*, which had been published in early 2004, was initiated sometime, probably late, that

---

[1] Anyone interested in the CDF's procedure of investigating works of theologians can consult the highly informative report by Bradford E. Hinze, "A Decade of Disciplining Theologians," in *When the Magisterium Intervenes: The Magisterium and Theologians in Today's Church*, ed. Richard Gaillardetz (Collegeville, MN: Liturgical Press, 2012), 3–39.

year when Ratzinger was still prefect (before his election as pope on April 19, 2005) but before William Levada, his successor as the CDF's prefect, took office in October 2005.

As to the process itself, apparently the procedure that was used in my case is the so-called ordinary process, as distinct from the urgent examination, which was used, for example, in the case of the Spanish and El Salvador–based Spanish Jesuit Jon Sobrino. This ordinary process includes, as one of its many steps, a decision by the cardinal prefect and the bishop members of the CDF in an "ordinary session" whether to approve the results of the investigation of a particular book (presumably by "consultors") and to communicate them to the bishop of the author (if he is a diocesan cleric) or the religious superior (if she or he is a religious). Their decision would subsequently be submitted to the Supreme Pontiff for his approval.

There is however something anomalous in the timing of the letter that raises the question of its authority. It was signed by Archbishop Angelo Amato, secretary of the CDF, on July 20, 2005, during the vacancy of the prefecture of the congregation. Joseph Ratzinger had been elected pope on April 19, 2005, and the position of prefect of the CDF was not filled until May 13, 2005, when William Levada, then-archbishop of San Francisco, was appointed to the post but did not officially assume office until October of that year. During the interregnum, when there was not yet a prefect at the CDF, was Archbishop Angelo Amato acting on his own—as the acting prefect?—or was he authorized to sign the letter in the name of Benedict XVI in an effort to complete the unfinished businesses of the former prefect? Or was Benedict still de facto the prefect of the congregation and did Amato sign in Benedict's name? The document was however signed after the announcement that William Levada had been appointed prefect of the CDF but before the appointee took office in October. Did Amato have the juridical authority to sign the CDF's document by himself in the interim, and was Levada informed of and did he approve Amato's action? Or was my case so minor that the signature of the secretary would suffice? At any rate, if the decision of the prefect and the bishop members of the CDF had been approved while Cardinal Ratzinger was prefect, the question of under whose authority Amato's action against *BRI* was taken is a moot point. (Angelo Amato was subsequently rewarded with a red hat, and Joseph Di Noia, OP, the undersecretary, who must have taken part in the investigation, was made an archbishop. Both have moved out of the CDF and would presumably no longer have an interest in the investigation.) By the time I responded to the CDF, Cardinal Levada was its prefect. In my letter to him dated April 4, 2006, I expressed my willingness to compose the article requested, provided that

1. The prohibition to reprint my book be lifted. Such prohibition, I contend, would be fair and just only *after* I have had the chance to explain and defend my views and only if my explanations were judged unsatisfactory.
2. Clarification be given on the nature and scope of the article since the CDF's observations were many and wide ranging.
3. Determination be made on the kind of theological journal in which it would be published. (Indeed, I doubt that any respected refereed journal would publish a diffuse article such as that demanded by the CDF.)
4. A fair and just financial remuneration be given for the work involved in the writing of such an article, since I would need to take unpaid leave from my job to write it.

I regard the first and fourth requests as matters of elementary justice and the second and third as canons of academic propriety. Whereas the first three requests seem obvious, the fourth has provoked some indignant eyebrow raising, and I will return to it below.

In addition, I informed the cardinal that I am by nature averse to publicity and that I was embarrassed by this undeserved notoriety. I also told him that I did not want to take advantage of this notoriety for financial gain, since an ecclesiastical censure might boost the sale of my quite obscure book. (In fact, to the chagrin of the publisher, there was only a very slight bump in sales!) Finally, I requested the cardinal to reconsider the whole investigation, since, in my opinion, it would further damage the already tattered credibility of the church.

To this date, the CDF has neither acknowledged receipt of my letter nor answered my four requests, positively or negatively.

In the meantime, I tried my best to keep the CDF investigation secret, even from members of my immediate family and my closest friends, so as not to cause them needless anxiety. I felt dishonest in answering "very well" to general questions about how I was doing and in lying with a "no" when I was pointedly and innocently asked by a close friend if I was having any "trouble" with the CDF. Up to this point in time, I had informed only those who needed to know of the investigation, namely, the president of Georgetown University (Dr. John DeGioia), the dean of Georgetown College (Dr. Jane McAuliffe), the chair of the Theology Department (Dr. Chester Gillis), and the highest administrators of Orbis Books (the last because of the prohibition to reprint *BRI*).

The Committee on Doctrine of the United States Conference of Catholic Bishops (USCCB)

Sometime in early 2007 (perhaps in March), I received a phone call at my office from Rev. Thomas Weinandy, OFM, Cap., executive director of the USCCB Committee on Doctrine (CD). I do not recall ever having met him, though I had heard his name and had read several of his works. I asked him in what capacity and on whose authority he was contacting me. He informed me that he was acting as executive director of the CD and that he was calling at the request of Donald Wuerl, the archbishop of Washington, DC (now cardinal), where Georgetown University is located. He reiterated the CDF's demand that I write the article in response to the CDF's observations. I informed him that I had stated to the CDF my willingness to write the requested essay provided that my four requests were granted. I suspected that Weinandy had access to my letter to Cardinal Levada, in which I explained the rationale of my four requests. I did not expect Weinandy to give answers to the first and fourth requests, since they were beyond his juridical competence. But I did expect him to give me clarifications on the nature and scope of the article and the kind of theological journal in which it was to be published, since he was asking to me to write it. Unfortunately, he did not provide any helpful answer at all. At any rate, I asked him to relay to whatever authority commissioning him to speak with me that I would be willing to write the article provided that the four requests I had made to the CDF be met.

A few weeks later, Weinandy called me again at my office, repeating my obligation to write the article. I told him that our conversation would go nowhere, since I would be reiterating the same remarks about my four requests to the CDF as conditions for my writing the article. He pointedly reminded me that I was dealing with the USCCB CD (presumably with canonical power over me) and not just a mere fellow academic. I again asked Weinandy about the nature and scope of the article I was asked to write and the kind of journal in which it was to be published, but again he did not provide helpful answers.

Subsequently, I received a letter from Bishop William Lori, chairman of the USCCB CD (now archbishop of Baltimore), dated May 15, 2007. The letter stated that since the CDF's *proposal* (Lori's reassuring euphemism for the CDF's order) that I write and publish an article to correct my theological positions in conformity with church teaching has been "unacceptable" to me (on the contrary, it was quite acceptable to me under certain conditions), "the Congregation for the Doctrine of the Faith has requested that the Committee on Doctrine examine *Being Religious Interreligiously*." (I fail to see the logical connection between my alleged refusal of the CDF's "proposal" and the CDF's request that the CD examine my book, since the CDF had already completed its investigation and had formulated its detailed "observations" on it.)

Bishop Lori's letter further stated that the CD had completed its work and "feels obliged to publish its own statement indicating the points on which the positions expressed in *Being Religious Interreligiously* diverge from that of the Catholic teaching." Prior to doing so, however, the CD, Lori said, would like to give me the opportunity to answer its concerns in "written arguments." Enclosed with the letter were three double-spaced pages listing the CD's concerns with three issues, namely, "the unique identity of Jesus Christ as the universal Savior, the salvific significance of non-Christian religions, and the role of the Church as the universal sacrament of salvation." The letter simply ignored the four requests I had made to the CDF.

It may be helpful at this point to briefly reconstruct the likely course of events so far. From the protocol number of the CDF's document on my case, it seems reasonably certain that the CDF started investigating *BRI* sometime in late 2004, when Cardinal Joseph Ratzinger was still prefect of the CDF, before his election as pope on April 19, 2005. On July 20, 2005, Archbishop Angelo Amato signed the CDF's document against my book, after William Levada was appointed prefect of the CDF but prior to his taking office in October 2005. The new prefect was apprised of my April 6, 2006, letter, but for whatever reason decided not to respond to me directly with regard to my four requests. He asked Donald Wuerl, the archbishop of Washington, DC, to help resolve my problem. Possibly, Cardinal Levada thought that my case was too insignificant to warrant his attention, or he thought that the whole procedure had been an embarrassing mistake, which he now wished to dispose of quietly by devolving it to the local level of the USCCB. In 2007, Thomas Weinandy in his capacity as executive director of the CD and at the request of Archbishop Donald Wuerl, contacted me regarding my obligation to write the article requested by the CDF. Failing to elicit my agreement to produce the article without a prior response to my four requests, he informed Wuerl of the impasse. At some point after this, the CD of the USCCB examined *BRI* under the direction of Bishop William Lori, then-chairman of the CD, who subsequently communicated with me in several letters. The CD composed a statement enumerating "the points on which the positions expressed in *Being Religious Interreligiously* diverge from that of the Catholic teaching." This statement was presumably written sometime between May and November of 2007, if not earlier.

This is, I submit, a reasonable reconstruction of the course of events. Clearly, there was nothing like a cloak-and-dagger mystery that can be turned into a pay-per-view blockbuster. It is just a boring, garden-variety bureaucratic maneuver to downgrade the investigation at the Vatican level and outsource it to minor local officials. The new prefect of the CDF signaled his willingness to let the local church resolve an issue that had been overblown by one of its Roman officials, perhaps with an ax to grind, and to have the whole affair forgotten, the sooner the better. I am too small a fish to fry at the Vatican level. This would explain why the USCCB CD undertook its own examination of my book, though of course basing itself on the CDF's "observations" on it.

In my response to Bishop Lori dated May 23, 2007, I pointed out that it was patently false to assert, as the CD's draft statement does, that the CDF's request for me to write an article was "unacceptable" to me. Indeed, I was most willing to write the article, but to do so without insisting on the first and fourth requests would be to act in complicity with injustice. Furthermore, I asked for the May 31, 2008, deadline to complete the "written arguments," given my many commitments.

Bishop Lori responded with a letter dated June 20, 2007, in which he stated that my preconditions "are beyond the competence of the Committee to grant." Furthermore, he noted that "it must be kept in mind that this committee's examination of the content of the book is distinct from your discussions with the Congregation for the Doctrine of the Faith." Finally, the bishop gave the September 1, 2007, deadline to submit my written arguments.

I responded to Bishop Lori with a letter dated August 16, 2007, in which I stated that it would be physically impossible to produce the requested "written arguments" before September 1, 2007, given my many assignments, especially in view of the beginning of a new academic year. I noted the irony of the CD's imposition of such a stringent and very short deadline on me while the CDF had not even deigned to acknowledge receipt of and respond to my letter of April 4, 2006. I also expressed my puzzlement regarding the "double jeopardy" to which my book has been subjected, since it was being simultaneously investigated by both the CDF and the USCCB's CD. Presumably, I still have to carry out discussions with the CDF, even after the CD publishes its statement on my book.

In his next letter to me dated September 10, 2007, Bishop Lori clarified many important points. He noted "the distinct roles" of the CDF and the CD in the investigations of *BRI*. He also mentioned the go-between intervention of Archbishop Donald Wuerl (as I have correctly guessed). More importantly, he added that "it is our impression that at this point the Congregation is not inclined to issue its own statement if the Committee on Doctrine publishes one, though the Congregation certainly has the authority to take actions at a later point if it deems this to be necessary." Furthermore, Lori specified that the CD's investigation is not "a juridical proceeding that could result in canonical sanctions." Finally, the bishop did not state whether the CDF's demand that I write an article, submit it to the CDF, and have it published in an appropriate journal had been rescinded. He simply said that what the CD required of me was not a publishable article, as the CDF had done, but a clarification of my positions in "a few thousand words."

This is both reassuring and ominous. Reassuring, because the CD's investigation was said not to constitute a juridical procedure with possible canonical sanctions. (I am not clear what possible canonical sanctions there might be.) Ominous, because the end of the CD's investigation might not be the end of the CDF's. There remains, even today, the sword of Damocles hanging over my head, to put it a bit melodramatically, since the CDF might not be satisfied with the CD's statement and might come back to me with the demand that I write an article, submit it to it for approval, have it published in an appropriate journal, and might even impose "canonical sanctions" should I fail to do so.

As of this writing (2016), the CDF has not notified me that it had found the CD's process and statement satisfactory and that as far as *BRI* is concerned, the case has been closed. I try not to lose sleep over this, but, truth to tell, Bishop Lori's statement that "the CDF certainly has the authority to take actions at a later point if it deems this to be necessary," with the possibility of canonical sanctions, is unnerving, like a cancer in remission but with the potential to come back. I think that it is highly unlikely that the CDF is still concerned with my case. There are much bigger theological fish to fry, and the clergy sex abuse scandal, financial mismanagement at the Vatican bank, and a host of other scandalous matters are taking up much of the CDF's time and energy. At worst, I am just a tiny index card in the CDF's file. However, even today, when friends ask me whether my "affair" with the Vatican has been settled, I have to honestly say that I do not know and that anything can happen. Be that as it may, I mightily resist the temptation of self-censuring when I teach, write, and lecture.

In the rest of the correspondences between me and Bishop Lori we negotiated for a mutually acceptable deadline, with Lori pushing for November 30, 2007, as the latest date, and me for May 31, 2008. My request for a later deadline (in fact about six months, excluding the holidays, which is the original length of time allowed by the CDF) was no delaying tactic on my part. Given the seriousness and the extensiveness of the observations of both the CDF and the CD, I was deeply concerned not to give a cursory clarification of my positions, "in a few thousand words," as Bishop Lori indicated. I do not think a few thousand words, however "few" is taken to mean, is an adequate space for a satisfactory exposition of my thought on the many themes on which both the CDF and the CD accuse me of being confused and confusing, unless what was wanted is a simple declaration of my intellectual submission and surrender to the two ecclesiastical bodies. As far as I know, most people whose works have been under investigation by the CDF (mainly priests or religious) could afford sabbaticals to write their responses, some even in book form, a luxury I did not have, both in terms of time and money. And even then their responses, lengthy and elaborate, have been judged insufficient by the church authorities concerned.

Prior to publishing the CD's statement on *BRI*, Bishop Lori wrote me a letter dated November 12, 2007, in which he urged that I subscribe to the CD's statement that I had "agreed that the book in its present form contains significant ambiguities on certain points" and that I "would rectify these ambiguities" in my "future publications and public presentations." I did not fully grasp all the legal implications of this suggested self-implicating acknowledgment. However, I pointed out to the bishop that since I had not been able to respond in detail to all the CDF's and the CD's observations on my book, it would not be ethically proper for me to affirm that I have agreed that my book in its present form contains "significant ambiguities on certain points."

As announced by Bishop Lori, on December 17, 2007, the CD published a fifteen-page document entitled "Clarifications Required by the Book *Being Religious Interreligiously: Asian Perspectives on Interfaith Dialogue* by Reverend Peter C. Phan" on the USCCB's website. It has three parts, divided into thirty-two points, which bear the following titles: "Jesus Christ as the Unique and Universal Savior of All Mankind"; "The Salvific Significance of Non-Christian Religions"; "The Church as the Unique and Universal Instrument of Salvation." These titles already indicate what the CD takes to be the central issues in which my views are judged ambiguous and/or erroneous.

As far as I can tell, the CD's statement attracted little if any public attention, appearing as it did during the week before Christmas, when most American Catholics were busy with shopping and thousands of other activities more enjoyable than worrying about theological orthodoxy. I pity those who have wasted so much time and energy composing that lengthy text that would have little or no impact on the "simple faithful" whose faith they ostensibly wanted to protect.

My controversy was, as I had suspected, no more than a tiny footnote on a page of local church newspapers. However, I do take seriously the CDF's and CD's accusation that *BRI* contains "significant ambiguities on certain points." The following chapters represent an attempt to clarify what readers of *BRI* might find ambiguous, confused, confusing, or downright erroneous. Given the complexity of the issues raised by both the CDF and the CD, I seriously doubt that I can adequately answer all their concerns in a "few thousand words," or even within the compass of a small book. I therefore beg readers for their indulgence if I substantially go beyond a few thousand words. I will try to be as succinct as possible, though at times, I fear, at the cost of the comprehensiveness and depth that are required for a full treatment of all the theological themes involved.

Perhaps it is not unusual that books that deal with complicated theological themes, such as *BRI*, contain "significant ambiguities on certain points." Even the author of 2 Peter warns that Paul's letters "contain some things that are hard to understand, which ignorant and unstable people distort, as they do on other Scriptures, to their own destruction" (3:16). It is unlikely that the author of 2 Peter was Peter, "the first pope," but it would be the height of irony if he were its author and wrote such dire warnings about Paul's letters.

*   *   *

I apologize to readers for burdening them above with an account, rather boring to boot, of the CDF's and the CD's dealings with me. But I must present this narrative for two reasons. The first is to fulfill my promise to a gentleman, a military officer, whom I do not know. He wrote to me, shortly after the publication of the CD's statement on *BRI*, that my arrogance in not responding to the magisterium would put the salvation of my eternal soul at risk. Apart from whether failure to respond to the magisterium, even out of arrogance, is tantamount to a mortal sin and would consign my soul to eternal flames, I promised him to show that a fair reading of all the documents between the CDF and the CD and me would demonstrate that I was more than willing to respond to church authorities. Whether asking for a six-month deadline to write a detailed response to the magisterium's weighty charges—amid multiple responsibilities—is reasonable, I leave it to him to judge.

The second reason is more delicate. It has been suggested that as an Asian living for so long in the United States, I had been so "inculturated" to its capitalistic ways that I have dared ask the CDF to "pay" for my work. Perhaps the best way to answer this insinuation is to quote from my letter to Cardinal Levada:

> There is another issue that I request the Congregation to consider, and that is just and fair remuneration. I am neither a curial official nor a priest engaged in pastoral ministry for which I would be provided with room and board, a salary, a paid vacation, and other benefits. Financially, I am completely and totally on my own. I have to pay for food and clothing, housing and transportation, health and life insurance and retirement benefits, and eventually my own funeral. In addition, I support my family, especially my mother, financially. To meet all these expenditures I have to work more than full-time, teaching, lecturing, and publishing vastly beyond what is normally expected of a professor.
>
> Nor do I belong to a religious order which would permit me to take an unpaid semester off to do research and write the article required by the Congregation. To write such article requires that I set aside time which I have already devoted to other paying tasks. I therefore request that the Congregation pay half of my

annual salary (six months, the amount of time that the Congregation originally allotted me to write the article). This is a matter of justice.

To those who have tut-tutted at my request for financial assistance, I would ask them to imagine the following scenario. Suppose you are the main or perhaps the sole breadwinner for your family. For some unknown reason, someone who is not your employer requires you to answer some charges you are deemed guilty of. The task imposed on you is so important that your reputation, career, and well-being, as well as the good of your family, will likely depend on how well you carry it out. Because of your professional responsibilities, you cannot perform this task successfully while also doing your full-time job. The only option is to take an unpaid leave. But then how will you pay rent, food and clothes, and other financial obligations, for yourself and your loved ones? Would you be justly charged with being a money-grabber if you ask your accuser to pay for the time it would take to answer the charges, not to mention compensation for psychological or physical damages these accusations may inflict on you and your family?

In all honesty, when asking for monetary compensation from the CDF, I was thinking not only of myself but also of lay theologians whose number is steadily increasing in the United States. Most of these are saddled with heavy family obligations. Throughout my dealings with the CDF and the CD, I had the distinct impression that church officials believe that we are at their beck and call and that we can easily take time off, or drop everything, to carry out whatever they bid us to do. As I have noted, most priests and religious (male and female) can afford doing that, with the financial help of their dioceses or orders, respectively. But this is not the case with lay theologians and a few clerics, like myself, who have to earn a living entirely on their own. Indeed, financial compensation is not something that the accused themselves should request as a favor but something that church authorities must, out of a sense of justice, voluntarily offer when they require theologians to write articles in response to what they consider ambiguities, confusions, and errors.

At the end of the day, the charge of money-grabbing, though utterly offensive, might perhaps have proved useful. It served to draw the attention of celibate church authorities to basic issues of justice and fairness. These simply escape them precisely because their celibate lifestyle and lack of family obligations would not alert them to such elementary details of life, especially when they normally have no financial worries and their material needs are fully provided for by their organizations.

Why This Book?

This small volume is part *apologia pro vita sua* (I apologize if this phrase sounds grandiose), part theological exposition. The timing for it is, at least for me, appropriate. Throughout my dealings with the CDF and the CD of the USCCB (June 2005–December 2007), I have consistently refused numerous requests by various communication media from different parts of the world to talk about the investigation of *BRI*. Now the lengthy interval affords enough distance, both temporal and emotional, for an unbiased account of what went on during the investigation and to harvest some practical lessons that may be useful to those whose writings might be subjected to similar investigations by church authorities.

More important than personal apologia and self-defense, it is an elaboration of "my theology," if the smattering of my various and sundry thoughts on the Christian faith deserves to be adorned with such a high-sounding sobriquet. I will confine myself only to the areas in which the CDF and the CD have found some of the ideas contained in *BRI* to be confused, confusing, and even erroneous. This elaboration has two goals. The first is to defend myself against the accusations that the two official teaching bodies have made against *BRI*. Here, it is very much the question of examining whether *BRI* in fact says what the CDF and the CD say it says.

This is of course no simple undertaking given the fact the CDF has no fewer than nineteen objections and the CD nearly twenty pages of observations against *BRI*. It would be impossible for me to answer in full each and every charge of the CDF and the CD within the limited space of this small book or even one of doorstopper size. However, it is necessary to show, albeit briefly, whether or not the CDF and the CD have correctly interpreted *BRI*, at least in fundamental theological issues. This is not a cheap rhetorical trick to dismiss the charges of the CDF and the CD out of hand by arguing that I do not recognize my work in their interpretations of it. Nor, if the past is prologue, do I entertain the hope that my answers, however detailed and elaborate, will be judged satisfactory by the Roman authorities. After all, the CDF has rejected as inadequate the lengthy, thorough, and learned responses to its charges by Jacques Dupuis,

Roger Haight, and Jon Sobrino, whose works have been investigated by the CDF, and in whose company I am but a dwarf, or, to reprise my earlier metaphor, a tiny minnow in the theological pond.[2]

Still, I believe that it is a matter of justice to show whether the CDF's and CD's interpretations of *BRI* are accurate since their judgment, true or false, carries a heavy weight within certain ecclesiastical circles. This was the case with Raymond Burke, then-archbishop of Saint Louis, later promoted to cardinal by Pope Benedict XVI and made prefect of the Apostolic Signatura, and unceremoniously demoted in 2014 to a sinecure by Pope Francis because of his overt opposition to the pope's reform agenda. Upon learning that I had been contracted to deliver the 2008 Aquinas Lecture at the Aquinas Institute of Theology, Burke pressured Rev. Richard Peddicord, OP, President of Aquinas Institute, to cancel my contract on the ground that, as the archbishop declared to the journalist Tim Townsend of *St. Louis Post-Dispatch*, I am not "a reliable teacher of the Catholic faith." The archbishop made this pronouncement, which could destroy the hard-earned reputation and career of a Catholic theologian, with total impunity—even with the possible reward of ecclesiastical preferment—not on the basis of having personally read *BRI*, in whole or in part, but simply and solely on the basis of the CD's statement on my book.

The second goal of my theological elaboration in this book is to explain, in nontechnical language as much as possible and with a minimum of scholarly apparatus, my way of doing theology and my thoughts on some of the key issues in which the CDF and the CD have judged *BRI* theologically objectionable. Unfortunately, my task here is a Catch-22. On the one hand, I need to show that I have remained within the pale of orthodoxy and am therefore *conservative*—in the etymological sense of the term—that is, *preserving* the tradition, in which Catholic theologians must be deeply rooted. On the other hand, an essential part of the theologian's

---

[2] Anyone interested in the rather sordid history of the investigation of Jacques Dupuis's book *Toward a Christian Theology of Religious Pluralism* can peruse the candid report of it by Gerald O'Collins entitled "A look back on Dupuis's Skirmish with the Vatican," http://www.ncronline.org/news/people/look-back-dupuis-skirmish-vatican. For a fuller history, see William R. Burrows, *Jacques Dupuis Faces the Inquisition: Two Essays by Jacques Dupuis on* Dominus Iesus *and the Roman Investigation* (Eugene, OR: Wipf & Stock, 2012). Pope (Saint) John Paul II is said to have "approved" three different versions of the "Notification" on Dupuis's book, a story fit for a late-night comedy shtick had it not caused extreme physical and psychological damage to the theologian.

task is to search for an understanding of the Christian faith that is appropriate to the contemporary context. This necessitates going beyond a mere reiteration of hallowed and magisterially approved formulas and answers. Indeed, repeating them in a situation different from the ones in which they were first formulated would not be a sign of fidelity but would betray their very meanings. Though I have never sought theological originality—highly prized in the academy, where nothing is worse than being dismissed as a derivative thinker—I hope nevertheless to have contributed more adequate answers, hence different from, the traditional ones, and to this extent *new*, to the theological issues confronting Christianity today.

Four Basic Issues

While the CDF's observations enumerate a disparate list of "serious ambiguities and doctrinal problems" allegedly present in *BRI*, the CD organizes them under three rubrics, that is, Christ, non-Christian religions, and church. To this triad of theological issues a fourth, which is intimately connected with them, may be added, namely, Christian mission. These four themes are of central importance in contemporary theology, especially in view of our current situation of religious pluralism, as I will argue in the next chapter.

However, I do not think that they—especially if treated in that order—offer the most fruitful venues to construct an adequate and appropriate theology to deal with religious pluralism, especially in Asia. For example, to fully appreciate the function of non-Christian religions in the history of salvation, it would be more helpful, for reasons that will be made clear in subsequent chapters, to begin with a theology of the Holy Spirit (pneumatology) rather than with a theology of Christ (Christology) and to discuss the rule/ reign/ kingdom of God (a kingdom-centered theology of religions) before broaching the church and its mission (ecclesiology and missiology). Nevertheless, given the fact that the CDF's and the CD's observations focus on the three themes of Christ, non-Christian religions, and church, I will deal with them, albeit in a different order. At any rate, the present book does not fully represent my own approach to religious pluralism but is mainly a brief reply to the agenda-setting concerns of the CDF and the CD.

As background to my theological elaborations, I have given above a brief account of the CDF's and the CD's investigations of *BRI* and my dealings with them. As mentioned above, the story has in itself nothing engrossing, except perhaps to those addicted to ecclesiastical politics. My account is accompanied by the CDF's and the CD's communications to me and my responses to them, which are provided in the Appendix. Since most often theological disagreements about particular issues are rooted in different ways of doing theology, I will offer reflections on different ways of doing theology, especially those that I think should undergird our approach to religious pluralism (Chapter 2). Though the CDF and the CD mentioned my understanding of the Holy Spirit only obliquely, that is, in connection with Jesus as the unique and universal Savior, an adequate pneumatology is a sine qua non basis for a theology of religions, Christology, ecclesiology, and missiology that can effectively respond to the challenges of religious pluralism. This theology of Divine Spirit and the Holy Spirit is outlined in Chapter 3.

With this pneumatological foundation in place, Chapter 4 provides an account of how I understand the role of Jesus as the "unique" and "universal" Savior. Chapter 5 discusses the role of non-Christian religions in the history of God's dealing with humanity. The last chapter discusses the church and in particular its mission.

What Was All the Fuss About?

To conclude, I would like to say something about the book that has received scrutiny and "observations" by the CDF and the CD. Why all the fuss about it? Why, indeed! In fact, after news of the investigation of my book broke, a well-known Catholic theologian, who also selectively reviewed theological books he deemed important, confessed that he had taken a glance at my book but did not think that it would deserve his time.

So, why all the fuss? Orbis Books would be much happier if I do not give a summary of *Being Religious Interreligiously* here, and would prefer, I am sure, that you readers purchase a copy of it for your reading pleasure. While I still hope that you will do so, it would be helpful to provide a summary of it, perhaps as a teaser to stimulate your buying interest.

BRI is part of a trilogy on Asian theology. (Oh dear, you have to buy all the three volumes now!) Asian theology, I must confess, is not my first scholarly interest. When I did my first doctorate in Rome, I researched the theology of the Russian Orthodox theologian Paul Evdokimov. The subject of my second doctorate from the University of London is the eschatology of the German Jesuit theologian Karl Rahner. For my third doctorate, from the University of London, the Doctor of Divinity, also known as the Higher Doctorate, I submitted my research on the history of Catholic missions in Asia, especially that of the seventeenth-century French Jesuit missionary Alexandre de Rhodes.

It was the latter research that pushed me in the direction of Asian theology in the 1990s. I began studying the statements of the Federation of Asian Bishops' Conferences (FABC) and the works of Asian, mostly Catholic, theologians. My frequent travels to Asia during this time exposed me to the realities of various Asian countries, notably India, the Philippines, Korea, Thailand, Hong Kong, Taiwan, Japan, and of course, Vietnam. From all these experiences, I learned that *dialogue* is the only modality for carrying out Christian mission in Asia, indeed, to use the language of the FABC, a "triple dialogue," that is, with the Asian poor, Asian cultures, and Asian religions.

Meanwhile I wrote a good number of essays on these three themes, some of them published in Asia and Europe, and therefore relatively inaccessible to the American public. I decided to gather these essays together and publish them in book form, under the rubric of the threefold dialogue. The first book, entitled *Christianity with an Asian Face: Asian-American Theology in the Making*, deals mainly with the dialogue with the Asian poor (liberation); the second, *In Our Own Tongues: Perspectives from Asia on Mission and Inculturation*, treats the dialogue with Asian cultures (inculturation); and the third, *Being Religious Interreligiously: Asian Perspectives on Interfaith Dialogue*, discusses dialogue with Asian religions (interreligious dialogue). Because the three volumes were not originally conceived from scratch but are collections of previously published essays, they do not exhibit a continuous argument, even though they are not a string of random and unconnected essays but develop the central themes (i.e., liberation, inculturation, and interreligious dialogue) from different angles. Of the three, I like the second volume best, as it is the easiest to read and the most interesting.

So, why so much fuss about *Being Religious Interreligiously*? A friend of mine, a preeminent theologian of interreligious dialogue, told me that if anyone should be condemned by the CDF, it should have been he, since his writings are much more radical than mine, which is true. I recall that Charles Curran had made the same argument when his writings on moral theology were condemned by the CDF: Other theologians were more "liberal" than he, he said. But I do not think that the CDF chooses to scrutinize and condemn books according to their degree of heterodoxy. The CDF's selection, I believe, is quite arbitrary, depending on how the book is delated to it, who does the delation, the "hotness" of the topic, and the potential influence of the author on the church or the academy.

As far as *BRI* is concerned, I do not know who delated it to the CDF and how. Potential influence on the church, I had none; on the academy, a little. As to the "hotness" of the theme, the book certainly has it, since, as the CDF's then-Prefect Cardinal Ratzinger had said, the greatest threat to the church was no longer liberation theology, which Ratzinger claimed to have defeated, but religious pluralism. My book came out at the time Jacques Dupuis's *Toward a Christian Theology of Religious Pluralism* was being censured; and the title of my book is a certainly a red flag.

So, what is all the fuss about? *BRI* is a dense book, not for popular consumption; it is certainly not a page turner, and it should have borne a warning: "Do Not Operate Machines While Reading This Book. It May Induce Slumber." It has three parts, all dealing with various aspects of interfaith dialogue. The first part is heavily philosophical, discussing what is often referred to as postmodernity. There I argue that the greatest challenge to the Christian faith today is the postmodern proposition that it is not possible to arrive at and claim absolute and universal truths through philosophic reason given the impossibility of "metanarratives." But I also argue that this postmodern claim, if true, opens the door to another way to truth, that is, through stories, and especially religious stories ("myths"). If the way to knowledge through "reason" is barred, since reason is always infected by "power," there is still open the way of "wisdom," or "holy foolishness." Furthermore, because no one religion can claim to have an exclusive, total, and comprehensive grasp on truth, as postmodern thought argues, then interreligious dialogue becomes an urgent necessity. In and through the telling of the stories of each religious tradition, it is possible to form a religious identity and a religious community, but this identity is now of necessity and by nature a "hybrid" one, consisting of "multiple religious belongings."

The second part forms the heart of the book, as I apply this modified postmodern epistemology—knowing the truth through interreligious dialogue—to the major Christian doctrines such as God, the Trinity, Christ, church, and peace-building. The third part carries out the same strategy for worship, liturgy, and the Eucharist.

The CDF and the CD focus on the essays contained in the second part and scrutinize them under four headings: the unicity and universality of Jesus as Savior, the unicity and universal mediation of the church as the sacrament of salvation, the role of non-Christian religions, and the necessity of mission. Needless to say, these themes are "hot" and controversial in the theology of religious pluralism, and what I wrote there is judged by the CDF and the CD to be confused, confusing, and erroneous, by the standards of *Dominus Iesus*. That is what all the fuss is about. The irony is that I was trying to "save" these Christian doctrines from the onslaughts of postmodernity and to make them honestly believable, though of course not rationally provable.

Whether I have succeeded in doing so, it is up to you to judge, after reading this book, and after you have bought *Being Religious Interreligiously* for yourself, and perhaps for all your friends (I am hearing the voice of my publisher whispering: "Do the commercial!").

CHAPTER 2

Different Ways of Doing Theology

*Why Do the Episcopal Magisterium and
the Theological Magisterium Often Disagree?*

[A friendly suggestion: Readers who are not interested—and justifiably so—in abstract methodological considerations may skip this chapter and proceed to the following ones. After perusing them, it will be helpful to return to this chapter to understand how theology is done in this book and why some bishops and some theologians, including myself, have taken diverse positions regarding the Holy Spirit, Christ, non-Christian religions, church, and mission. The reason, in a nutshell, is that we have employed different theological methods.]

Differences of opinions in matters of life and death cannot be explained simply by appealing to taste. There is something deeply inappropriate to refer to someone's religion as religious "preference," as is often done on census forms, as if religious conviction were a choice between vanilla and chocolate. Of course, whether a person is a Buddhist or a Christian is often a matter of birthplace or family tradition. But if a person consciously chooses to be one or the other, such a decision cannot be accounted for by the preference for a particular doctrine (for example, the Trinity vs. nontheism) or ritual (for example, Mass vs. meditation)—though it may involve that—but by how one sees the world as a whole: in a word, by one's way of knowing things or, to use philosophical terms, one's "epistemology" or "methodology."

Similarly, theological views on particular doctrines (for example, that Jesus is divine) are often rooted in different ways of doing theology or theological methodologies. Disputes about particular doctrines will ultimately turn into disputes about *how* these doctrines are and should be derived from the sources of the faith of the community. Unfortunately—with due apologies to René Descartes—there is nothing that draws a yawn and an eye-rolling faster than a *discours sur la méthode* (discourse on method), the title of a work by the celebrated seventeenth-century French philosopher and mathematician. Yet, it is necessary to reflect on the different way*s* (note the plural!) in which theology is done today in order to understand how and why the Congregation for the Doctrine of the Faith (CDF) and the Committee on Doctrine (CD) have made certain judgments about my (and other theologians') works and how I myself have arrived at my own positions, some of which the CDF and the CD find either confusing and/or erroneous.

At the risk of putting nonspecialist readers into a deep slumber, I have decided to begin with reflections on theological methods. I am prompted to do so not only by their immediate relevance for my book but also by the March 24, 2011, statement of the CD of the United States Conference of Catholic Bishops (USCCB) on Elizabeth Johnson's 2007 book *Quest for the Living God: Mapping Frontiers in the Theology of God.*[1]

The statement alleges that Johnson's book contains "misrepresentations, ambiguities, and errors that bear upon the faith of the Catholic Church as found in Sacred Scripture, and as it is authentically taught by the Church's universal magisterium" (183). It states unequivocally, front and center, that a *faulty theological method* is responsible for Johnson's many errors. Her theory of human knowledge of and language about God, her understanding of God's suffering and immutability, her feminist theology of God, her view of God's presence in non-Christian religions, and her theology of the Holy Spirit, human evolution, and the Trinity, according to the CD, "do not accord with authentic Catholic teaching on essential points" (199).

Clearly, this is a very serious charge. What is of greatest interest to me, however, is that all of these alleged errors are said to stem from Johnson's

---

[1] The statement of the CD is available on the USCCB's website: http://www.usccb.org/doctrine/statement-quest-for-the-living-god-2011-03-24.pdf. The whole Johnson dossier is conveniently available in a recent volume *When the Magisterium Intervenes: The Magisterium and Theologians in Today's Church*, ed. Richard R. Gaillardetz (Collegeville, MN: Liturgical Press, 2012), 213–75. Citations of the CD's statement and Johnson's responses come from this book. The page number of the book is given in parenthesis. Incidentally, the choice of the CD's document on Johnson's book is highly opportune, since it is almost certain that both it and the CD's statement on my book are composed by the same person, namely, Thomas Weinandy, executive secretary of the CD of the USCCB.

failure to observe "the method proper to Catholic theology." "It is here," the statement goes on to say, "*at the level of method*, that the book rests upon a false presupposition, *an error that undermines the very nature of the study and so skews many of its arguments, rendering many of its conclusions theologically unacceptable*" (183, emphasis added). Clearly, in the CD's judgment, method is paramount: a wrong method is poison; the right method, panacea. Hence, the necessity of a preliminary methodological discussion, even though it is a perfect pill for insomnia!

My intention here is not to assess the accuracy of the CD's evaluation of Johnson's book, though it would indeed be the height of irony if its presentation of Johnson's theological views ends up containing "misrepresentations, ambiguities, and errors," the very things it condemns her work for.[2] Nor does Johnson need my or anyone else's defense of her views. She is widely acknowledged as being more than capable of holding her own.[3] I am simply noting that for the CD, theological method plays a pivotal role in theological elaborations, a view that can hardly be gainsaid if by "method" is meant not merely technique or recipe but a "way" of doing things, as the etymology of the term implies (*meta* with, along + *hodos* way). The way one makes things inevitably shapes the things made.

With regard to method, the CD's statement charges that Johnson does not follow "the method proper to Catholic theology." Citing Pope John Paul II's encyclical *Fides et Ratio* (no. 65), the statement describes this method as composed of two acts, namely, *auditus fidei* (hearing the faith) and *intellectus fidei* (understanding the faith). "With the first," says John Paul II, "theology makes its own the content of revelation as this has been gradually expounded in Sacred Tradition, Sacred Scripture and the Church's living Magisterium. With the second, theology seeks to respond through speculative inquiry to the specific demands of disciplined thought" (184). Clearly, theological method

---

[2] Johnson's one-sentence evaluation of the CD's statement says it all: "Numerous omissions, distortions, and outright misstatements of fact riddle the reading" (247).

[3] For Johnson's lucid, cogent, and devastating critique of the "misrepresentations, misinterpretations and incorrect picture" of her book contained in the CD's statement, see http://www.ncronline.org/news/faith-parish/johnson-us-bishops-doctrine-committee or *When the Magisterium Intervenes* (213–51). Compared to Johnson's magisterial and elegant text, the CD's statement reads like a beginning graduate student's badly written book report that could benefit from the services of a competent literary and theological editor. The fact that it is signed by nine bishops does not of course guarantee its scholarly and literary quality.

is central to and a sine qua non for true theology. The question is whether there is and should be only one *proper* method for Catholic theology.

"The Method Proper to Catholic Theology"?

In saying that the way of doing theology as taught by John Paul II is "the method proper to Catholic theology" (183), does the CD intend to affirm that this is the *only* correct method to do Catholic theology and therefore other methods are "improper"? Though the statement does not explicitly say so, the answer seems to be a peremptory yes, especially if stress is laid on "*the*" and "*proper*" in the cited phrase. In its conclusion, the CD's statement tersely specifies what it considers the proper theological method for Catholic theology:

> The basic problem with *Quest for the Living God* as a work of Catholic theology is that the book does not take *the faith of the Church as its starting point.* Instead, the author employs standards from outside the faith to criticize and to revise in a radical fashion the conception of God in Scripture and *taught by the Magisterium.* (199, emphasis added)

Again, my point here is not to assess the validity of the CD's description of Johnson's theological method, that is, whether she actually "employs standards from outside the faith"—whatever they are—in doing her theology.[4] Rather, my question is merely whether the theological method *as described by the CD* can be claimed to be the *only valid* or even *proper* way of doing Catholic theology. My answer is a decisive no.

The pivotal question is of course what is meant by "the faith of the Church" and whether it must be used as "the starting point" for doing Catholic theology, and in this connection, what is meant by "starting point." In its introductory paragraph, already cited above, the statement speaks of "the faith of the Catholic Church as found in Sacred Scripture, and as it is authentically taught by the Church's universal magisterium"(183).[5] It seems

---

[4] In her response to the CD's statement, Johnson cogently argues that "not only does *Quest for the Living God* begin with the faith of the church, but it also ends there as well" (216).

[5] As will be explained in detail later, in Catholic theology "authentic (teaching)" is

that according to the CD, the teachings of the church ("as taught by the Magisterium"), without exception, must—methodologically speaking—be where one begins one's theologizing (the "starting point"), and in terms of content, they must also function as the principles and the criteria of truth of Catholic theology ("as taught by the Church's universal magisterium").

"Faith of the Church" and Teachings of the
Magisterium as Starting Point of Theology?

If this is the point of the CD's statement on theological methodology, one must wonder in what theological world its redactor or ghost writer has been living. (Of course, the bishops who signed the document did not write it themselves; indeed, it may be wondered if each and every one of them has read it in its entirety or understood each and every point of it.) Most contemporary Catholic theologians, liberal or not, do not begin their theologizing in this way, taking "the faith of the Church" as taught by the magisterium (perhaps as formulated in *Catechism of the Catholic Church*?) as their methodological *starting point*. Historically, Catholic theology, especially neoscholastic theology, has long been done in this way, but there are good reasons for abandoning this method, and indeed it has been almost universally abandoned! At any rate, the theological method proposed by the CD's document against Johnson as "the method proper to Catholic theology" is defective in at least four aspects, which I elaborate below.

Interpreting as "Proof-Texting"

This method promotes a thinking process known as proof-texting, in which later church teachings are used to frame and control the interpretation of the Bible and tradition. Indeed, it jeopardizes the very act of *auditus*

---

distinguished from "infallible (teaching)." The former teaches in a binding and authoritative way, but without the claim of infallibility, and is therefore in principle not free from error. The latter is free from error and occurs when a teaching is made by (1) the pope *ex cathedra*, or (2) the bishops assembled with the pope at an ecumenical council (extraordinary and universal magisterium), or (3) the totality of all the bishops with the pope outside of an ecumenical council (ordinary and universal magisterium). As it stands, the CD's statement ("as it is authentically taught by the Church's universal magisterium") wrongly conflates all these important distinctions and makes the magisterium in all its modes of teaching the "starting point" of theology.

fidei, which the CD's statement fervently recommends, that is, listening to the texts of the Bible and the tradition and allowing them to speak to us in their strange, disconcerting, multiple, often mutually contradictory, voices, without trying to domesticate them with dogmatic concerns, even those of the papal and episcopal magisterium. Only then can we perceive and retrieve those aspects or themes of the Bible and tradition that have been ignored, misunderstood, suppressed, or only partially understood by the church, not least by the magisterium.

But even if a theologian chooses to begin with the teachings of the magisterium, she or he is faced with the decision about which magisterial teaching to use as the starting point. A glance at church history will show that the "magisterium" is not, and has never been, a monolithic organ or bureaucracy with an official spokes*man* (the male gender is appropriate here) and a unanimous corpus of teachings on every doctrine and practice. Rather, the episcopal magisterium is composed of various flesh–and–blood bishops (including popes) with widely divergent views and perspectives; with much, little, or no theological learning; with much, little, or no holiness of life, as the history of the church has amply shown. In spite of all this, according to Catholic teaching, these men (again, the male gender is appropriate here for the Catholic Church) can teach, under very strict and well-specified conditions, what the Bible has taught (and only this!) without error.[6] By no means, however, does this mean that their teachings, and the formulations in which these teachings are couched, are the best, or the only possible, or beyond correction and improvement. Consequently, when using magisterial documents, one must proceed not only with trust and faith but also with caution and prudence, and if and when necessary, there is the duty to propose ways to correct, modify, improve, and expand their teachings. This is no subversive claim; in fact, it simply describes the way theology has always been done.

---

[6] For a lucid exposition of the Catholic teaching on the magisterium, see Francis Sullivan, *Magisterium: Teaching Authority in the Catholic Church* (Mahwah, NJ: Paulist Press, 1983); Richard Gaillardetz, *Teaching with Authority: A Theology of the Magisterium in the Church* (Collegeville, MN: Liturgical Press, 1997); Richard Gaillardetz, *By What Authority? A Primer on Scripture, the Magisterium and the Sense of the Faithful* (Collegeville, MN: Liturgical Press, 2003).

Act of Personal Faith and Critical and
Reflective Intelligence in the *Auditus Fidei*

In the theological method espoused by the CD's statement, the *auditus fidei*, the first step of theological work, is apparently understood as an uncomplicated and uncritical acceptance in faith of God's revelation and, ultimately, of what the church teaches, as if this divine revelation were an obvious and self-evident matter: "Theologians must, therefore, first lay hold of the content of God's revelation, the *auditus fidei*, as proclaimed in Scripture and taught within the Church, through an act of personal faith" (184).[7]

Important as this personal acceptance of faith is for doing theology, it is no mere act of the will that can be done fundamentalistically, without critical and reflective thinking, to determine what God has said and differentiate it from what God is said to have said, even by church authorities. In the process of the *auditus fidei*, critical intelligence cannot and must not be sacrificed in favor of the magisterium. The *auditus fidei* is not a passive hearing of the divine voice that comes directly from above or through the episcopal magisterium. Rather, it is an attentive and active listening to God's self-manifestation, here and now, in the community of faith and elsewhere that requires a filtering out of the extraneous noises and accretions that have been added to God's speech throughout the ages and have at times drowned it out. It is a real "obedience"—from the Latin *oboedire,* which means "give ear to," that is, listening with deep attention and critical intelligence.

This does not of course mean that the *auditus fidei* is done individualistically, in isolation and in private, for example, in the library or in one's study. On the contrary, this act of critical appropriation of the content of

---

[7] Speaking of "an act of personal faith," in my experience, this acceptance of God's revelation is common and profound among lay theologians, who by choice undertake a long and arduous course of study as part of their Christian vocation, often at great personal and financial costs, and with no guarantee of a well-paying job. By contrast, a clerical student (seminarian) may take theological courses simply as a requirement, perhaps even as a hurdle, for the priesthood, with all expenses paid, in a comfortable environment, and is guaranteed a lifetime job and all kinds of honor, unless he is found out to have grievously misbehaved, especially in sexual matters. Furthermore, it may not be assumed that when a bishop, or a member of a committee of an episcopal conference, issues a theological document, he has personally laid "hold of the content of God's revelation . . . through an act of personal faith" and through a life of deep prayer and Christian discipleship.

faith must be performed in and with the community of all Christians (and not just Catholics!), both lay and clerical, not only intellectually but, more crucially, in the daily living and practice of the faith, from which alone an authentic understanding of things divine will result. In this community of faith, the teaching office of popes and bishops is endowed with a special authority—and in well-defined cases, with infallibility—but it is not the only "magisterium." In the church, in addition to (1) this hierarchical magisterium, there are also (2) the magisterium of the theologians by virtue of their hard-earned scholarly competence, (3) the magisterium of all Christians by virtue of the *sensus fidei* (sense/instinct of faith), and, as I will argue, also (4) the magisterium of the poor with whom God identifies Godself in a preferential way, and (5) the magisterium of non-Christian believers by virtue of their religions. It is in and through these five mutually enriching and correcting magisteria that theologians must "lay hold of the content of God's revelation," since God speaks to us in all five of them. Given the importance of this theme, I will come back to it below.

Thus, critical intelligence and systematic thinking are exercised in both the *auditus fidei* and the *intellectus fidei* alike. The former cannot be done just by an act of pure and simple faith, without philosophical and theological presuppositions, nor does the latter operate by "speculative inquiry" apart from faith.[8] By opposing the *auditus fidei* to the *intellectus fidei* and dividing them into two successive steps, each operating with its own medium, namely, faith in the former and reason in the latter, the CD falls into a fundamentalistic position not unlike that of the Evangelicals and Pentecostals, with the only difference that here the hierarchical magisterium rather than the Bible functions as the ultimate criterion of truth.

Other Theological Methods Already at Work

The CD's statement seems to be innocent of the fact that not every doctrinally orthodox and spiritually fruitful Catholic theology has been constructed by taking "the faith of the Church as its starting point." To

---

[8] The document assigns to the *intellectus fidei* the role of "speculative inquiry," in distinction from the "act of personal faith" operating in the *auditus fidei*. The CD does not seem to be aware of the awkwardness of this expression, given the fact that in contemporary English, "speculative" suggests fanciful conjecture rather than evidential knowledge, which of course is not what theology attempts to do!

be sure, by its very nature, Catholic theology, in distinction—not opposition—to religious studies, is done in, with, and for the church. By vocation, and ideally, a Christian theologian is one who has undergone, to use the Canadian Jesuit theologian Bernard Lonergan's expression, a fourfold "conversion," namely, intellectual, affective, moral, and religious, of course in various degrees.

By intellectual conversion I mean a single-minded commitment to pursue the truth, without relativism but also without absolutism, and when the truth is found, to express it forthrightly and humbly, no matter what the cost (including the penalties imposed by church authorities). In this intellectual conversion, one begins by asking (1) what the data of one's experience are; (2) what their meaning is; (3) whether they are true, and lastly; (4) what one must do in light of these data, their meaning, their truth, and their value. In this process of discovery and knowledge, not only one's intellect but also, and above all, one's "heart" are engaged, because faith concerns matters of life and death and the whole person. Not rarely is the discovery of truth accompanied by an affective conversion, made up of excited eurekas, deep joy, profound gratitude, intellectual humility, and inner peace. These intellectual and affective conversions generally, though not always, lead to a moral transformation of one's life, and for a Christian, to a life modeled on that of Jesus and lived out as his disciple. One begins cultivating certain virtues congruent with one's vision of truth and the community to which one chooses to belong. These three conversions are brought to their fulfillment by the religious conversion to God, that is, by God's gift of faith, hope, and love. Indeed, it is divine grace that precedes, gives rise to, accompanies, and fulfills all the other three conversions.

Integral to this fourfold conversion is communion with the community of fellow believers, which in Christian parlance is called church. Ordinarily, this conversion is followed by baptism, and by his or her baptismal vocation, the theologian seeks to serve the church by means of intellectual work to advance the understanding and practice of faith. This ecclesial, that is, church-related character of theology, however, by no means requires that the theologian take the teachings of the magisterium, much less its specific dogmatic formulations, as the "starting point" of her or his theologizing, as the CD's statement requires. Examples of theologies that do not do so abound in the post–Vatican II era, as any competent survey of contemporary Catholic theology will show.

No doubt, the Bible must be, as Vatican II says, the "soul" of theology. But this does not at all mean that *methodologically* Catholic theology must *start* from the Bible, especially *as interpreted by* the episcopal magisterium, or that it may not begin "with a critique of the Church's faith," which the CD has accused Elizabeth Johnson of doing (184).[9] On the contrary, many contemporary Catholic theologies, taking a cue from Vatican II's Pastoral Constitution on the Church in the Modern World, start by "reading the signs of the times" and then "interpreting them in the light of the Gospel" (*Gaudium et Spes*, no. 4). Nor does this interpretation of the signs of the times dispense the theologian from examining whether any of the episcopal magisterium's past interpretations of the Bible is inadequate, misleading, or erroneous, and even whether certain biblical teaching is no longer appropriate in the light of the signs of our times.

At any rate, doing theology by starting from "the faith of Church," especially *as taught* by the episcopal magisterium, significantly narrows the scope of discovery and understanding. It is tantamount to doing scientific research by limiting oneself to textbooks; the experiment may confirm what has been known, but nothing new is discovered. By contrast, doing theology with starting points other than the faith of the church as taught by the hierarchical magisterium affords the theologian opportunities to see the faith of the church in a new light, to recover forgotten, overlooked, or suppressed ideas, and even to discover hitherto unknown aspects of the incomprehensible mystery of God.

In so doing, one need not appeal to what the CD's statement calls "standards from outside the faith," since the criteria of justice and racial, ethnic, and gender equality, though prominent in the modern discourse on human rights, are intrinsic to the Bible itself and are by no means "standards from outside the faith." Thus, for instance, when theologians, feminist and otherwise, Catholic and non-Catholic, argue for the ordination of women to the priesthood and the episcopacy, they do not simply appeal to "standards from outside the faith," as the CD's document against Johnson implies, such as gender equality (which is not in itself a bad argument!). Rather, they

---

[9] In her response to the CD, Johnson notes that her book explicitly "starts and finishes with the faith of the church, defining itself in that light" (216). I would like to add that "starting with the faith of the church" is not equivalent to starting from the teachings of the episcopal magisterium, which seems to be the at least implied position of the CD's statement.

derive their arguments from the very heart of the Christian faith, which affirms the creation of woman and man in God's image and likeness, baptismal conformation of all to Christ the priest in whom there is no male and female, and the universal call to ministry in the church.

Necessity of Many Magisteria for Today's Church

The "faith of the Church" is vastly more than *what* has been "taught by the Magisterium," much less "*as* taught by the Magisterium." To be sure, the office of "authentic" or better, "authoritative" teaching is reserved to the bishops (among them the pope), with various degrees of authority and corresponding levels of assent. However, bishops, singly or as a collective, are neither the only nor the most effective and persuasive teachers in the church. Just as the church is not to be identified with popes and bishops, so must the teaching of the church not be regarded as identical with the episcopal magisterium.

Unfortunately, today the word *magisterium* is commonly used, especially in official church documents, to refer exclusively to the teaching function of bishops, as if they alone can or are allowed to teach. This is theologically wrong and leads to an impoverishment of the "faith of the Church." The unthinking habit of using the term *magisterium* to refer exclusively to the magisterium of bishops (here called the episcopal or hierarchical magisterium) tends to belittle and even ignore the other magisteria that, though not "authoritative" in the juridical sense, are no less "authentic" and enriching and can be used as a fruitful "starting point" for theology.

As mentioned above, there are other magisteria in the church beside the episcopal magisterium. Vatican II, in its dogmatic constitution on divine revelation (*Dei Verbum*), affirms that there is growth in the understanding of God's revelation and that this happens mainly in three ways: "through the contemplation and study made by believers, who treasure these things in their hearts [Lk 2:19, 51], through the intimate understanding of spiritual things they experience, and through the preaching of those who have received through episcopal succession the sure gift of truth" (no. 8). These three ways may be said to correspond broadly to the magisterium of the theologians, the magisterium of the faithful, and the magisterium of the bishops respectively. Let's call the magisterium of bishops episcopal magisterium, that of the theologians theological magisterium, that of the faithful lay magisterium. A word about each is in order.

Episcopal Magisterium

Of course, these three magisteria do not operate with the same authority and in the same manner. The "authority" of each is derived from different sources and competences. The episcopal magisterium teaches in virtue of the "apostolic succession," whereby the bishops carry out their teaching or "prophetic" role to safeguard the truth in matters related to our salvation, or "faith and morals." They can do so in the following four ways:

1. When a bishop, or a group of bishops, or the pope enjoins a particular religious practice, adopts a practical policy, or takes a disciplinary decision as the best response to a here-and-now situation in the church, they do not teach a binding doctrine but try to find a concrete application of the Christian principles to solve a particular problem. The proper response is compliance with prudence, obeying it only to the extent that it contributes to the common good of the church and society.

2. When a bishop, or a group of bishops, or the pope teaches in an *ordinary* manner, they teach truthfully but with no guarantee of infallibility and therefore with the possibility of error; this teaching is technically called an authentic teaching. The expected response to this kind of teaching is "religious docility (*obsequium*) of will and intellect" (*Lumen Gentium*, no. 25).[10]

3. The episcopal magisterium is exercised in an *extraordinary* way when the college of bishops defines a teaching concerning faith and morals in an ecumenical council or when the pope teaches *ex cathedra*, that is, when he teaches as the supreme teacher and pastor of the church on matters of faith and morals to be held by the universal church. Then they teach truthfully and infallibly; the teaching is called a dogma. The proper response to this extraordinary magisterium is an act of assent of faith.

4. The episcopal magisterium is exercised in an *ordinary universal* way when the whole college of bishops, while scattered throughout the world, agrees that a certain doctrine concerning faith and morals is *to be held definitively*. In this case, they teach truthfully and infallibly,

---

[10] The Latin *obsequium* can be translated, in increasing order of force, as respect, docility, submission, assent, obedience.

and the teaching is called a definitive teaching. The proper response to the ordinary universal magisterium is an act of firm assent, though not of faith since it is not a dogma.[11]

No doubt, for most Catholics and perhaps even for many theologians, these hair-splitting distinctions of the four types of teaching by the episcopal magisterium and the required corresponding responses, namely, prudent compliance to practical policies, religious docility of will and intellect (*obsequium*) to "authentic teaching," assent of faith to "dogma," and firm assent to "definitive teaching," sound like a mental Rubik's Cube. However, on another level, they are of great importance, especially with regard to the issues treated in this book, in view of the fact that there has recently been a creeping infallibility by which every declaration and document emanating from the pope and the Roman Curia, especially the CDF, or even a statement of the CD of the USCCB, is taken to be the final and infallible word. In this ecclesiastical atmosphere, it is useful to be able to discern the degree of binding authority of each act of the episcopal magisterium.

Important as this theological discernment between different types of teaching may be, the ultimate point about the hierarchical magisterium is that, according to the Catholic faith, the Holy Spirit has given to the *church as a whole*, made up of laity and hierarchy, the "sure gift of truth" (*Dei Verbum*, no. 8), by which the people of God as a whole believe and teach truthfully. It is only by virtue of this "sure gift of truth" and on the basis of the church's common faith (*sensus fidei*) that, with the assistance of the Holy Spirit, the hierarchical magisterium—the pope by himself, the pope and the college of bishops of which the pope is a member, a group of bishops (for example, episcopal conferences), or the individual bishop—can teach truthfully. This divine assistance, however, is not and must not be understood as an "inspiration"—to put it crudely, a whispering in episcopal ears by the Holy Spirit—so that the bishops can know what to teach and how to teach it. On the contrary, the Spirit assists the bishops in and through their teachers who today are a multitude and variety of people. What bishops know, they know it by learning from others, and not through some private revelation or "infused knowledge" that is available exclusively to them through ordination. It is important to remember this mundane fact since

---

[11] For a clear exposition of this standard theology of the episcopal magisterium, see Gaillardetz, *By What Authority?*, 74–89.

the current use of the term *magisterium* often conjures up a secret source of knowledge or a privileged access to the "deposit of the faith."

As is true of everyone else, the principle that one cannot teach what one does not know applies to bishops as well. In this context, it is useful to recall how most if not all bishops learn about God's self-revelation and how on the basis of that knowledge, they can fulfill their teaching ministry.[12] Like any Catholic, bishops first learn about the Christian faith from their parents, religion teachers, and pastors, who may or may not be theologically well informed. Later, in seminaries, they study theology from their professors, who may or may not be great theologians. Academically speaking, very few of the seminaries, including those in Western countries, are centers of scholarly excellence; most are mediocre; not a few are quite below university standards.[13] In their defense it may be claimed that their purpose is not to produce scholars but pastors.[14] Whatever their qualities, seminaries are the places where most bishops get their theological education.

---

[12] Catholic theology textbooks, even the more liberal ones, tend to treat the episcopal magisterium abstractly, as if bishops, as individuals and as a group, are endowed with special knowledge and skills and therefore can teach truthfully and effectively, merely by virtue of their ordination and membership in the episcopal college, without asking the rather embarrassing question of whether or how a flesh-and-blood bishop who has little theological training beyond what he has learned in the seminary (and that was years ago!) can effectively perform his teaching office *by himself and on his own*. Just three anecdotes to illustrate my point. A number of years ago a young nun from China confided to me that her bishop could barely write Chinese characters correctly. (To his immense credit, he did send her abroad to study theology). During the decades of Communist control of North Vietnam, several bishops were appointed who had little more than a lay catechist's rudimentary knowledge of the faith. Saintly they might be, but teachers of faith they were not, in the usual sense of the term. Several years ago, a high-ranking German cardinal, who is also an acclaimed theologian, expressed his dismay at the fact that so few American bishops hold a doctorate in theology.

[13] Obviously, seminaries in the so-called Global South do not possess the same faculty and library resources as those in the Global North and cannot be expected to produce future bishops with adequate theological competence. It is not an accident that bishops in Asia, for instance, rely heavily on their theologians to carry out their teaching office. See the Office of Theological Concerns of the Federation of Asian Bishops' Conferences (FABC).

[14] Intellectually-gifted clerics of the Global South—Africa, Asia, and Latin America—are often sent to Rome to pursue graduate studies in theology, and a Roman degree is often a stepping-stone to the episcopacy. Those of us who have studied in Rome know well the quality of its pontifical universities, most of which function more like seminaries than research-oriented universities. Only a few of them match the majority of US university-related divinity schools in terms of faculty, library collections, and financial resources.

After ordination, it is a rare priest who keeps up with serious and prolonged theological updating, an arduous and time-consuming work that does not always bring ecclesiastical promotions. It would be instructive to survey the library collections in rectories and discover how much time pastors spend reading serious theological works a day. Besides the annual clergy continuing education conference (where this is mandatory), there does not seem to be much else, except the individual priest's personal efforts at theological self-improvement beyond what he has learned in the seminary. Lack of theological depth, in particular in biblical scholarship, among many priests engaged in pastoral ministry is confirmed by poll after poll showing the widespread dissatisfaction of the parishioners with Sunday homilies and other forms of religious instruction. Yet, it is from the ranks of these priests that normally candidates for the episcopacy are chosen. Furthermore, when the candidate is vetted, the litmus test is not his depth of theological knowledge but unswerving "orthodoxy" in matters regarding priestly celibacy, contraception, ordination of women, and, more recently, same-sex marriage.

It is in this context of how bishops are theologically educated that episcopal magisterium must be broached. It is important that when speaking of episcopal magisterium, we not depict it abstractly, as a body of *magistri* (teachers) who are magically bestowed, through ordination, advanced theological knowledge and pedagogical skills. Rather, we must look at bishops as teachers *concretely*, that is, we must pay heed to how much they in fact know what they teach and how well they teach what they know.[15] This is all the more necessary in the United States, where there is the odd custom of bishops adorning their names with D.D. (Doctor of Divinity), as if

---

[15] Elizabeth Johnson gently lets the cat out of the bag when she asks: "Did each of the nine bishop members or their theologians read the book and draw up notes? Did they discuss the points to be made and debate them *pro* and *con*?" (248). I would go further: Assuming that the nine bishops had the time and the willingness to read Johnson's book, did their theological background enable them to understand it fully, or, more ironically, even their own statement, which discusses modern theism, Aquinas, Kant, Metz, Schillebeeckx, Moltmann, Soelle, evolution, and Trinitarian theology? Have they read at least the key works of these authors and theological movements to be able to issue and sign a truthful and credible statement on Johnson's book? Will they say publicly, as politicians do these days in their campaign ads, "I am (so and so) and I approve this message" and be ready to be challenged on accuracy and fairness? The issue here is not simply about the theological qualifications of the nine bishops who signed the statement but about the process of exercising the episcopal magisterium itself.

episcopal ordination confers theological expertise through some kind of magical epistemological infusion.

Let it be noted in passing that of the three offices of the bishop—priest, teacher, and pastor—the first and third can be fulfilled, strictly speaking, without a high degree of professional competence. As for the priestly office, according to the Catholic tradition, the sacraments performed by the bishop (or priest and deacon) are valid *ex opere operato* (from the work being done), irrespective of his personal holiness. That is, the sacraments "work," or are valid, as long as he intends to do and does correctly what the church requires him to do, which usually involves little more than reading from the sacramentary and executing the rubrics properly, under the watchful eyes of the master of ceremonies whose main task is making sure that nothing essential is omitted. (In pre–Vatican II days, liturgical courses consisted of little more than learning how to perform the rituals correctly.) With regard to the pastoring role, canonically, by virtue of his appointment, the bishop has the *juridical* power to govern the diocese, no matter how much administrative skill he has. Not so with the teaching function. No one can teach what one does not know, nor can one teach well what one knows without assiduous training and well-honed skills. In other words, effective teaching cannot be fulfilled effectively simply on the basis of ordination.

The question then is, how can an individual bishop, or a group of bishops, or even the entire episcopacy teach the faith truthfully and competently, given the current state of their theological knowledge? I am not at all suggesting that bishops are all innocent of theological learning—indeed, a number of them are first-rate theologians—or that a doctorate in theological sciences makes a competent teacher of the faith. I am only saying that the average seminary theological education, which most bishops have, is far from sufficient to exercise the episcopal magisterium truthfully and competently in today's world.[16] Even possession of a doctorate in theology

---

[16] It may be argued that despite their relative lack of theological learning, bishops can exercise their magisterium competently because they function as, to use a metaphor proposed by Cardinal Donald Wuerl, "referees and umpires" (205) directing the "game" of theology. No doubt bishops are "judges" of the faith. But the cardinal's metaphor limps badly and is self-defeating, first because bishops must also be competent theological players and not just direct the game from above or from outside; second, a competent referee must know all the rules of the game well, which cannot be said of bishops in general with regard to theology; and third, the decisions of referees and umpires can be and sometimes are reversed thanks to technologies more accurate than the human

is no guarantee of continuing theological competence, especially if there have been no efforts at regular updating, as is done in any other profession. In saying this, I do not deny the bishops' right and duty to teach, or the authoritative character of their teaching, or the assistance of the Holy Spirit. Rather, the issue is whether the bishops, individually and as a body, can teach truthfully, effectively, persuasively *by themselves* and *on their own*, especially on complex doctrinal, ethical, sociopolitical, and economic issues facing contemporary society. The answer is that they cannot, unless they learn from and collaborate with the other four magisteria.

Theological Magisterium

That theologians have always played an important and indispensable role in the church needs no elaboration. Thomas Aquinas recognizes the importance of the teaching function and authority of theologians by calling it *magisterium cathedrae magisterialis* (teaching function of the magisterial chair) to distinguish it from *magisterium cathedrae pastoralis* (teaching function of the pastoral chair). That Thomas himself played a key role in the life of the church is demonstrated by the fact that he died in 1274 on his way to attend the Council of Lyons. Both before and after Aquinas, the contributions of theologians to the understanding of faith in general and to the episcopal magisterium have been paramount. In fact, no document of ecumenical councils has been composed without the extensive handiwork of theologians, just as most episcopal, including papal, documents have been ghostwritten by theologians, though of course the pope and the bishops bear ultimate responsibility and authorship for them.

Notwithstanding the indispensable role of theologians in assisting the episcopal magisterium, it is wrong to see it simply as an ancillary function. The service of theologians is not being a mouthpiece for the bishops. Nor is the theologian merely an apologist for church teachings. It is no longer accepted today that, as Pius IX said, and reaffirmed by Pius XII (*Humani Generis*, no. 21), "the noblest office of theology is to show how a doctrine defined by the Church is contained in the sources of revelation." Undergirding this conception of theology is the view that theologians stand under

---

eye! Are there mechanisms that would help bishops exercise their magisterium competently and truthfully and, when necessary, to correct the errors and misjudgments of the episcopal magisterium? I believe there are, and they are *the other magisteria*.

the bishops, more precisely, between the bishops and the laity in a one-way descending line of teaching authority, with the theologians mediating, communicating, explaining, and defending the former to the latter.

It is also implicit in the requirement by Canon 812 and Pope John Paul's *Ex Corde Ecclesiae* (1990) that Catholic theologians teaching the "sacred sciences" in Catholic colleges and universities obtain a *mandatum* from the local bishop in which the professor recognizes his or her "commitment and responsibility to teach authentic Catholic doctrine and refrain from putting forth as Catholic teaching anything contrary to the Church's magisterium" and by which the bishop acknowledges that the professor is "a teacher within the full communion with the Catholic Church."[17] Clearly, in this view of the teaching ministry of the church, the most important quality of the theologian is fidelity to the Christian faith *as taught by* the episcopal magisterium.

Any Catholic theologian worthy of the name will acknowledge the responsibility to "teach authentic Catholic doctrine" and will "refrain from putting forth as Catholic teaching anything contrary to the Church's magisterium." "Putting forth as Catholic teaching anything contrary to the Church's magisterium" is proof of lack of academic competence and moral integrity and constitutes probable cause for dismissal, with or without the *mandatum*. However, after having explained accurately and respectfully the "authentic Catholic doctrine," the Catholic theologian is duty-bound to raise the question of whether such "authentic Catholic doctrine," which of course was formulated in and for a particular place and time, has obscured, neglected, and even suppressed other aspects of the Christian faith; whether

---

[17] United States Conference of Catholic Bishops, *Guidelines Concerning the Academic Mandatum in Catholic Universities* (Washington, DC: USCCB, 2001). It is interesting to note how this statement equates the "Church's magisterium" with the episcopal magisterium simply and without remainder. Here again it is essential that we take the local bishop as a flesh-and-blood person. If the local bishop is taken as a particular individual with a certain level of theological formation and not as a member of an abstract magisterium who is assumed to be ex officio a competent theologian, one wonders how he is competent to judge truthfully whether a professor of theology at the local university deserves to be granted, or refused, the *mandatum* and whether he or she is "within the full communion with the Catholic Church." Which process of evidence gathering and evidence assessment will be adopted by the local bishop in making a decision that may destroy a theologian's career and reputation? Can it be fairly assumed that a local bishop, even of a big diocese, has sufficient resources to carry out this task? Will the bishop be held legally and financially accountable for his erroneous or unjust decision?

in its current expression it is fully and universally applicable today; and whether it requires a different formulation that is more appropriate for our social, cultural, and religious contexts, and, if so, how. Such critical questions are far from being a lack of fidelity to the Christian faith, but rather the only way to remain faithful to it—for and in our age.

As has been explained above, the theologian's task is to promote an *intellectus fidei* (understanding of the faith), a process requiring not only gathering and experiencing of data (ascertaining the precise teaching of the Christian faith on the matter at hand) but also understanding the data (determining their meaning), evaluating their truth claims (judging the data), and acting on their moral and spiritual demands (putting the truths into practice). Thus, the theologian is not situated *between* the episcopal magisterium and the laity but functions as a magisterium itself, with its own proper method and ways of knowing. However, it is vitally important to emphasize that this task of *intellectus fidei* is not carried out by the theologian in isolation but within the circle of interaction and dialogue, both by teaching and learning, with the other four magisteria, namely, episcopal magisterium, lay magisterium, the magisterium of the poor, and the magisterium of believers of other religions.[18]

Lay Magisterium

Of the three magisteria, namely, of bishops, theologians, and lay faithful, the last, which I call lay magisterium, is the least studied. Admittedly, the expression *lay magisterium* has not been used by ecclesiastical documents or by, as far as I know, other theologians, to designate the teaching or prophetic function of the laypeople who constitute the overwhelming majority of the Christian faithful (*Christifideles*) whereby God's revealed truth is received, communicated, and lived in the church. This teaching role of the laity is fundamental, and by "fundamental" I mean "at the foundation or root." Without it, neither the episcopal magisterium nor the theological magisterium can exist or function. Both must be deeply rooted within and draw their teachings from it.[19]

---

[18] On this model of teaching in the church, see Richard Gaillardetz, *By What Authority?*, 136–41. As I will argue later, in fact there are not three but (at least) five magisteria. In addition to the three mentioned, there are the magisterium of the poor and the magisterium of non-Christian believers.

[19] Vatican I explicitly says that the Holy Spirit was not promised to the successors of Peter so that "they might disclose a new doctrine by His revelation, but rather, that,

What I call lay magisterium is an essential part of what Vatican II refers to as the *sensus fidei* (instinct of the faith) and *sensus fidelium* (instinct of the faithful). The possessor of this instinct of the faith is *the church as a whole*, that is, all the Christian faithful (*Christifideles*), who are made up of the hierarchy and the laity (among the latter are included the religious). The key text on this *sensus fidei* is Vatican II's *Lumen Gentium*, no. 12:

> The holy people of God shares also in Christ's prophetic office; it spreads abroad a living witness to him, especially by a life of faith and love and by offering to God a sacrifice of praise, the fruit of lips confessing his name (see Heb 13:15). The whole body of the faithful, who have received an anointing which comes from the holy one, (see 1 Jn 2:20 and 27) cannot be mistaken in belief. It shows this characteristic through the entire people's supernatural sense of the faith, when "from the bishops to the last of the faithful" it manifests a universal consensus in matters of faith and morals. By this sense of the faith, aroused and sustained by the Spirit of truth, the people of God, guided by the sacred magisterium which it faithfully obeys, receives not the word of human beings, but truly the word of God (see 1 Th 2:13, "the faith once for all delivered to the saints" (Jude 3). The people unfailingly adheres to this faith, penetrates it more deeply through right judgment, and applies it more fully in daily life.[20]

A few observations on this *sensus fidei/fidelium* are in order. First, it is God's gift to the whole people of God in baptism, and not just to bishops and theologians. Second, though bishops and theologians are *Christifideles* and exercise a magisterium of their own, their number is almost next to nothing compared to that of the laity. Therefore, when we refer to the *sensus fidei/fidelium* we must give due attention to the laity, both women and men. Third, the *sensus fidei/fidelium* is animated and directed ("aroused and sustained") by the Holy Spirit. Fourth, it is not a purely passive reception of the

---

with His assistance, they might jealously guard and faithfully explain the revelation or deposit of faith that was handed down through the apostles." See J. Neuner and Jacques Dupuis, eds., *The Christian Faith in the Doctrinal Documents of the Catholic Church* (New York: Alba House, 1982), 233. Consequently, the episcopal magisterium as well as the theological magisterium must listen to and learn from the lay magisterium.

[20] English translation of Vatican II's documents is taken from Austin Flannery, ed., *Vatican II: The Basic Sixteen Documents* (Northport, NY: Costello Publishing, 1996).

faith but an active process of appropriating and teaching the faith by means of a "living witness," "a life of faith and love," a "sacrifice of praise," "adherence" to the Christian faith, a deeper penetration into it through "right judgment," and an ever-fuller application of it to daily life. As a consequence, in my view, the teaching role of the laity deserves to be called magisterium. Fifth, the episcopal magisterium (the "sacred magisterium") serves as "guide" of this sense of faith of the people of God. Sixth, though not explicitly mentioned in the text, the theological magisterium also functions as guide, albeit without the authority of the episcopal magisterium. Seventh, when this sense of the faith manifests "a universal consensus in matters of faith and morals," it is free from error ("cannot be mistaken in belief"). Eighth, it is from this infallibility of the *sensus fidei* of the whole church—including the laity—that the episcopal magisterium derives its infallibility and not vice versa. Indeed, Vatican I, when defining the papal infallibility, explicitly states that the pope when teaching infallibly "possesses the infallibility with which the divine Redeemer willed *His Church to be endowed*" (emphasis added).[21]

My above exposition of the three magisteria in the Catholic Church should not be controversial. That popes and bishops must learn from the lay magisterium sounds objectionable only to those who still use the term *magisterium* to refer exclusively to the teaching of the pope, the Roman Curia, and the bishops (which is false), or who view the hierarchical magisterium as if it were sitting on top of a pyramid and working top-down and unidirectionally, from the bishops to the laity through the mediation of the theologians (which is theologically unsustainable).

To those who are scandalized by the view that the pope and bishops have the obligation to learn from the theologians and the laity, who are the *Christifideles* and share in the *sensus fidelium*, the following words of the third-century bishop and martyr Saint Cyprian of Carthage should be reassuring:

> But it happens by the practice of presumption and of insolence that each one defends more his own depraved and false view than he consents to the rights and truths of another. Foreseeing this matter, the blessed apostle Paul writes to Timothy and warns that the bishop ought not to be quarrelsome or contentious, but gentle and *teachable*. Now he who is meek and mild in the patience of *learning* is teachable.

---

[21] Neuner and Dupuis, *The Christian Faith in the Doctrinal Documents of the Catholic Church*, 234.

*For bishops ought not only to teach, but also to learn because he who grows
daily and profits by learning better things teaches better* (emphasis added).[22]

With regard to the relationship among bishops, theologians, and laity, who
all share in and contribute to the *sensus fidei*, albeit in different forms and
ways, it is to be conceived not as a pyramid descending from bishops to
theologians to laity, but as a circular process of mutual learning and teaching of bishops, theologians and laity in receiving the *sensus fidelium*, and this
dynamic process of "reception" begins again, as a spiraling loop, in ever-
new contexts, thus expanding and deepening the *sensus fidelium*.[23] In this
view, the special and unique role of the episcopal magisterium as guardian
(in the etymological sense of "conservative") and when necessary, judge of
the faith, is not only preserved but also made truthful and persuasive by
being placed within a humble dialogue of learning and teaching with the
theological magisterium and the lay magisterium, which in turn can teach
and when necessary, correct the episcopal magisterium.

How this learning-and-teaching dialogue is absolutely necessary for the
magisterium of the church can be illustrated with one example. There is
no doubt that the laity, and especially lay women, can teach bishops almost
everything about marriage, sexuality, and family. It strains credibility to
suggest that celibate old men can teach married people in these matters
without first being taught by them, and I do not mean merely "consulting"
them. How else can the current chasm between the episcopal magisterium
and the lay magisterium be explained in matters regarding contraception,
divorce and remarriage, and more recently, same-sex marriage, except by
the fact that bishops are willing to "consult" the laity but are not *learning*
and being *taught* by them?

The Magisterium of the Poor

In addition to these three traditional magisteria I suggest two further
magisteria, those of the poor and of non-Christian believers. Admittedly,
it sounds offensive to pious ears to claim that these two groups of persons

---

[22] Saint Cyprian, *Letters,* 74, 10, trans. Sister Rose Bernard Donna (Washington,
DC: Catholic University of America Press, 1964), 292–93. One can also appeal to
Blessed Cardinal John Henry Newman, *On Consulting the Faithful in Matters of Doctrine*
(1859; reprint, Kansas City: Sheed & Ward, 1961).

[23] On this *communio*-model of reception, see Gaillardetz, *By What Authority?*, 115–17.

are teachers for Christians, including bishops, especially the latter since they themselves are not Christian. However, the necessity of these two magisteria has been emphasized in recent theology, the former by liberation theologians of all provenances and types, and the latter especially by Asian theologians.

With regard to the poor as teachers of the faith, liberation theologians in Latin America, particularly Jon Sobrino, and in Asia, notably the Sri Lankan Jesuit Aloysius Pieris, have argued that it is the "magisterium of the poor"—Christians and non-Christians—that can teach us, more effectively and persuasively than any other church magisterium, how to be a disciple of Jesus today. Teachers of the faith, such as popes, bishops, and theologians, generally are not poor and do not live like the poor, at least in the West, in spite of the dramatic example and exhortation of Pope Francis. Given this economic situation, it is hard to imagine how the meaning and the truth of the Beatitudes—the very heart of the Gospel, especially Luke 4:20: "Blessed are you who are poor, for yours is the kingdom of God"—can be taught persuasively by people wearing costly miter, crosier, pectoral cross, ring, and other princely accouterments adorned with lace, gold, and precious stones. (Lately, the cappa magna is making a splashy comeback.) Can the message of the Beatitudes be credibly conveyed by professors of theology enjoying tenure, the *mandatum*, and a comfortable income? It is hard to see how the lavish lifestyle of those exercising the hierarchical and theological magisteria can help them bear a credible witness to the Son of Man who has nowhere to lay his head (Matthew 8:20) and who came not to be served but to serve (Mark 10:45).[24]

My point is not to do away with high-priced ecclesiastical vestments— clerical haberdashers like the Gammarelli in Rome have to make a living— and salary for theology professors who—unlike bishops—have bills to pay and families to support. Rather, it is to affirm that without the magisterium of the poor, Christian as well as non-Christian, who are the living icons of Jesus the Crucified and the object of God's preferential love, the teachings of bishops and theologians about God and the Crucified will be no more than noisy gong and clanging cymbal.

In this context, it is necessary to highlight the intrinsic connection between "orthodoxy" and "orthopraxis." Church authorities are deeply

---

[24] It is salutary to note that even theologians as they live and work in the West, like myself, run a serious risk of bearing a counterwitness to the Jesus of the Gospel!

concerned with the teaching of true doctrines and are quick to condemn what they perceive to be confused, confusing, and erroneous writings of theologians. However, it is to be noted that, unlike mathematics for instance, the validity of religious truths cannot be separated from how they can transform lives and whether they are practiced by those who teach them. Not only does this imply that teachers of the faith who do not practice what they preach are not credible, it also means that doctrines are formed and normed by practice (orthopraxis), just as practice is normed and formed by doctrine (orthodoxy). Applying this principle to the magisterium of the poor, it may be said that the poor are the teachers of bishops and theologians, not by their theological scholarship (orthodoxy), which often they cannot afford to acquire, but by their voluntary or enforced practice of Jesus's own poverty and self-emptying (orthopraxis).

The Magisterium of Believers of Other Religions

Lastly, there is the magisterium of non-Christian believers. Like the magisterium of the poor, it has only recently been proposed and advocated, especially by Asian theologians. This proposal no doubt seems outlandish to those for whom answers to all the problems of life are already and exclusively contained in the Bible, which is believed to contain answers to everything, even scientific questions, such as when the world came to be and whether there is evolution. Above all, in religious matters, according to these Christians, the church need not, and even must not, dialogue with non-Christians to learn from them. Why bother with interreligious dialogue if, as asserted by the Declaration of the CDF, *Dominus Iesus*, the church already possesses "the fullness and definitiveness of the revelation of Jesus Christ"; religions other than Christianity are not "ways of salvation"; non-Christian religions have at best "belief" (*credulitas*) and not "faith" (*fides*); and their sacred scriptures cannot be said to be "inspired"?[25]

Suppose that instead of starting from church teachings on religious pluralism that were formulated in contexts marked by claims of universality, uniqueness, and superiority, claims that were not rarely enforced by conquest, colonialization, and violence, the CDF's theologians who wrote

---

[25] See Congregation for the Doctrine of the Faith, *Declaration* Dominus Iesus *on the Unicity and Salvific Universality of Jesus Christ and the Church* (London: Catholic Truth Society 2000), especially nos. 5, 7, and 8.

Dominus Iesus sit at the feet of the spiritual teachers and believers of other religions and learn from them. Of the authors of this Declaration, how many have been taught by non-Christians; have deep friendship with non-Christians whose lives manifest holiness far superior to theirs; have prayed with them using their holy books and in their sacred temples; have practiced in the company of non-Christian monks and nuns spiritual discipline, which is much stricter than that of Christian monasticism; have mother, father, brothers, sisters, or relatives who have declined to become Christian because they find the teachings of their religion conducive to holy life; and have lived in countries where Christians are a minority and where saying all those things would cost them their lives?

Without these and many other life-changing experiences of *learning* from and being *taught* by the magisterium of non-Christians, it is impossible to appreciate the spiritual ("salvific") values of their religions. Those who accept with humility and gratitude the magisterium of the *pagans* can bear witness to their goodness and holiness of life, the truth of their teachings, the nobility of their ethics, and the transformative power of their spirituality. Of course, we must not idealize non-Christians and their religions. They are sinners and their religions on occasions reprobate, but so are Christians and Christianity. But there is no denying that Christians, and hence Christianity itself, have a great deal to learn from these non-Christians and their religions, and it is theologically legitimate to refer to their teaching as "the magisterium of believers of other religions." In our increasingly globalized and religiously pluralistic world, the acknowledgment of this magisterium, in addition to the other four magisteria, and of its necessity for the church today, is all the more urgent, precisely in order to secure the truthfulness and effectiveness of the episcopal, theological, and lay magisteria.

* * *

After perusing these rather lengthy, at times technical, reflections on theological method and the five kinds of magisterium (especially on the episcopal magisterium) readers may ask, what is the point of all this? The point is simple: it tries to answer the question of the subtitle of this chapter: "Why Do the Episcopal Magisterium and the Theological Magisterium Often Disagree?" As I have noted at the beginning of this chapter, theological views on particular doctrines are more often than not rooted in different ways of doing theology or theological methodologies. Disputes about particular doctrines will ultimately turn into disputes about *how* these doctrines should be derived from the sources of the faith of the community (which method?) and by *whom* (which magisterium?).

Clearly, whether one holds that "the method proper to Catholic theology" is to start from the faith of the church, especially as it has been taught by the hierarchical magisterium—as the CD's statement does—or whether one thinks that theology should begin with the "signs of the times" and interpret them in light of God's self-revelation and then, conversely, interpret God's self-revelation in terms of the signs of the times—as the majority of contemporary Catholic theologians do—the choice of method can obviously lead to very different interpretations of a certain Christian belief. Furthermore, whether one uses *magisterium* to refer exclusively to the hierarchical or episcopal magisterium, and, worse, conflates all the different ways in which it is exercised and assigns them equal authority—as the CD's statement does—or whether one holds that there are five magisteria—the bishops, the theologians, the laity, the poor, and the believers of other religions—all functioning in reciprocal teaching and learning, albeit in different manners and degrees of authority, as I have suggested, the decision will profoundly impact the way theology is done and its elaborations.

Given these fundamental differences in method and approach, it is sometimes frustrating to dispute about differences on a particular doctrine rather than examining how it has been derived from which sources. When I was studying theology in Rome in the early 1970s, a Spanish professor kept reminding us that when doing theology, we should get down to the foundation rather than staying on the upper floors. In the following chapters, as I try to respond to the concerns of the CDF and the CD of the USCCB about my little book, I will get down to the foundation.

Asian Theology and Its Method

I would like to conclude these reflections on theological method by showing that this way of doing theology is by no means an idiosyncratic invention of mine.[26] In fact, it has been expounded at great length and strongly recommended by the Federation of Asian Bishops' Conferences

---

[26] For further information on this method, see Chapter 10, "Doing Theology, Asian Style," in my *In Our Own Tongues: Perspectives from Asia on Mission and Inculturation* (Maryknoll, NY: Orbis Books, 2014), 174–200.

(FABC).[27] In 2000, the FABC's Office of Theological Concerns (OTC) produced a lengthy document entitled *Methodology: Asian Christian Theology*.[28] In introducing this method, the OTC states that Asian theology will use "conceptual tools and a philosophical approach arising from the various Asian cultures." One of the overriding values of Asian cultures is "harmony," which looks for "a language of reconciled diversity that will enable people of different communities to work together for peace and the building of a more just society." To promote harmony, the OTC goes on to say:

> Asian Christians will be looking for ways to integrate the experiences of Asia, the experiences of their own forbears and hence of their own psyche, into their Christian faith. The Asian way is one of integration and inclusion. Rather than saying "A is true, so B must be false," the Asian tends to say "A is true, and B is also true in some sense." This is not to say that truth is relative. There is but one Truth; but Truth is a Mystery which we approach reverently, while we try to understand its various aspects and dimensions. Hence, the Asian Christian is open to dialogue, a dialogue based on profound respect for individuals, communities and their religious traditions.[29]

---

[27] The FABC was founded in 1970, on the occasion of Pope Paul VI's visit to Manila, Philippines. Its statutes, approved by the Holy See *ad experimentum* in 1972, were amended several times and were also approved again each time by the Holy See. For the documents of the FABC and its various institutes, see Gaudencio Rosales & C. G. Arévalo, eds., *For All the Peoples of Asia: Federation of Asian Bishops' Conferences. Documents from 1970 to 1991*, vol. 1 (Maryknoll, NY/Quezon City: Orbis Books/Claretian Publications, 1992); Franz-Josef Eilers, ed., *For All the Peoples of Asia: Federation of Asian Bishops' Conferences. Documents from 1992 to1996*, vol. 2 (Quezon City: Claretian Publications, 1997); Franz-Josef Eilers, ed., *For All the Peoples of Asia: Federation of Asian Bishops' Conferences. Documents from 1997 to 2002*, vol. 3 (Quezon City: Claretian Publications, 2002); Franz-Josef Eilers, ed., *For All the Peoples of Asia: Federation of Asian Bishops' Conferences. Documents from 2002–2006*, vol. 4 (Quezon City: Claretian Publications, 2007); and Vimal Tirimanna, ed., *For All the Peoples of Asia: Federation of Asian Bishops' Conferences. Documents from 2007 to 2012*, vol. 5 (Quezon City: Claretian Publications, 2014). For fuller information on the FABC, see its website: http://www.fabc.org. For a history of the FABC's first three decades, see Edmund Chia, *Thirty Years of FABC: History, Foundation, Context, and Theology*, FABC Paper 106 (Hong Kong: FABC, 2003).

[28] See the text in FAPA, vol. 3, 328–419.

[29] Ibid., 331.

The OTC is deeply aware that there have been in the history of the church several theological methods. It describes the particularities of the Syriac (especially as practiced by the St. Thomas Christians in India), Greek, and Latin methods. Of special relevance is what the OTC says about the method of neoscholastic theology that dominated Roman Catholic theology since Pope Leo XIII's attempt to revive Thomism in 1879 with the encyclical *Aeterni Patris* until the Second Vatican Council:

> The best thing for theologians to do was to revive the teachings of great theologians of the past, giving priority to St. Thomas Aquinas. New insights into theological problems were seen as logical developments of the data contained in the dogmatic formulations of past councils. Genuine development of dogma seemed restricted to minor issues. In this theology, history, the lived experiences of the faithful as well as economic, political and cultural factors, did not play much of a role. Relying on abstract philosophical principles, which were assumed to contain universal truths, this deductive theology considered itself to be, in its form and conclusions, of universal validity. The idea that historical circumstances could and should play a role in the theologizing process was rejected: this was seen only as a danger for the universal validity of Christian dogma.[30]

In contrast to this method that takes the faith of the church as taught by the episcopal magisterium as its staring point, the OTC proposes a "theological method in an Asian context." By *context* the OTC does not mean the *background* or venue in which theology is done. Rather,

> context or contextual realities are considered resources for theology (*loci theologici*) together with the Christian sources of Scripture and Tradition. Contextual realities becomes resources of theology in so far as they embody and manifest the presence and action of God and his Spirit. This is recognized through discernment and interpretation. It calls for theological criteria to recognize and assess the loci.[31]

---

[30] Ibid., 351. In many ways, these observations offer a devastating critique of the "method proper to Catholic theology" proposed by the CD's statement.

[31] Ibid., 356.

The OTC goes on listing the resources that Asian theologians must make use of: cultural resources; social movements, especially women's movements, tribal movements, ecological movements, reality of the poor, and people's movements; and religious resources, especially Hinduism, Buddhism, Islam, Confucianism, and Daoism.[32] This use of Asian contextual resources does not of course lessen the importance of specifically Christian sources, namely, Scripture and tradition, which for *Christians* "enjoy normativity and fundamental importance for theology."[33] However, as *Asian* Christians, these Asian resources must be "integrated into theology together with the Christian sources of faith which guide our theological enterprise decisively, though not exclusively."[34] The OTC justifies the use of Asian resources as *loci theologici* for Asian theology on two bases. First, "Christian faith considers the whole universe, all of creation, as a manifestation of God's glory and goodness."[35] Secondly,

> God is the Lord of history. This means that God, who created the universe and humankind, is present and active in and through His Spirit in the whole gamut of human history leading all to the eschaton of God's Kingdom. God as Redeemer reveals His salvific plan which is one for all humankind. This salvific plan explains the presence of God's saving grace in religions, cultures, movements, history of peoples, their struggles.[36]

Clearly, the OTC's reflections on theological method go far beyond what the CD's document calls the "method proper to Catholic theology." After perusing the above pages on theological method—dry and technical as they might sound—readers, I hope, will understand the basic reasons why there are diversity of opinions—not faith—between the CDF and the CD, on the one hand, and the FABC and those who follow its theological method, on the other hand, regarding Christ, religions, church, and mission.

---

[32] See ibid., 355–405.
[33] Ibid., 362.
[34] Ibid., 363.
[35] Ibid.
[36] Ibid., 364.

CHAPTER 3

Divine Spirit

Is He / She / It Present Always and Everywhere in Human History?

As I have noted in Chapter 1, in condemning *Being Religious Interreligiously* (*BRI*), both the Congregation for the Doctrine of the Faith (CDF) and the Committee on Doctrine (CD) of the United States Conference of Catholic Bishops highlight four areas in which they judge the book confused, confusing, and erroneous: the role of Jesus Christ as the unique and universal Savior (Christology), the function of non-Christians in the history of salvation (theology of religions), the necessity of the church as the sacrament—sign and instrument—of salvation (ecclesiology), and the task of mission (missiology). In Chapters 4–6, I will discuss these themes and show where and why my views are different from those of the CDF and the CD. In line with what I have said in the previous chapter, before broaching those four themes, which, as it were, occupy four above-ground stories of the theological building, I would like to go down to its foundation and dig around to find the concrete slab supporting Christian beliefs about Jesus Christ, non-Christian religions, the church, and mission. The foundation stone, I suggest, is. Divine Spirit: In the beginning, before Christ, religions, church, and mission, there is Divine Spirit.

Unfortunately, for people living in the scientific age, where nothing is real unless it can be quantified and measured, the term *Spirit*, especially with the lower-case *spirit* and its plural *spirits*, conjures up fantastical beings such as ghosts, demons, angels, fairies, and monsters, or superstitious activities such as spirit possession, psychic medium, channeling, séance, and so on.

51

Thus, to invoke Divine Spirit to account for Christian beliefs seems like trying to explain obscure things by means of more obscure things, or, to put it in the elegant Latin phrase, *obscurum per obscurius*.

Divine Spirit:
God as Spirit and the Holy Spirit

If there is anything common to all religions, it is the belief that there exists a reality that transcends the material world, a being that is by nature inaccessible to the five senses, and for which, though interpreted very differently by various religions, the term *spirit* seems to be an appropriate cipher. In Western languages spirit, like the word *god*, is often written with a capital letter to highlight the sacred nature of this reality. When referring to this Spirit in Western languages both personal (He/She/Him/Her) and impersonal (It) pronouns are used, though the former is more common, and both the masculine and the feminine genders are employed as well, though the use of the masculine is—so far at least—more widespread. That's why in the subtitle of this chapter, I refer to Spirit as "He/She/It." This use of both personal and impersonal pronouns and of both the masculine and the feminine genders in speaking of "Spirit" is not just a grammatical convention but reflects the various ways "Spirit" is conceived in different religions, that is, as personal and impersonal and as male and female, sometimes even within a single religion. Finally, "Divine" is attached to "Spirit" in order to differentiate this one transcendent "Spirit" from a multitude of finite "spirits" such as angels, demons, gods, and goddesses. However, its use does not imply that "divine" has the same meaning in all religions. On the contrary, as will be shown below, it has extremely diverse connotations that cannot be homogenized into one single common meaning.

God as "Spirit"

I have suggested above that Divine Spirit is the foundation upon which the Christian theology of Christ, religions, church, and mission is built. Before arguing this point, I would like to draw attention to the double meaning of the expression *Divine Spirit* in Christian theology. First, "Divine Spirit" can refer to God as spirit (with the lower-case s). John 4:24 says, "God is spirit (*pneuma tô theos*)." Note that in the original Greek, there is no article before *pneuma* (spirit). (The King James Version translates the phrase as *God is a spirit,* adding the indefinite article *a.*) Second, there is no verb *is;* it is implied. Third, *pneuma* stands at the beginning of the sentence, putting emphasis on the immaterial nature of God as spirit. What is meant by "God is spirit" is not spelled out but must be determined by examining the biblical usage of the term *pneuma.* At a minimum, however, if by "spirit" (note the lower-case of s) is meant "non-material," then many religions, if they are theistic, can agree with John 4:24 that "God is spirit."

Secondly, in Christian theology, it is believed that there is only one God (one "substance" or "essence" or "nature") but that this one God is Father, Son, and Spirit (three "persons").[1] The terms "substance," "essence," and "nature" on the one hand, and "person" on the other, are not used in the Bible to distinguish between God's substance or nature and the three divine persons. Rather, bishops and theologians, especially at the ecumenical council at Chalcedon (451), took over profane Greek terms such as *ousia* (being) and *physis* (nature) to refer to God's essence (*what* God is) and *prosopon* (mask) and *hypostasis* (substance) to refer to the three "persons" in God (*who* God is).

Using these terms, early Christian theologians want to express the fact that Christians experience the one divine "being" acting in the world in three distinct "persons": as Father (whose children they are), as Son incarnated in Jesus (whose brothers and sisters they are), and as Spirit (by whose grace and power they are made children of the Father and brothers and sisters of Jesus). Christians are convinced that "Father," "Son," and "Spirit" are not merely impersonal "ways" or "modes" of God's self-expression and activities in the world, as if they were interchangeable "masks" (like the actor's) worn by the one and same God. Rather they are experienced as distinct "realities" of the one God. Thus, Christians relate to the Father as

---

[1] I am much aware of the argument of feminist theologians against the exclusive use of the masculine gender and images in speaking about God in general and especially about the Trinity in which two out of three images are masculine, namely, "Father" and "Son," the other ("Spirit") being neuter. Of course, no orthodox Christian theologian attributes sexuality to God, even though, following the Christian tradition, she or he may continue to employ the gender-based language and imagery in speaking of God. Furthermore, there is in Christian tradition a bias for personal language in speaking about God, even though the Bible does use ample impersonal terms and images to refer to God, such as rock, fortress, bird, living water, and so on. This is not the place to enter into a debate on the complex issue of language about God. For convenience's sake I will use the traditional language about the Trinity.

his sons and daughters, not as his brothers and sisters; similarly, they relate to the Son Jesus as his brothers and sisters, and not his sons and daughters; and they relate to the Spirit not as "his" sons and daughters, nor as "his" brothers and sisters, but as the power enabling them to be what they are in relation to the Father and the Son. (I put "his" in quotation marks when referring to the Spirit because whereas "Father" and "Son" are masculine in Greek, and therefore "his" is grammatically appropriate, in Greek Spirit (*pneuma*) is neuter and therefore, grammatically speaking, the impersonal "it" would be more appropriate. It was not until the council of Constantinople in 381 that the "personality" of the Spirit was officially affirmed.) Greek theologians use the terms *hypostasis* or *prosopon,* whereas Latin theologians use the term *persona,* to refer to the Father, the Son, and the Spirit, even though their secular usage may be misleading if applied to the Trinity without careful modifications. (Etymologically, *hypostasis* means "substance" and *prosopon* "mask," which is the opposite of distinct "person.")

In sum, in Christian theology "Divine Spirit" can refer either to God as "spirit" (with the lower-case s) and to the "Third Person" in God, the Spirit (with the upper-case S), often with the adjective "Holy" attached: The Holy Spirit. These two references of "God Spirit" must be kept in mind as we proceed to explore the foundation of Christian theology: God as spirit and the Holy Spirit. It is God as spirit that is the foundation of Christian theology.

The "Holy Spirit" in the Trinity

One final preliminary remark: in order to explain the one nature of God (unity) and the three divine persons (plurality) or the "Trinity," there are two main approaches, broadly (albeit not with total accuracy) categorized as Western/Latin and Eastern/Greek. The Western approach, championed by the African bishop Augustine of Hippo (354–430) and Thomas Aquinas (c. 1224–74), starts with the one divine substance or nature (the one God), and then moves on to explain how the Father, the Son, and the Holy Spirit are identical with this one nature (and hence, they are equally divine) and how they are three *distinct* "persons" by virtue of their real "relations" to one another. These eternal relations within the Godhead are constituted by the originations of the Son and the Holy Spirit from the Father. The Father, who alone is unoriginated, is Father because he generates the Son; the Son is Son because he is generated/born from the Father; and the Holy Spirit is Spirit because he/she/it "proceeds" or comes out of, or is "spirated" by the Father (and the Son).

A widely used analogy for the divine unity and plurality (Trinity) is the human subject, favored especially by Augustine. The human subject, who has a human nature, has, or more precisely, *is* a mind (Latin: *mens*). In this one human nature (which stands for the one divine substance), the mind (which stands for the Father) "knows" itself by generating the "idea" or "inner word" (which stands for the Son), and the mind also "loves" itself, producing "love" (which stands for the Holy Spirit). Thus, in the one divine "substance," the mind, the intellect, and the will stand for the three divine "persons": Father, Son, and Holy Spirit, respectively.

The second approach starts with the fact that when the Bible uses the term *God*, it does not refer to a divine "substance" but to the Father. One example among hundreds is Galatians 1:3–5: "Grace to you and peace from *God our Father* and the Lord Jesus Christ, who gave himself for our sins to set us free from the present evil age, according to the will of *our God and Father*, to whom be the glory for ever and ever. Amen" (emphasis added). For the Bible, the unity of God is not rooted in the one divine "substance," "essence," or "nature" but in the Father who is one. It is the Father, and not the common divine essence, who assures the oneness of God. Furthermore, the Son and the Holy Spirit are divine not because they share equally in the divine substance like the Father, as the Western approach thinks. Rather, they are divine because they "receive" divinity as gift from the Father. The Father is the "source" or "giver" of the divinity of the Son and the Holy Spirit.

Furthermore, Christians experience this one God-Father ("Divine Spirit") acting in history in and through two "agents," namely, the Son and the Holy Spirit. They have access to the Father in the Son and through the Holy Spirit, as Ephesians 2:14 puts it succinctly: "Through him [Christ] both of us [Jews and gentiles] have access in one Spirit to the Father." How and where these two agents act in history will be explained in detail in Chapter 4, when we speak of Jesus Christ. Suffice to recall here an arresting image proposed by a second-century bishop, St. Irenaeus (c.130–c.200), who, though he was bishop of Lyon, France, was born in the East (probably in Smyrna, now Izmir, on the west coast of Turkey) and wrote in Greek. Irenaeus suggests that the two distinct personal agents, Jesus and the Holy Spirit, function like the "two hands" of the Father.[2] His purpose is not to

---

[2] Irenaeus repeatedly says that God creates the world with his "hands," that is, his Son and his Spirit. See especially his *Adversus Haereses*, bk. V. For example, he says in

describe in detail how the two hands actually work in history, whether independently, dependently, or in collaboration with each other, a topic that is of great relevance for this book. Rather, Irenaeus's concern is to affirm against the Gnostics that God the Father has only one plan of action. This unity of God's plan to save humanity had been strongly rejected by Marcion (d. c. 160), who teaches that the God of the Old Testament (the "God of Law") is evil, in contrast to the good God preached by Jesus in the New Testament ("God of Love"). Against Marcion and the Gnostics, Irenaeus strongly affirms that God's plan of salvation is one and is revealed in both the Old and the New Testaments.

Irenaeus's important point is that even though there are two agents ("hands") who carry out the Father's plan of salvation, Jesus and the Holy Spirit do not have a plan of salvation each, distinct from each other. Rather, they fulfill only *one* plan of salvation: that of the Father. It is not theologically correct to say that the Son has a plan ("economy") of salvation and that the Holy Spirit has another "economy," different from that of the Son. Of course, as I will argue later, the fact that there is only one economy of salvation does not entail that the two "hands"—Son and Holy Spirit—act in the same way, at the same time, in the same place, with the same people, and in total dependence on each other. This point is of fundamental importance for my theological argument throughout this book.

The Greek term for plan of action is *oikonomia*, and using this term, theologians, such as the German Jesuit Karl Rahner (1904–84), name the Trinity of Father, Son, and Holy Spirit as they act in history, each in his own distinct way, the "economic Trinity," whereas the Trinity of Father, Son, and Holy Spirit as they are in themselves eternally is called the "immanent Trinity."[3] Because in and through his action in the world, God the Father gives us God's own self, indeed, his own Son and Holy Spirit, and not just some part of God, what we know and experience of the economic Trinity can be "extrapolated" to the immanent Trinity. Thus, from the fact

---

book V, 6, 1: "God will be glorified in his own creation, conforming and conjoining it to his Son. For by the hands of the Father, that is, the Son and the Spirit, the entire human person is made after the image and likeness of God, and not just a part of the human person" (my translation).

[3] On Karl Rahner's theology of the Trinity, which shapes my own, see Peter C. Phan, "Mystery of Grace and Salvation: Karl Rahner's Theology of the Trinity," in Peter C. Phan, ed., *The Cambridge Companion to the Trinity* (Cambridge: Cambridge University Press, 2011), 192–207.

that we experience God the Father acting in the world through his two "hands," that is, his Son and his Holy Spirit, we can say that in the immanent Trinity there are three eternal "persons," namely, Father, Son, and Holy Spirit. Consequently, we do not need to speak first of a common divine "substance" (one God) and subsequently speak of the three persons, Father, Son, and the Holy Spirit, who are identical with this substance, as Thomas Aquinas does. This approach, prevalent in the West since Augustine, is of course not wrong; in fact, it explains well the equality of the three divine persons. However, it is not the way the Bible speaks of God and of God's action with us in the world. Nor is the anthropological or "psychological" model of the immanent Trinity, in the image of mind, intellect, and will, the most helpful and illuminating. In fact, it is overly abstract and ahistorical. The better model to understand the immanent Trinity is one that is formulated on the basis of how the economic Trinity has acted in history, and this is the model followed here.

All the foregoing reflections on Divine Spirit and on the Trinity of Father, Son, and Holy Spirit will serve to bolster my argument that the foundation of Christian theology is Divine Spirit or God as spirit (with the lower-case s). Of course, to understand what/who Divine Spirit is, it is possible to start with the teaching of the episcopal magisterium, especially the first seven ecumenical councils, and the CD's statement insists that we must. However, in line with what is said in the previous chapter, I will show that there is another much more fruitful approach to understand God as spirit, one that starts from vastly richer and wider resources, which have been listed at the end of the last chapter, and one that responds to our present context of religious pluralism. This is the approach adopted by the Federation of Asian Bishops' Conferences (FABC), one that I fully and gratefully appropriate.

Active Presence of Divine Spirit and the Holy Spirit in Asia

Perhaps the most convenient way to expound an Asian perspective on Divine Spirit is to provide a commentary on the document issued by the Office of Theological Concern (OTC) of the FABC in 1997, entitled *The Spirit at Work in Asia Today* (*SWAT*).[4] The document is remarkable for its

---

[4] The FABC was founded in 1970, on the occasion of Pope Paul VI's visit to Manila, Philippines. Its statutes, approved by the Holy See *ad experimentum* in 1972,

unusual length (about a hundred pages), comprehensiveness, and insightful-ness. It intends to elaborate the pneumatology (theology of the Holy Spirit) implicit in the FABC's previous documents that deal with interreligious dialogue, the local church, church and politics, and harmony.

At the outset, we must note the ambiguity in the term *Spirit* in the title of the document *The Spirit at Work in Asia Today*. It can refer to Divine Spirit (God as spirit) or the Holy Spirit (the "Third Person" of the Trinity). As a matter of fact, it is the second meaning that dominates throughout the document. The two meanings are of course not self-contradictory. Indeed, for our present purpose, they help clarify what we mean by saying that the foundation of the Christian beliefs on Christ, religions, church, and mission is Divine Spirit. As explained above, the Father, and not the generic divine substance, is active in history in and through his Son and Holy Spirit, each in distinct, albeit not mutually exclusive, ways. Thus, in speaking of the "Spirit" at work in Asia, the OTC is describing none other than Divine Spirit insofar as He/She/It is present and active in Asia under the personal agency of the Holy Spirit, who is one of Divine Spirit's two "hands."

What is highly extraordinary about the OTC's document on the Spirit is that, in contrast to the method prescribed by the CD, *The Spirit at Work in Asia Today* does not begin with the teaching of the episcopal magisterium on the Holy Spirit, though there exists a huge amount of materials span-ning seventeen centuries, from the First Council of Constantinople (381) to Pope John Paul II (1920–2005). Rather, true to its method, as explained in the previous chapter, it begins with a description of how the "Spirit" is active in Asia's religio-cultural traditions and sociopolitical realities. Only

---

were amended several times and were also approved again each time by the Holy See. For the documents of the FABC and its various institutes, see Gaudencio Rosales & C. G. Arévalo, eds., *For All the Peoples of Asia: Federation of Asian Bishops' Conferences. Documents from 1970 to 1991*, vol. 1 (Maryknoll, NY/Quezon City, Manila: Orbis Books/ Claretian Publications, 1992); Franz-Josef Eilers, ed., *For All the Peoples of Asia: Federation of Asian Bishops' Conferences. Documents from 1992 to 1996*, vol. 2 (Quezon City, Manila: Claretian Publications, 1997); Franz-Josef Eilers, ed., *For All the Peoples of Asia: Federa-tion of Asian Bishops' Conferences. Documents from 1997 to 2002*, vol. 3 (Quezon City, Manila: Claretian Publications, 2002); Franz-Josef Eilers, ed., *For All the Peoples of Asia: Federation of Asian Bishops' Conferences. Documents from 2002–2006*, vol.4 (Quezon City, Manila: Claretian Publications, 2007; and Vimal Tirimanna, ed., *For All the Peoples of Asia: Federation of Asian Bishops' Conferences. Documents from 2007–2012*, vol. 5 (Quezon City, Manila: Claretian Publications, 2014). These volumes will be cited as *FAPA*, fol-lowed by the number of the volume and the pages.

then does it discuss the work of the Spirit in the Bible and the church, followed by an attempt at formulating an Asian theology of the Spirit. The main focus of *SWAT* is the Holy Spirit's action in Asia, but it carefully notes that the work of the Spirit and that of Christ, far from opposing each other, are mutually complementary: "The more we follow the leading of the Spirit, the deeper and closer will also be our understanding of the mystery of Jesus Christ."[5] *SWAT* is composed of six parts.[6] I will not summarize the entire document but only highlight those aspects that are germane to my theme of the foundation of Christian theology.

The Spirit at Work in Various Religio-Cultural Traditions in Asia

Theologically speaking, it is highly significant that *SWAT* begins its treatment of the Holy Spirit with a lengthy exposition on the presence and activity of the Spirit in Asian cultures, religious and socio-political realities rather than with biblical and magisterial teachings, as is usually done in official church documents and Western theological texts.[7] Implicit in this methodology is the theological conviction that Divine Spirit is actively present in non-Christian religions in and through the Holy Spirit and that to this extent these religions may be regarded as "ways of salvation." In reflecting on the Spirit in Asian religious traditions, the authors of *SWAT* declare their intention to "discern the presence of the Spirit as expressed, believed, imaged and symbolized by believers themselves in these traditions."[8]

Note that *SWAT* does not say that Divine Spirit or the Holy Spirit as believed by Christians is *identical* with the realities spoken of in other religions, or that the Christian theology of Divine Spirit or the Holy Spirit and the teachings of other religions on the various realities mentioned below are simply different ways of referring to the same thing. That would be a superficial and intellectually lazy comparison. On the contrary, *SWAT* is

---

[5] FAPA, III, 238.

[6] *SWAT's* six sections: (1) the Spirit at work in various religio-cultural traditions of Asia, (2) the Spirit at work in sociopolitical realities, (3) the Spirit at work in the biblical traditions, (4) the Spirit at work in the church, (5) toward an Asian theology of the Spirit, and (6) pastoral recommendations.

[7] See Parts I and II, comprising forty-three pages, almost half of total number of pages of the document.

[8] *FAPA*, III, 239.

deeply aware of the *radical differences* between some of the Christian beliefs and those of other religions. What it affirms is simply that there are *deep resonances* between them, which a sympathetic, open-minded, and humble-hearted listening-in-dialogue can discern.

SWAT goes on to highlight these "resonances" between the Spirit and various realities present in Asian religions. In Hinduism, the document mentions the Hindu concepts of *atman* (the self), *prana* (breath), *antarayamin* (inner controller/indweller), *ananda* (bliss/joy), *sakti* (power/energy, especially as female), *agni* (fire), and *pavaka* (purifier). After pointing out a "deep resonance" between these Hindu concepts and the Christian concepts and images of the Holy Spirit, such as breath, wind, fire, power, life-giving force, and so on, *SWAT* asks, "Was the Spirit (apart from concepts congenial with the Spirit) present in the Indian Tradition?," and it answers unequivocally, "Yes. If we are able to discern the signs of the Spirit we can read the history of Hinduism as a holy history, where the Spirit has led our brothers and sisters to the depths of the mystery of God and leads them towards Christ."[9] The difficult challenge of course is for Christians to discern "the signs of the Spirit" in Hinduism.

Buddhism, with its explicitly nontheistic religious stance, presents a daunting challenge to the project of elaborating a theology of Divine Spirit. *SWAT* is well aware that "if one sets out to 'find God' in Buddhism, the result will be either frustrated disappointment or distortion of tradition."[10] In particular, *SWAT* notes two significant differences between Buddhism and Christianity. First, Buddhism does not believe that there is a permanent "self" that perdures unchanging and identical throughout time and after death. Rather the "self" is nothing but a continuous coming-into-being and going-out-of-being of five "aggregates" (form, sensation, perception, mental formation, and consciousness) for which the term *nonself* (*anatta* or *anatman*) would be more appropriate. Secondly, Buddhism does not speak of a personal God; not that the Buddha explicitly denies the existence of God (atheism), but he simply regards the question about God as distracting people from their task of alleviating suffering (nontheism or atheism).

In spite of profound differences between Buddhism and Christianity, *SWAT* affirms that an encounter between the two religions is possible. Such

---

[9] *FAPA*, III, 241–42.
[10] *FAPA*, III, 243.

an encounter is possible, the document says, not at the level of concepts, which are quite different, but

> on the level of experience of human life and the human quest for the transcendent. The fact that a Christian also belongs to a tradition which affirms the transcendent, the existence of a spiritual world beyond the world of physical senses and the rational mind, should make the Christian open to a different conception and experience of that reality.[11]

The thesis of *SWAT* is that it is at the level of experiencing the Four Noble Truths, that is, by *practicing* and not merely discussing them, that an encounter between Buddhism and Christianity, vastly different though they are as conceptual systems, is possible. To put it in Christian terms, the experience of Divine Spirit, or the Holy Spirit, can be obtained in the experience of the Four Noble Truths.

This experience of the transcendent is open to Christians as they undergo for themselves the Buddha's experience of enlightenment, which is embodied in the so-called Four Noble Truths, namely, (1) that all existence is "suffering" (*dukkha*), (2) that the cause (*samudaya*) of suffering is "desire" or "craving," (*tanha*) (3) that it is possible to "cease" (*nirodha*) this desire, and (4) that there is an "eightfold path" (*magga*) to achieve liberation from suffering (*nirvana*).

In addition, *SWAT* points out, as a person practices the Four Noble Truths, he or she will experience the "Four Sublime States," namely, *upeksa* (equanimity); *karuna* (compassion); *mudita* (sympathetic joy); and, above all, *maitri* (love). Of the four, love is central, "for without love, compassion turns to contempt, sympathetic joy to vicarious satisfaction, and equanimity to heartless indifference." This universal love is the hallmark of the enlightened person (*bodhisattva*) in Mahayana Buddhism, who vows to save all beings, destroy all evil passions, learn truth and teach others, and lead all beings toward Buddhahood. Later schools of Buddhism, especially in China, Korea, Japan, and Vietnam, stress devotion to a series of *bodhisattvas*, especially the Amitabha Buddha and Avalokitesvara (who becomes the female Kwan Yin in China and Kannon in Japan). At the end of its exposition of Buddhism, *SWAT* raises the all-important question about the experience of Divine

---

[11] Ibid.

Spirit or the Holy Spirit: "As Christians come to share something of the
vision and experience of the Buddha as lived out in the lives of the people
with whom they share the Asian heritage, what can they perceive but the
work of the Spirit which they too have experienced?"[12]

SWAT moves on to consider the two Chinese religious traditions, that
is, Confucianism and Daoism. Unlike Buddhism, these traditions are not
explicitly nontheistic. However, the Transcendent Being (e.g., Heaven or
the Dao) does not play a central role in their beliefs and practices, the overriding purpose of which is to bring humanity to full flourishing. Nevertheless, *SWAT* praises Confucius's respectful attitude toward Heaven who is
believed to intervene in human affairs to bring about goodness and justice.
Given the preeminence of Confucius as a sage and teacher of wisdom in
East Asia, the document does not hesitate to regard him as "an agent of the
Spirit before the coming of Christ."[13]

Whereas Confucius remains rather reluctant to speak of Heaven, the
Daodejing discourses at length on the *Dao* (Way or Path) that paradoxically
cannot be spoken of and whose name cannot be named. The ineffable *Dao*,
which is absolute mystery, has two aspects: as transcendent, it is *wu* (nonbe-
ing) and hence beyond human understanding and language. As immanent,
it is *yu* and is manifested in the *yin* and *yang* whose interactions produce
the *qi* (air, breath, life-giving force, spirit) that animates the "ten thousand
things" of the cosmos. In addition to the "deep resonances" between the
Daoist doctrine of the *Dao* and the Christian doctrine of Divine Spirit and
the Holy Spirit, there is another aspect of Daoism that provides a place
where, according to *SWAT*, the Spirit is active in Asia, and that is its spirituality. Daoism commends a way of life that brings about mystical union
with the *Dao*, harmony with nature, and transformation of the entire body
into immortality. In practical conduct, Daoism prescribes *wu wei* (nonaction
or "nothing-doing"), which is neither physical withdrawal from the world
nor moral passivity, but a way of doing good for others effectively and
effortlessly but without violence, competition, interference, and manipula-
tion, like flowing water smoothing hard rocks, or *qi* circulating in all the
different parts of the universe. This *wu wei* way of doing things or "nothing-
doing" recognizes the relativity, interconnectedness, and interdependence of

---

[12] *FAPA*, III, 248.
[13] *FAPA*, III, 251.

all things. Like *yin* and *yang*, all opposites do not negate each other but are mutually complementary. Living in harmony with opposites requires the cultivation of the attitude of nonattachment and nondesire.

In assessing Confucianism and Daoism in terms of Divine Spirit and the Holy Spirit, *SWAT* concludes categorically:

> In many ways, they [Confucianism and Daoism] reflect the work-ings of the Holy Spirit in the cosmos and particularly in humanity and its history. The Taoist virtues of docility, trust, humility, non-violence, detachment, equanimous love; and the Confucianist virtues of responsibility, honesty, loyalty and fidelity are but manifestations of the fruits of the one Spirit of God working in all sorts of different ways in different people in the world.[14]

The next object of discussion is what has been referred to under the umbrella category of "primal religions." *SWAT* sees them as characterized by two basic beliefs, namely, in a supreme divine being (the Great Spirit), and in what has been called the "excluded middle" (the spirits). Primal religions (*SWAT* includes under this category Shamanism and Shintoism) are found primarily among indigenous peoples, also referred to as *tribals* or *aborigines*, terms that often have a pejorative connotation of cultural backwardness. The document notes that the attitude fostered by primal religions toward the Great Spirit and spirits, of which some are benign and others evil, is both awe and fear. With regard to whether the Holy Spirit is active in primal religions, *SWAT* frankly recognizes that until Vatican II these religious traditions had been condemned as idolatry and supersti-tions. However, since the council, a more positive appreciation of primal religions has been advocated, and the document notes that "much of the indigenous people's world view and ethos is compatible with the Christian faith" and that "traditional beliefs, rites, myths and symbols of indigenous peoples provide material for developing indigenous theologies and liturgi-cal ceremonies."[15] Clearly, *SWAT* acknowledges the presence of the Holy Spirit in primal religions, albeit with some reservation, given their belief in evil spirits and practices to appease them.

---

[14] *FAPA*, III, 257.
[15] *FAPA*, III, 261.

No such qualm is to be found in *SWAT*'s discernment of the presence of the Spirit in Islam. The document opens its presentation of Islam with a categorical affirmation:

> The Divine Spirit, who works unceasingly to renew the face of the universe, is also active in the religion of Islam to produce the Spirit's inimitable fruits in the lives of Muslims. . . . A study of the Qur'an, the Sacred Book of Islam, shows a constant effort to sow in the lives of believing Muslims those qualities that Christians recognize as the fruits of the Spirit.[16]

The document singles out for admiration the Islamic teaching on love, compassion, and submission to God's will and the practices these virtues entail. The document is convinced that "by forming friendships with Muslims, by coming to know better their faith and practices, and by working together with them for good, it is God's Holy Spirit who is praised and worshiped."[17]

The Spirit at Work in Sociopolitical Realities

Whereas it is a common practice to discern the presence of the Spirit in religions, it is rather unusual to do so with reference to sociopolitical events and movements. By so doing *SWAT* provides a basis for dialogue not only between Christianity and other religions but also between religions and nonreligious ideologies and movements (e.g., socialism and communism) that are dominant in many Asian countries.

Acknowledging the extreme variety of Asian sociopolitical realities, *SWAT* mentions sociopolitical movements (e.g., the *Swaraj* and *ahimsa* movements in India, the anticolonialism struggle and the Communist ideology in China, Korea and Vietnam, the *pancasila* ideology in Indonesia, and the "People's Power" in the Philippines), ecological movements, women's movements, workers' movements, political ideologies (e.g., atheistic Marxism, antitheistic capitalism, fundamentalism, communalism, national security ideology), and youth movements. *SWAT* urges Christians to discern the work of the Spirit in all these dizzyingly diverse realities as they combine biblical and church teachings on the Holy Spirit with the Asian religious,

---

[16] *FAPA*, III, 261–62.
[17] *FAPA*, III, 266.

cultural, and sociopolitical heritage in the attempt to elaborate "an Asian pneumatology which might provide elements to discern the various spirits at work in Asia today."[18]

The Spirit at Work in the Biblical Tradition

SWAT presents a masterful summary of the teaching of the Bible on the Spirit and the Spirit's presence from creation to Jesus. *SWAT* lists ten activities of the Spirit as described by the Bible: The Spirit draws people to the truth, begets people into the kingdom of God, teaches, witnesses, accuses by rousing a sense of sin, liberates, effects growth, prays, leads, and renews.[19] Of this summary four points deserve highlighting. First, the document strongly insists on the unity and inseparability between Word and Spirit throughout human history: "There is no Spirit without the Word and there is no Word without the Spirit."[20] Secondly, there is *mutual* dependence between Word and Spirit; one cannot operate without the other. On the one hand, the Spirit is presented as "the Spirit of Jesus" and as Jesus's gift; on the other, "the Spirit is at work in Christ."[21] Thirdly, the Spirit operates with utter freedom; it blows where it wills. One place where *SWAT* discerns the activity of the Spirit is the sacred scriptures of non-Christian religions: "The Sacred Scriptures of the other religions are also reflections of the presence and activity of the Spirit in the non-Christian religious institutions."[22] Fourthly, there is a need of discernment between the Spirit, on one hand, and evil spirits and false claims to have the Spirit, on the other. This raises the question of criteria for discernment, and the document lists three: fruits of the Spirit, values of the kingdom of God, and the sense of faith of the church.

The Spirit at Work in the Church

Again, *SWAT* offers an insightful overview of the theology of the presence and activity of the Spirit in the church that can be termed *pneumatological ecclesiology*. In particular, the document insists on the unity between the Spirit and the church, of which the Spirit is the soul, as it were. It

---

[18] *FAPA*, III, 281.
[19] See *FAPA*, III, 294–97.
[20] *FAPA*, III, 298.
[21] *FAPA*, III, 288.
[22] Ibid.

laments the danger of excessive institutionalization of the church's structures to the detriment of the charisms. It welcomes the rebirth of Spirit-centered spirituality in Protestant Pentecostalism, Catholic Charismatic Renewal, and other movements that celebrate the gifts of the Spirit (e.g., glossolalia, healing, prophecy, etc.) for the building up of the body of Christ.

SWAT highlights some of the ways in which the Spirit is present in the church, the first of which is the giving of gifts or charisms such as those mentioned above. Another activity of the Spirit is leading the church to the fullness of truth. The third is renewing and revitalizing the church through Pentecostal and Charismatic movements; the expansion of ministries to the laity, in particular women; the formation of small ecclesial communities with their emphasis on prayer, Bible study, work for peace and justice, and reception of the fruits of the Spirit. Lastly, *SWAT* links the work of the Spirit in the church to interreligious dialogue. Paradoxically, the Spirit's presence *in* the church enables the recognition of the Spirit's presence *outside* the church. It is the presence of the Spirit in the church that impels Christians toward dialogue with other religions and enables them to see in the "deeper meanings and intentions of people of other faiths . . . the voice of the Spirit bearing witness to the marvelous variety of God's self-revelation to man."[23]

After this rapid survey of how the FABC's document *The Spirit at Work in Asia Today* views the presence of Divine Spirit and/or the Holy Spirit in Asian religions and sociopolitical movements as well as in the Bible and the church, it would be helpful to show how *SWAT* is relevant to the basic argument of this book. I have argued in the last chapter that it would be futile for me to answer all the objections of the CDF and the CD to what they allege to be confused, confusing, and erroneous in *BRI* by examining each of them by itself (and for that matter, for Elizabeth Johnson to respond to the CD's statement on her book *Quest for the Living God* by rebutting each of its accusations by itself, though she has done it devastatingly). The alleged reason is, as the CD has explicitly pointed out, that Johnson, and presumably myself, have not followed "the method proper to Catholic theology." In the last chapter, I have shown that the method that the CD claims to be "proper" to Catholic theology is nothing of the sort.

In this chapter, I introduce another, very different method of doing theology, one in which the "contextual realities"—in this case, Asian religions

---

[23] *FAPA*, III, 307.

and Asian sociopolitical movements—function, in addition to the Bible and church teachings, as *resources* for theology or the *loci theologici*. Once this methodological step is taken, one need not take the teachings of the episcopal magisterium as the starting point of theology, as the CD prescribes. On the contrary, one may, and indeed must, begin with the signs of the times, or to use *SWAT*'s pregnant expression, "signs of the Spirit," which are to be interpreted in light of the Gospel, and vice versa in whose light the Gospel (and magisterial teachings) are to be interpreted. Indeed, reversing the traditional order, *SWAT* examines the presence of the Spirit in Asian religio-cultural traditions and sociopolitical movements *before* speaking of the Spirit in the Bible and the church, a procedure I suspect the CDF and the CD would reject as not "proper" to Catholic theology. In other words, the disputes between the CDF and the CD and my little book should not be first engaged on issues of Christology, theology of religion, church, and mission—the metaphorical above-ground floors of Christian theology—but at the foundation, which is method.

I have further argued in this chapter that if the FABC's theological method is adopted, the reality that Asian theologians have discovered at the foundation of the Christian faith, and hence of theology, is not Christ, religions, church, and mission—themes on which the CDF and the CD focus in condemning *BRI*—but Divine Spirit. From the Christian point of view, I have shown that Divine Spirit can be understood as God as spirit (with the lower-case s, and more specifically, as God the Father) and as the Holy Spirit (with the upper-case S), the "Third Person" of the Trinity, one of the two "hands" of God the Father. *SWAT* argues that Divine Spirit or the Holy Spirit is actively present in Hinduism, Buddhism, Confucianism, Daoism, Asian primal religions, and Islam. One may of course disagree with *SWAT*'s claim of a "resonance" between a specific Christian doctrine and a teaching of these religions, but it is impossible to gainsay the radical significance of this procedure for Christian theology as a whole.

Toward an Asian Theology of Divine Spirit/the Holy Spirit

In the light of *SWAT*'s discernment of the "signs of the Spirit" in Asian cultures and religions, Asian sociopolitical movements, the Bible, and the church, I will attempt in this concluding part an "Asian pneumatology." It lies at the foundation of my responses to some of the charges of the CDF and the CD against *BRI*. Of course, what is presented here is but a sketch and not a systematic and comprehensive treatise of the theology of Divine Spirit/the Holy Spirit. Only its basic features are mentioned here. I begin with a summary of *SWAT*'s outline of an Asian pneumatology and then will develop it with further insights of my own.

An Asian Pneumatology:
From the Holy Spirit to the Son to the Father

First, methodologically, an Asian pneumatology starts "from below," that is, from reflections on Asian cultures, religions, and sociopolitical movements. As *SWAT* rightly claims, this starting point "offers a broader theological framework in which we are able to relate the Spirit with the mystery of God's reign, and consequently understand and interpret our Asian experiences in a pluri-cultural and multi-religious context."[24]

Second, the Spirit is viewed primarily as mystery, that is, as that which cannot be fully and exhaustively expressed in anything finite, hence as Divine Spirit, and yet is present and active in all finite things. As *SWAT* puts it beautifully, "Whatever has been manifest and expressed has been viewed as the mirror of the unmanifest, the unexpressed; the revealed as a fragment of the unrevealed."[25]

Third, of the myriad ways the Spirit is active in the world, an Asian pneumatology emphasizes three, that is, ecological unity (binding humans with the cosmos), movement (crossing over all types of boundaries and divisions), and freedom (liberation from attachment and egoism and struggle for social justice and peace).

Fourth, since Asia is characterized by deep pluralism in all aspects of life, "the approach to the Spirit as the author of plurality strikes a highly responsive chord in the Asian hearts."[26] Consequently, an Asian pneumatology will intentionally and explicitly cultivate what the FABC terms *receptive pluralism*, that is, the many and diverse ways in which Asian people respond to the Spirit: "We value pluralism as a great gift of the Spirit . . . The many ways of responding to the prompting of the Holy Spirit must be continually in conversation with one another."[27]

---

[24] *FAPA*, III, 318.
[25] Ibid.
[26] *FAPA*, III, 321.
[27] Ibid.

Finally, such pneumatology carries profound implications for being church in Asia. In particular, it requires of Christians struggling in effective solidarity with the powerless, according primacy to charisms over institutions, and becoming a participative community of equals.[28]

Distinction-in-Unity and
Mutual Dependence between the Holy Spirit and the Son

While concurring fully with *SWAT*'s Asian pneumatology, I propose further reflections on the relationships between the Holy Spirit and the Son to formulate an Asian pneumatology—the theology of Divine Spirit as spirit (with a lower-case s) and as the Holy Spirit (with an upper-case S)—that serves as the most appropriate and fruitful foundation for a theology of Christ, religions, church, and mission contained in *BRI*.

1. The Spirit—understood as the "Third Person" of the Trinity—is the *first* transcendent reality that humans, Christians included, experience, both chronologically and theologically. In any religious experience, it is the Spirit who is the first reality known and loved. From the Christian perspective, the proper *ordo* of both Christian living and Christian theology is "*from* or *by the power of* the Spirit *in* the Son *to* the Father." In other words, the proper and necessary structure of Christian life, and also religious experience in general, is *from* the Spirit *in* the Son *to* the Father. This is the "sequence," if you will, temporal as well as theological, of how we know and love God. The Father is the ultimate reality and the goal toward whom we tend, and we can do so only in and through his two hands working in history.

Moreover, with regard to the Father's two hands, we first experience the Spirit and then the Son, for without the Spirit, we cannot know the Son, whereas a person, because of certain circumstances such as living *before* the incarnation of the Son in Jesus, or *after* the incarnation of the Son but in a country to which the good news has not been preached, may know the Spirit, in and through his or her religion, as we have seen above, without actually knowing Jesus. In fact, this is the case with the overwhelming majority of human beings! This "order" in knowing the Father in and through the Spirit and the Son reflects the structure of the economic Trinity. In history, we cannot move *from* the Father, then *to* the Son, and then *to* the Spirit, as in the immanent Trinity, for the Father is known and

---

[28] For a brief exposition of an Asian pneumatology, see *FAPA*, III, 317–25.

loved only in and through the Spirit and the Son, in that order. Much less, strictly speaking, do we know and love the Father *and* the Son *and* the Spirit, as we say in the doxology: "Glory be to the Father *and* to the Son *and* to the Holy Spirit," if by that we mean that there is no "order" in our specific relationships to the three divine persons. All these reflections serve to underline the fact that from the Christian perspective, the Spirit is the starting point and foundation of our encounter with Divine Spirit, as the Holy Spirit leads us to the Son who leads us to the Father.

2. It is generally acknowledged that a separation, or worse, opposition between Christ and the Holy Spirit would postulate two distinct divine economies (plans of salvation) for the world: that of the Son and that of the Holy Spirit. As we have seen above, St. Irenaeus argues against Marcion that a duality of plans of salvation would destroy unity in God. Instead, he suggests that there is only one plan of salvation, namely, that of God the Father, but that it is carried out in the world by the Father's two hands or agents, the Son, and the Holy Spirit.

While I fully subscribe to Irenaeus's teaching on the unity of God's plan of salvation, I think further precisions are needed to understand the relation of unity-in-distinction between the Son and the Holy Spirit correctly. It is possible and necessary to distinguish between the activities of the Son and those of the Holy Spirit as well as between their modes and venues of operation. There is a *mutual* dependence and conditioning between the Son and the Holy Spirit. The Holy Spirit cannot function without the Son, a truth that is often insisted upon in Western theology. But it must be no less strongly emphasized that the Son cannot function without the Holy Spirit. (In the same vein, it must be said that the Father cannot function without the Son and the Holy Spirit, and vice versa.) This mutual dependence among the three divine persons in being and action is a corollary of the Trinitarian structure of the Christian God and is expressed by the Greek term *perichoresis* (literally go forward around, or more poetically, dance around) and the equivalent Latin terms *circumincessio* or *circuminsessio* (literally go or step around).

Unfortunately, this truth of the *mutual* dependence between the Son and the Holy Spirit was obscured in classical Western/Latin theology of the Trinity. Western theology, from Augustine to Thomas, explains the relations among the three divine persons in terms of the distinct originations of the Son and the Holy Spirit from the Father who alone is "unoriginated."

The Son is originated from the Father by way of "birth" or "generation," whereas the Holy Spirit is originated from the Father by way of "procession" (Greek: *ekporeusis*). This term is taken from John 15:26 ("When the Advocate comes, whom I will send to you from the Father, the Spirit of truth who comes [proceeds] from the Father") and is used to differentiate the Holy Spirit from the Son. The Son and the Holy Spirit equally originate from the Father, but their modes of origination are different: the Father "generates" or "gives birth" to the Son, whereas he "spirates" or breathes forth the Holy Spirit.

"Generation" and "spiration" are little more than metaphors taken from human experiences of giving birth and breathing forth to articulate the biblical teaching about how Divine Spirit acts in himself (the immanent Trinity) and in the world (the economic Trinity). There is of course nothing wrong with this way of speaking of God, as long as we remember that these are metaphors or analogies, albeit authorized by the Scripture. A serious problem however arises when this origination is understood as sequential originations, that is, from the Father to the Son to the Holy Spirit—in descending and linear order—in spite of assertions of the divine *perichoresis* to the contrary. This results in the total, one-way dependence of the Holy Spirit not only on the Father but also on the Son. Thus, we have the oft-repeated formulas: "the Spirit of the Son," "the Spirit of Jesus," and the "Spirit of the Father." Implicit in these formulas is a denial of the dependence of the Son and the Father on the Spirit. As a consequence, there are no such official formulas as "the Father of the Spirit," "the Son of the Spirit," and "Jesus of the Spirit." Similarly, we say, "In the name of the Father, and the Son, and the Holy Spirit," as in the sign of the cross, and never "In the name of the Holy Spirit, the Son, and the Father," or "In the name of the Son, the Father, and the Holy Spirit," or "In the name of the Father, the Holy Spirit, and the Son," even though, strictly speaking, given the *perichoresis* in the Trinity, such formulas are theologically legitimate. As a consequence, the perichoretic structure of the Christian God, with the image of the three divine persons dancing round holding each other's hands, is jeopardized.

An illustration of the way the Holy Spirit is made dependent on the Son, and not the other way round, is the obscure but fierce debate between the Greek and the Latin churches about the "procession" of the Holy Spirit. The creed that was promulgated at the First Council of Constantinople (381), known as the Niceno-Constantinopolitan Creed, declares, "We believe in the Holy Spirit, the Lord, the giver of life, who proceeds from the Father." In the West, at the Third Council of Toledo (589), to combat the Arian heresy that denies the divinity of the Son, added the expression "and the Son" (in Latin, *Filioque*) to "from the Father." Though emendation of the creed is canonically unlawful, the expression *Filioque,* as well as the alternative expression "through the Son," has been widely accepted, since it is intended to preserve the truth of the divinity of the Son. Later, however, in the ninth century, the patriarch of Constantinople, Photios, adamantly condemned it as heretical and went so far as to say that the Spirit proceeds from the Father *alone*.

There is no need to follow the tortuous history of the controversy on the *Filioque*, which was dictated by ecclesiastical politics as much as by doctrinal concern for orthodoxy. What is of interest here is the unintended effect of the *Filioque* on the understanding of the function of the Holy Spirit in history. Because the Holy Spirit is made totally dependent on the Son (as well as the Father), it is difficult if not impossible to see how the Holy Spirit can be actively present in history where the Son is not known. This "Christocentric" perspective has led to a "forgetfulness" of the Holy Spirit, of which Western/Latin theology has often been accused. This lack of a robust pneumatology can be reversed only if it is admitted that just as the Father cannot "spirate" the Holy Spirit without the Son (*Filioque*), the Father cannot "generate" the Son without the Holy Spirit (*Spirituque*, literally "and the Spirit").[29] Only when *Filioque* and *Spirituque* are kept together, that is, only when we affirm that (1) the Father generates the Son in, through, and with the Holy Spirit, (2) that the Father spirates the Spirit in, through, and with the Son, and (3) that the Father cannot be Father except in, through, and with the Son and the Holy Spirit, is the triadic/Trinitarian structure of the Trinity fully preserved. This theology of Divine Spirit is not, I submit, an irrelevant mumbo-jumbo but has vast implications for our understanding of how the Holy Spirit and the Son are present in history, as I will show in the following chapters.

3. Mutual dependence among the three divine persons does not however negate, but rather requires, a certain "autonomy" in being and acting

---

[29] Among theologians who have proposed this perspective with the expression *Spirituque* is the Russian Orthodox theologian Paul Evdokimov (1901–70), on whose thought I wrote my first dissertation (*Culture and Eschatology: The Iconographical Vision of Paul Evdokimov* [New York: Peter Lang, 1985]).

of each divine person, inasmuch as they have irreducibly *different* manners of being and acting. Otherwise the divine persons cannot be distinguished among themselves, and we would end up with modalism rather than Trinitarianism. These differences entail that each Person can and does function "autonomously." As mentioned above, after the incarnation of the Son, or the Word, of God in Jesus of Nazareth by the power of the Holy Spirit, anyone who knows the Son also knows the Spirit. However, before the incarnation and even after the incarnation, in times and places where the Jesus of history could not personally reach due to his historical limitations as a Jew living in the first century of the Common Era, and in places where he has not been preached and known, the Holy Spirit can be and has been actively present, as *SWAT* has shown.

This "autonomous" action of the Spirit, which is not opposed to that of the Son but distinct and in a certain true sense, independent of it, allows us to fully recognize the work of the Spirit outside Jesus, before the incarnation of the Son in him, and even after it, and outside Christianity, especially in other religions, whose spiritual or salvific value and function can be affirmed in itself, and therefore without the need to reduce them to being simply "preparation" for or "stepping stones" to Christianity (*praeparatio evangelica*), or to being "fulfilled" or "superseded" by it, thereby denying their integrity and otherness. As a person can perform a single task well, sometimes using both hands at the same time and equally, at times, better with one hand than with the other, and still at other times, one rather than the other, so analogously the Holy Spirit and the Son, God the Father's two hands, can operate in similar ways in carrying out his single plan of salvation, in Christianity as well as in other religions.

4. In the dialogue with Asian religions, it is helpful to recall that "Spirit" has been conceptualized in diverse, at times diametrically opposed, ways. It has been interpreted in theistic, monotheistic, polytheistic, monistic, non-dualistic, dualistic, humanistic, and even atheistic terms, as has been shown above. This is not the place nor is it possible to go over all these philosophical and theological possibilities.

The point of this chapter is simply that before speaking of Jesus, religions, church, and mission we need to go to the foundation of the theological edifice. Divine Spirit and the Holy Spirit can serve as the most useful starting point and foundation for interreligious dialogue in places with religious diversity as vast as in Asia. As *SWAT* puts it concisely,

The "Spirit" could be understood as the human or the divine Spirit. In non-theistic religions, such as Buddhism, Jainism or Taoism, it stands for the "given" human potentiality to speak, seek and find total human liberation. But in the biblical, and some other theistic, traditions, this potentiality tends to be regarded as the divine Spirit operating immanently in the human person. In either case the diversity of tongues which defines the activity of the Spirit argues for religious pluralism.[30]

---

[30] *FAPA*, 274.

CHAPTER 4

Jesus Christ, the Unique and Universal Savior

Possibility of an Interreligious Christology?

As I was typing the title and subtitle of this chapter at Narita International Airport in Tokyo, a little Japanese American girl, perhaps no more than ten years old, glanced over my laptop screen, saw the words "Jesus Christ, the Unique and Universal Savior?" read them aloud, and asked me point-blank: "Do you believe in Jesus?" Discombobulated by this public and in-your-face inquiry into one of the most personal aspects of my life, I blurted out, "Yes, I do." Then, unprompted, she declared, "I do too." Her mother and her younger brother shot her a sharp disapproving look, signaling that she must not talk to a stranger, especially about matters as deeply personal as faith. I was glad that the conversation ended there. Thank God, the girl did not have the chance to inquire what "Interreligious Christology" in the subtitle of the chapter means. On my part, I regretted not having the opportunity to ask her if her faith in Jesus included the belief that he is the unique, exclusive, and universal Savior. Of course, she wouldn't have a clue what I was talking about.

The Many and Varied Contexts of Christology

I was on my way back to the United States after spending two weeks teaching at the East Asian Pastoral Institute, part of the Jesuit Ateneo de Manila University, located in the capital of the Philippines, and at the Euntes Asian Center, an institute for mission formation run by the Pontificio Istituto Missioni Estere (PIME) Fathers, located in Zamboanga City,

Mindanao, in the southern part of the country. Both academic institutions offered courses promoting, as stated in their self-descriptions, "a new way of being church," a common shorthand for the Asian churches' commitment to a dialogue with the Asian poor, cultures, and religions as an essential part of the mission of the church.

With the exception of tiny East Timor, the Philippines is the only country in Asia with a largely Christian population (of its 103 million, about 83 percent are Catholic and 10 percent are Protestant and Evangelical). Muslims (mostly Sunni) make up about 5 percent of the population. In Mindanao, however, an estimated 40 percent of the island's population is Muslim. While I was in the Philippines, in Mindanao, there were eruptions of violence between the government army and the Moro National Liberation Front, an armed conflict dating back to the 1970s. Though the war was economically and politically motivated, it was threatening to turn into a bloody conflict between Catholics and Muslims, given the demographic composition of Mindanao. There had been many killings, and thousands of Catholics and Muslims were forced to flee from their villages.

Besides violence, there is widespread, dehumanizing poverty in the Philippines. The highway leading from the Manila International Airport to Quezon City, where the East Asian Pastoral Institute is located, is lined on both sides by rows upon rows of ramshackle cottages of utter destitution. During my stay in Zamboanga, Angelo Calvo, an Italian Claretian priest and missionary, gave me a tour of the city. He took me to a Muslim area known as Rio Hondo and Mariqui where there were thousands of huts on stilts, with corrugated-iron or thatch roofs, spreading for miles on the sea. There was no running water, no electricity, no sanitation, no paved roads, and no sewage systems, with dogs and goats and children scampering everywhere. The water was thick with garbage and human wastes, and swarms of children were swimming in it! Only God, Fr. Calvo, whose mission includes work for urban youth, murmured with ill-concealed sorrow, knows how these children could have survived hunger and filth.

A couple of miles away from this Muslim *barangay* (village), in the center of the city, right across from a luxurious shopping mall, a brand-new, two-story church, richly decorated with stained-glass windows, shoots up to the heavens, majestic and mighty. Sunday Mass was being celebrated, with the attending faithful spilling into the churchyard. Attached to the church are the five-story, well-appointed parish office and priests' residence. Both the church and the residence, I was told, were built by a monsignor of the archdiocese, who was running for mayor of the city and whose family owns a five-star hotel and restaurant overlooking the sea. (The candidate, whose image, dressed in bright red, was plastered on ubiquitous banners, lost the election, in spite of his family's powerful connections.) Fr. Calvo was anxious for me to see the opulence of the priests' residence. We rode the elevator up to the fifth story, took a furtive look, and immediately went down, since we did not want to be caught in the empty building. The scandalous wealth that separates the Catholic quarter from the Muslim barrio is too painful to bear. I was then reminded of a sentence in a book I had read a couple days earlier: "If Christianity was not good news for the poor, it would not be good news for anyone."[1]

After lunch, Fr. Calvo took me to a village named *Katalingban* (community), where he had helped two hundred Muslim families build their own houses after being evicted from their squat huts. In the middle of the barrio, there is an open multipurpose building for religious celebrations and community activities. In front of the building, there is a basketball court where children were playing. All the kids, most of whom are Muslim, greeted Fr. Calvo affectionately. Fr. Calvo also showed me another nearby community of one hundred families called *Kalinaw* (peace). These two villages are not wealthy, but they do have running water, electricity, and sanitation. And, there, true to the names of the villages, Christians and Muslims live together in harmony and peace. Fr. Calvo said that another community of three hundred families was being planned, and he insisted that all the villages had been built by intent without the canonical supervision of the local archbishop.

On another day, I was invited by Fr. Sebastiano D'Ambra, an Italian PIME missionary, to visit the Harmony Village of the Silsilah (Arabic for "chain" or "connection") Dialogue Movement, some six miles outside Zamboanga City. The Silsilah Dialogue Movement was founded in 1984 by D'Ambra to build bridges between the Catholic and Muslim communities when their relations were being frayed by the military conflicts between the Muslim separatist movement, the Moro National Liberation Front, and the Marcos government. Fr. D'Ambra told me that one of his confreres, Fr. Salvatore Carzedda, had been killed by the Moro National Liberation Front in 1992. Part of the movement is the Harmony Village, which is located on a thirty-five-acre property of rolling hills and woodlands. Fr. D'Amba gave

---

[1] Sebastian C. H. Kim, ed., *Christian Theology in Asia* (Cambridge: Cambridge University Press, 2008), 12.

me a tour of the main buildings and described the various activities of the village. At the heart of the village is the chapel where Muslims and Christians pray together. During my visit I attended the evening prayer service, with readings from the Bible and the Qur'an, punctuated by periods of silence and meditation. The evening prayer was followed by a simple dinner where Christians and Muslims shared food together.

Jesus, the Unique and Universal Savior?

The above brief narrative is not an attempt at self-indulgent nostalgia; rather, it is meant to serve as the contexts—in both senses of the term, namely, location and theological resource—for speaking of Jesus Christ today, at least in Asia. Some of these contexts are familiar to the Western academy: university, theological and pastoral institute, students of theology, ministerial formation, church and politics, parish life, and religious orders. Others are totally unexpected and strange: the airport, a young girl's spontaneous profession of faith to a total stranger, a Muslim slum of dehumanizing poverty, a Catholic clergy luxurious residence, a settlement village for evicted Muslims founded by a Catholic priest, a center of interreligious worship for Christians and Muslims also founded by a Catholic priest, deadly military conflicts, activities for justice and peace, expatriate missionaries, and even martyrdom.

It is in these traditional and uncanny contexts that I would like to examine the claim that Jesus is the "unique" and "universal" Savior. I choose to do so because it is my views as expressed in *Being Religious Interreligiously* (*BRI*) on these two characteristics of Jesus as Savior, namely, uniqueness and universality that both the Congregation for the Doctrine of the Faith (CDF) and the Committee on Doctrine (CD) condemn as confusing and even erroneous. My intention here is not—indeed cannot be—to present an exhaustive exposition of Christology as the background against which the statements of both the CDF and the CD and my own admittedly jejune understanding of who Jesus Christ is are to be evaluated. To do this adequately requires a masterful command of contemporary Christological literature, which I do not possess, even though I have spent as much time and energy as afforded by the leisurely life of a university professor almost exclusively on reading and studying during my waking hours, having no other earthly hobbies. Yet, I would be telling a bald lie were I to claim to have read all the most recent significant works on Christology.

The most convenient way to remedy a lack of mastery of the Christo-logical literature in discussing the uniqueness and universality of Jesus Christ as Savior is to examine the Declaration of the CDF entitled *Dominus Iesus*: *On the Unicity and Salvific Universality of Jesus Christ and the Church* (August 6, 2000; *DI*).[2] On the heels of its publication there were first a storm of protests, especially on the part of the Jews, and then a flood of popular and scholarly commentaries, both supportive and critical.[3] The main objections are to *DI*'s statement that only Christians have "*theological faith*," whereas the followers of other religions have only "*belief*" (no. 7) and that though "the followers of other religions can receive divine grace, it is also certain that *objectively speaking* they are in a gravely deficient situation in comparison with those who, in the Church, have the fullness of the means of salvation" (no. 22).

In response, several high-placed curial cardinals clarified that *DI* does not include Judaism in its evaluation of non-Christian religions and that it is intended for internal consumption only, a shot across the bow to warn Catholic theologians against doctrinal errors, and not as an instrument for interreligious dialogue. Indeed, it was rumored that the target of the docu-ment was the Jesuit theologian Jacques Dupuis (1923–2004), whose work the CDF had condemned, and those theologians, mostly Asian, who adopt his theology of religious pluralism.[4]

Be that as it may, it is unnecessary to detail here the history of the reception of *DI* in and outside the Catholic Church, since our focus here is only on the uniqueness and universality of Jesus Christ as Savior. To focus on *DI* is also strategically useful since its teaching has been used as the litmus test for orthodoxy. Indeed, in judging my book to be "notably confused on a number of points of Catholic doctrine" and also containing "serious ambiguities," the CDF states that "taken as a whole, it is in open contrast with almost all the teachings of the Declaration *Dominus Iesus*." A critical analysis of the teaching of the document would then serve as a response to the various "observations" of the CDF and the CD on *BRI*.

Before embarking upon this task, three preliminary remarks are in order. First, *DI* uses the term *unicity*, not *uniqueness*. It is a transliteration

---

[2] The English text of *DI* is available on the Vatican website at http://www.vatican.va.

[3] For a single-volume well-crafted commentary, see Stephen J. Pope and Charles Hefling, eds., Sic et Non: *Encountering* Dominus Iesus (Maryknoll, NY: Orbis Books, 2002).

[4] See Jacques Dupuis, *Toward a Christian Theology of Religious Pluralism* (Maryknoll, NY: Orbis Books, 1997).

of the Latin *unicitas*, a term rarely if ever used by the average English-speaking person. But it expresses more precisely than "uniqueness" the *numerical* connotation of the term *unique*. In popular parlance, Jesus is not simply "number one" (meaning "the best") savior (with lower-case s); rather he is the only *one* Savior (with capital S). Secondly, "Salvific Universality" means that Jesus is the Savior for the whole humankind. That is, if anyone is saved, he or she is said to have been saved by Jesus. Coupled with "unicity" the phrase means that humans are saved by Jesus and by no one else. Thirdly, unicity and salvific universality are also attributed to the church; it is affirmed that the church and nothing else is the numerically *one* instrument of salvation for all humanity. This is a distinct claim from that of Jesus's unicity and universality requiring a separate examination, which I will do in Chapter 6.

"Unicity" of Jesus as Savior

The claim of the unicity of Jesus as Savior in the numerical and exclusive sense as explained above, if taken as an *empirical* statement that would be in principle verifiable on public criteria of evidence, necessarily presupposes a competent and exhaustive comparison among all claimants, past, present, and future, to the title of "Savior." Obviously, *DI* cannot and must not make such a claim. The reasons are many, and five will be mentioned here. First, the CDF—or any other organization for that matter—does not have the requisite knowledge of all the religions of the world to make a well-informed judgment on the merits of the claim of unicity by a particular religion. Second, even if miraculously it does have the requisite knowledge of all religions, still it cannot make a judgment on future, not-yet-existing claimants in comparison to whom Jesus is asserted to be the only one Savior since it does not know who these future claimants may be. Third, a set of public and mutually agreed-upon criteria for deciding one claimant against another is currently unavailable, and thus a judgment for or against a claimant is necessarily arbitrary and indefensible. Fourth, there is no common understanding of what is meant by "salvation," even among Christians, let alone among diverse religions, about which the claim of unicity is made. Even if a person is conclusively proved to be unique, still it is not yet clear in what matter he or she is unique since not everyone agrees with what is meant by "salvation." Last, not all religions have "salvation" of their adherents as their aims. This would make the claim of unicity for an individual as Savior, even if proved to be true, totally irrelevant for those religions that do not have salvation as understood by Christians as their goals.

I have lingered at some length on the logical impossibility of the claim for the unicity of Jesus as Savior as an *empirically verifiable* claim, *not* in order to deny its alleged truth but to highlight its nature as a *profession of faith*. By their very nature, affirmations of faith cannot be proved rationally; otherwise they would not be truths of faith but of reason. However, because they are asserted so often and so adamantly by church authorities, not rarely with threats of canonical penalties for those who deny them, they are generally assumed by the rank-and-file (and perhaps even by not a few members of the hierarchy themselves) as a plainly *obvious* and rationally *provable* truth. Their certainty about the truth of the unicity and universality of Jesus as Savior would remain absolute and unshakeable until they meet people of other faiths who, too, claim, with equal certainty and matching conviction, unicity and universality for *their* religious founder and/or religion. (Of course not all religions make or feel the need to make such a claim.)

Such an encounter with people with religious views diametrically opposite to one's own, to whom one is challenged to prove the truth of one's faith, is rare in the Vatican's corridors of powers, where people would risk losing their jobs, and would not have been appointed to such jobs in the first place, if they publicly voice doubts about, or even merely raise doubts for discussion, what the hierarchical magisterium teaches about Jesus (and other forbidden subjects such as women's ordination and gay marriage). By contrast, in places, such as Asia, it is a daily fact of life that the Christian claim for the unicity and universality of Christ as Savior is routinely disputed and unceremoniously dismissed, if not ridiculed. This is especially the case when such claims are made for the church, given its history of at times sinful and scandalous behaviors.

In addition to this common hazard of misunderstanding a profession of faith about the unicity and universality of Jesus as Savior as empirically verifiable truth claims, there is also the danger of theological stagnation. With the episcopal magisterium's vigorous insistence on the use of hallowed phrases, such as *unicity* and *salvific universality*, to speak of Jesus as the litmus test of orthodoxy, theologians are strongly discouraged from examining whether such a language, forged during Christianity's religious dominance, is still appropriate to the contemporary context of religious pluralism and to places, such as Asia, where Christianity is a minority. I will come back to this point below after I discuss the "salvific universality" of Jesus.

"Salvific Universality" of Jesus

The claim that Jesus is the Savior of all human beings, like that of his unicity, is not an empirical claim but a profession of faith. As a claim of faith, it cannot on principle be empirically proved, and as an empirical claim, it cannot be verified either. The reasons are many. First, the impact, good or bad, of a person's words and deeds is of necessity limited primarily to the people of that person's place and time, depending on their reaction to him or her. In the case of Jesus, we may think of the people who had a direct and personal contact with him and responded, positively or negatively, to his actions and teachings such as his parents, disciples, friends and enemies, the Pharisees and the Sadducees, and the crowd who followed him. Secondarily, a person can also be said to have an impact on the people, either contemporary or posterior to that person, who do not personally know him or her but who are influenced, for good or for ill, by that person's deeds and words. In the case of Jesus, we may think of, for instance, the Pharisee Nicodemus or the apostle Paul, who, albeit contemporaries of Jesus, did not know him personally but were influenced by him, and of all the Christians who live after Jesus down the centuries.

However, in no case can a person be said to have a positive or negative impact ("universality") on those who lived *before* him or her. This is a metaphysical impossibility, unless that person has a "preexistence," that is, a real "existence" before his or her historical existence in a particular place and at a particular time. It makes no sense, for example, to say that I have an impact on the people who had lived before I was born. Efficient causality cannot work retroactively, even for God. In the case of Jesus, who was a Jew living in Palestine in the first century of the Common Era, limited as he was by a particular place and a particular time, it equally makes no sense to say that he exercised a positive impact ("salvific universality") on, for example, Gautama the Buddha, Confucius, Plato, or Aristotle, who all preceded him by several centuries, or on billions of people who lived before him—unless, of course, Jesus is *professed* to be identical with the eternal Son, the Word (Logos), or the Wisdom of God. But this is precisely my point, namely, that the claim of "salvific universality" for Jesus as the Savior is a profession of *faith*, and not an empirical statement.

This being the case, it is possible and necessary to distinguish between the Word of God *before* his incarnation in/as Jesus of Nazareth and the Word of God *after* his incarnation in/as Jesus of Nazareth. The unincarnated Word of God (in Greek, *Logos asarkikos*), as one of the two hands of the Father (Divine Spirit), to use St. Irenaeus's celebrated image again, was actively present in history *outside and without* Jesus of Nazareth and was not restricted by place and time. By contrast, the active presence of the incarnated Word of God in/as Jesus of Nazareth (in Greek, *Logos sarkikos*) was limited by place (Palestine) and time (some thirty-five years of his lifespan). This Jesus of Nazareth could and did have an impact on his contemporaries and those who live *after* him, if they accept him as their Savior. However, during his lifetime he could not exercise an impact on those who lived *before* him. In this sense he did not have "salvific universality" on them.

This point is made imaginatively in 1 Peter 3:19–20, where it is said that *after* his death Jesus "went and made a proclamation to the spirits in prison, who in former times did not obey, when God waited patiently in the days of Noah, during the building of the ark." This extremely obscure passage is commonly interpreted to mean that after his death Jesus descended into "hell," that is, the abode of the dead, to proclaim the good news of salvation to those who had died in disobedience to God before him ("the spirits in prison"). It is precisely only *after* his death, when he was no longer bound by space and time, that Jesus could have a salvific impact on those who had lived before him and who now accepted Jesus's preaching and were thus saved. This does not mean that between Noah and the death of Jesus there were no people saved. It is most likely that there were, but their salvation is not and cannot be caused by Jesus retroactively but must be attributed to another agent of God. To anticipate my answer, this agent is one of the two hands, or both hands of God, the Son of God and/or the Holy Spirit.

If it is claimed that Jesus has "salvific universality" on those who predated him, the only possible rationale for such a claim is that Jesus is identical with the eternal Word of God who is beyond space and time. Technically, it is said that Jesus has two "natures," that is, human and divine, but is only one "person," that is, the Word of God. In this case, the claim of the salvific universality for Jesus as Savior is not an empirically verifiable affirmation but a rationally unprovable profession of faith.

There is an added reason why such a claim is an affirmation of faith. The claim here is about *salvation*. However "salvation" is understood, it is not some physical quality such as heat or cold, and hence measurable and verifiable. Indeed, to say that Jesus is the Savior, regardless of whether for all or only for some, is essentially a profession or proclamation of faith, not an *empirical* assertion of fact. Of course, if Jesus saves, then his saving action is factual or real, that is, it is not a fiction of the imagination, but this "fact" is not empirically verifiable precisely because it is about "salvation."

As with the claim for the "unicity" of Jesus as Savior, my thesis on the logical impossibility of the claim for Jesus's "salvific universality" on humans who lived *before* him is not intended to deny Jesus's role as Savior of the whole humanity. Rather it is to highlight the fact that it is a profession of faith and not an empirically verifiable assertion. It is perfectly legitimate for Christians to believe and to confess publicly that Jesus is the Savior of all, past, present, and future. However, they cannot and must not affirm this faith statement about the salvific universality of Jesus as a statement analogous to the statement that water boils at 212 degrees Fahrenheit. To do so, they risk exposing the Christian faith to ridicule, since they would affirm as ontologically possible a logical impossibility.

By the same token, Christians must be prepared to accept the possibility that believers of other religions, too, affirm that their religious founders possess a "unique" and "universal" role of their own, albeit not in terms of "salvation" as Christians understand it. For instance, Buddhists do claim that the Buddha has taught a "unique" way to achieve freedom from suffering (the Four Noble Truths to achieve nirvana), that indeed his is the "only" way to achieve this goal, and that his teaching is "universally" valid, that is, efficacious for all people in all places and at all times. Furthermore, Buddhists may argue that because the Buddha predated Jesus by several centuries, the Christian affirmation that through his "salvific universality" Jesus "saved" the Buddha is logically impossible as an empirical statement. By contrast, the opposite may be true. Without subscribing to the highly improbable theory that Jesus went to India sometime before his public ministry (during the so-called "lost years of Jesus"), it is not a historical impossibility that the Buddha might have had an impact on Jesus, since he existed before Jesus, and that his teaching might have been known to Jesus, as there was an extensive network of communication between India and Palestine in the first century. But even for Buddhists, this empirical affirmation remains only a possible but unprovable historical assertion.

On the other hand, not unlike Christians who profess in faith the "salvific universality" of Jesus thanks to their faith in Jesus as the Word of God made flesh (the *logos sarkikos*), Buddhists, at least in the Mahāyāna tradition, may claim in faith that the Buddha has "liberationist universality" thanks to the doctrine of the "Triple Body" (Sanskrit, *trikāya*) according to which the Buddha has a three distinct modes of existence. The first, and the most fundamental of the three, is the "Body of Dharma" (*Dharmakāya*), which has absolute existence and is undifferentiated, free from all determinations, formless, omniscient, omnipotent, and infinitely compassionate (not unlike Jesus's divine nature). The second is the "Body of Transformation" (*Nirmānakāya*), which is the "incarnation" or appearance of the *Dharmakāya* in the historical human form of Siddhārtha Gautama (not unlike Jesus of Nazareth), as well as in countless other earthly, possibly nonhuman manifestations, everywhere and at all times. The third is the "Body of Bliss" (*Sambhogakāya*), which is the manifestation of the *Dharmakāya* in a heavenly form (in contrast to the earthy form of *Nirmānakāya*); it is an intermediate body, that is, the "Body of Transformation" in transition to the absolute "Body of Dharma" (not unlike Jesus's risen body).

My point here is not to argue for a similarity or parallel between the Christian doctrine of the Incarnation of the Word of God in Jesus of Nazareth and the Buddhist doctrine of the "incarnation" of the *Dharmakāya* in Siddhārtha Gautama of India. Rather, it is to point out that just as Christians can claim "unicity" and "salvific universality" for Jesus, thanks to their belief in the incarnation of the Word of God in him, so, too, Buddhists can equally claim "unicity" and "liberationist universality" for the historical Buddha thanks to their doctrine of the Triple Body. It is to be noted that both claims are claims of faith, and not empirical statements, and both are valid and true within their own universes of faith. This is something that Christians must be mindful of and respectfully acknowledge, even as they proclaim Jesus as the unique and universal Savior.

Before examining whether the Christian formulation of the "unicity" and "salvific universality" of Jesus as Savior is appropriate to the Asian context of religious pluralism, I would like to recall very briefly what is said in the previous chapter about the presence of the Holy Spirit, the other hand of God the Father. Whereas the historical Jesus was limited in his actions by place and time, no such restriction is imposed on the activities of the Holy Spirit. As John 3:8 puts it, "The wind [Spirit] blows where it chooses, and you hear the sound of it, but you do not know where it comes from or where it goes." Thus, the "salvific universality" of the Holy Spirit is unlimited, whereas that of Jesus was limited. Before the incarnation of the Word of God in/as Jesus, during Jesus's lifetime, and after Jesus's death and resurrection, the Holy Spirit is active throughout the world and at all times, outside and independently, albeit in collaboration with Jesus, and the venues of the Holy Spirit's activities are, as the Federation of Asian Bishops' Conferences (FABC) indicates, the sociopolitical movements, cultures, and religions of all peoples. It is therefore imperative that when speaking of the "unicity" and "salvific universality" of Jesus as Savior, we must also affirm— if I may use a true albeit somewhat awkward expression—the much more universal universality of the Holy Spirit. Thanks to Divine Spirit working with its two hands, and more specifically with the Holy Spirit in this case, we may and must acknowledge in principle (to use a Latin expression, *de iure*) the real possibility that historical figures other than Jesus of Nazareth function as agents of Divine Spirit in peoples' socialpolitical movements, cultures, and of course, religions.

It is in the light of what has been said above that certain statements of *DI* must be evaluated. It states that

> therefore, the theory of the limited, incomplete, or imperfect charac-
> ter of the revelation of Jesus Christ, which would be complementary
> to that found in other religions, is contrary to the Christian faith.
> Such a position would claim to be based on the notion that the
> truth about God cannot be grasped and manifested in its globality
> [sic; totality?] and completeness by any historical religion, neither by
> Christianity nor by Jesus Christ. (no. 6).

First, I find *DI*'s implicit claim that Christianity as a "historical religion" can "grasp" and "manifest" "the truth about God" "in its globality and completeness" utterly unfounded and even contrary to what the church professes about God. If God is absolute mystery, is it not blasphemous to claim that "the truth about God" can be "grasped" and "manifested" in "its globality and completeness" by Christianity, which is a historical religion? Is there not a long and venerable tradition of "apophatic" or "negative theology," so prevalent among the mystics, which insists on adoring silence before God rather than grasping and manifesting the truth about God in globality and completeness?

Nothing expresses more forcefully and beautifully the impossibility of grasping and manifesting the truth about God in its totality and complete-ness than the first stanza of Thomas Aquinas's celebrated Eucharistic hymn, which is sung during Benediction:

Adoro te devote, latens Deitas,
Quæ sub his figuris vere latitas;
Tibi se cor meum totum subjicit,
Quia te contemplans totum deficit.

Devoutly I adore Thee, O hidden Deity,
Truly hidden beneath these visible things,
My whole heart submits to Thee,
Because it fails completely in contemplating Thee (my translation).

How can human language about God, which is nothing more than stuttering and stammering, do what *DI* claims that Christianity does, namely, *grasp and manifest the truth about God in its globality and completeness*? Can *DI* point to any church teaching or papal encyclical or theological work that does this? Where is the *latens Deitas* that Thomas adores devoutly? Where is the submission of the whole heart and the acknowledgment of complete intellectual failure before God that he commends?

Second, even if God has totally revealed Godself to us—and I believe God has—as I have argued in the last chapter, it does not at all follow that the church as a whole, much less the hierarchical magisterium by itself alone, can grasp what God has revealed in its globality and completeness. Even the Fourth Gospel concludes with these words: "But there are also many other things that Jesus did, if every one of them were written down, I suppose that the world itself could not contain the books that would be written" (John 21:25). John's disclaimer is not just a rhetorical device to forestall future attacks against his lack of "globality" and "completeness"; rather it is a humble acknowledgment of the infinite riches of God's revelation in Jesus that nothing ("the world itself") can contain or "grasp" and "manifest." Where is the teaching of St. John of the Cross in his *Ascent to Mount Carmel,* in which he makes the soul exclaim *nada, nada, nada* (nothing, nothing, nothing) at the moment it reaches the top of the mountain because God is "Pure Darkness" that our finite intellect can never fully grasp and manifest?

Third, to say that Jesus as a Jew living in Palestine in the first century of the Common Era was limited in his ability to reveal God is not the same as saying that his revelation is "limited, incomplete, or imperfect." Jesus, as the eschatological (last) prophet, truthfully tells us what we need to know about who God is, and therefore we do not need to wait for another prophet who would presumably give a fuller revelation of God; *in this sense*

Jesus's revelation of God is complete, perfect, and final. But this does not mean that Jesus has said everything and exhaustively and in every perfect way possible what he could have said about God. (How can the CDF tell if this is the case?). After all, Jesus's linguistic skills were limited (he knew Hebrew and Aramaic, and possibly a smattering of Greek and Latin words); his formal education was minimal; his cultural horizon was severely limited (Jewish, and a bit of Greek and Roman); his religious background was monolithic (Judaism); his life was relatively brief (a little over thirty years).

In short, in no way can Jesus be regarded as a "cultured" person by today's standards. (With regard to the end of time he explicitly admits, "But about that day and hour no one knows, neither the angels in heaven, nor the Son, but only the Father" [Matthew 24:36].) With all these and other limitations, he could but reveal God with whatever limited means he had at his disposal. *In this sense* Jesus's revelation of God remains "limited," "incomplete," or "imperfect"; to say this is *not*, pace *DI*, "contrary to the Church's faith." This being the case, there can be no objection to saying that if there is a holy and wise religious teacher in India (for example, the Buddha), in China (for example, Laozi or Confucius), or in Arabia (for example, Mohammad) whose teaching and practice can help us know and love God better, they "complement" the revelation of Jesus, as least in the sense that they can teach us new insights about God using Indian, Chinese, or Arab cultures and religious ideas, which of course Jesus could not do.

Fourth, that the church as a *historical religion*, which is made up of sinful people from top to bottom, needs the help ("complement") of non-Christians to put into perfect practice Jesus's teaching, requires no demonstration. (How could the CDF deny this with a straight face when as it was composing *DI*, it was handling cases of clergy sex abuse, which would have been buried under episcopal protection had it not been for the media?) Furthermore, there are abundant examples of how the church has been enriched by other religions in areas such as spirituality, monasticism, non-violence, respect for nature, without which it cannot grasp and manifest "the truth about God in its globality and completeness."

The Asian Faces of Jesus

It comes as no surprise then that there have been in recent years a huge number of works that try to understand who Jesus was as a Jew[5]

---

[5] Although studies of Jesus as a Jew, by both Christian and Jewish biblical schol-

as well as who Jesus is from the perspective of the peoples of the Third World, or Two-Thirds World, or the Majority World, or the Global South (Africa, Asia, and Latin America). In addition, there are myriad studies of how Jesus can be represented differently in terms of race, ethnicity, gender, class, culture, nationality, and religion, most often from the vantage point of excluded and marginalized people. It is not my interest here, nor it is feasible, to expound all of these liberationist Christologies.[6] Rather my focus here is on how Asian theologians have painted Jesus's face, so to speak, with Asian features and to see what importance they have attached to the issue of the unicity and salvific universality of Jesus as Savior.

Briefly, in the early stages of Asian theological development, inculturation or contextualization of the Christian faith was done primarily by making use of dominant cultural symbols, classical philosophy, and religious beliefs and practices to depict an Asian face of Christ. Thus, for instance, in India, extensive use is made of Hinduism, especially as expressed in the Vedanta; in China, it is Confucianism; and in other countries, such as Japan, Korea, and Sri Lanka, it is Buddhism. While such approach is admittedly legitimate and fruitful, it has been severely criticized for being elitist and above all, for neglecting other cultural and religious traditions, especially those that have been marginalized and oppressed by the economic, political, and religious ruling class. Ironically, Jesus, whom inculturationists attempt to render meaningful to particular contexts, ends up being made complicit to such domination of the poor and the marginalized people.[7]

In response to this critique, recent Asian Christologies have turned to the cultures and religions of the oppressed groups and made use of them

---

ars, are not directly connected with my concern here, nevertheless they are of huge importance because they retrieve Jesus's historical, sociopolitical, cultural, and religious particularities—and thus his manifold limitedness—that have been eclipsed either by dogmatic concerns to emphasize his divinity and universality or by overt and covert anti-Judaism that has been an undercurrent in Christian tradition.

[6] See, for instance, Martien E. Brinkman, *The Non-Western Jesus: Jesus as Bodhisattva, Avatara, Guru, Prophet, Ancestor or Healer?* (London: Equinox, 2007); Clinton Bennett, *In Search of Jesus: Insider and Outsider Images* (London: Continuum, 2001); Volker Küster, *The Many Faces of Jesus Christ* (Maryknoll, NY: Orbis Books, 2001); Gregory A. Barker, ed., *Jesus in the World's Faiths: Leading Thinkers from Five Religions Reflect on His Meaning* (Maryknoll, NY: Orbis Books, 2005); and Gene L. Green, Stephen T. Pardue, and K. K. Yeo, *Jesus without Borders: Christology in the Majority World* (Grand Rapids, MI: Eerdmans, 2014).

[7] See Aloysius Pieris, *An Asian Theology of Liberation* (Maryknoll, NY: Orbis Books, 1988), 87–96.

to represent Christ the Savior as the liberator from any and every form
of oppression. Thus, in India, there are Dalit (the "broken" outcasts) and
Tribal Christs; in Korea, there is Christ the Minjung (the people); and in
patriarchal cultures, there is Christ the Woman, and so on.[8]

Here I will give a rapid survey of these two trends of Asian Christology,
the inculturationist and the liberationist, by summarizing a book by the
Indian Jesuit Michael Amaladoss, whose writings have also come under the
CDF's scrutinizing eyes.[9] In his book *The Asian Jesus*, Amaladoss is careful
to point out that he is not constructing a dogmatic-systematic Christology
through a comparative study of the Christian doctrines about Christ and
the religious concepts of other religions.[10] Rather he intends to explore
the possibility of understanding better who Jesus is through the use of the
religious symbols of other religions. He begins by surveying the images of
Jesus used in the Bible and the Christian Tradition, such as the incarnated
Logos, Lord, Suffering Servant, High Priest, Word of God, and Liberator.
He then lists the images that non-Christian Asian religious thinkers have
drawn from their own religions to describe who Christ is for them: moral
teacher, avatar (incarnation of God), *satyagrahi* (fighter for truth), *advaitin*
(one who has a nondual relationship with God), and bodhisattva (the Buddha of mercy).

The major part of the book is dedicated to developing images of Jesus
that are rooted in both the Christian faith and Asian cultural and religious traditions, namely, Jesus as the Sage, the Way, the Guru, the *Satyagrahi*,
the Avatar, the Servant, the Compassionate, the Dancer, and the Pilgrim.
Amaladoss is well aware of the profound differences in the understandings
of these images between the Christian tradition and the Asian religions. He
is not proposing a simplistic identification between the Christian understandings of Christ and these images, much less some kind of dogmatic

---

[8] For a helpful introduction to Asian Christologies, see Vimal Tirimanna, ed., *Asian
Faces of Christ* (Bangalore: Asian Trading Corporation, 2005).

[9] For Amaladoss's brief statement of his theology of religion written in response
to the CDF's request, see his "Other Religions and the Salvific Mystery of Christ,"
Vidyajotti Journal of Theological Reflections 70 (2006) 8–26.

[10] See Michael Amaladoss, *The Asian Jesus* (Maryknoll, NY: Orbis Books, 2006).
Of course, some type of comparison is unavoidable, but Amaladoss avers: "I would like
to keep this comparison at the level of language and symbol and not get into the area
of philosophical and theological reflection where it becomes comparative theology"
(ibid., 7).

syncretistic synthesis. Rather, "symbols," he recalls the French philosopher Paul Ricoeur's celebrated saying, "give rise to thought," and thus they invite us to discover and test correspondences among things that at first sight appear to have no connections among themselves, and thus promote a deeper understanding of them.

Underlying Amaladoss's cross-cultural and interreligious explorations in Christology for Asia, as well as other Asian theologians' attempts at inculturating the Christian beliefs in Jesus Christ into the Asian contexts is the conviction that Jesus, a Jew of the first century of the Common Era, and his words and deeds have meaning and relevance for the Asian peoples. One would not undertake such a task if one believes that Jesus is so unique that he cannot be understood by anyone except Christians. In this sense, these Asian theologians acknowledge that Jesus and his message of salvation have a universal relevance and impact on the followers of other religions as well as unbelievers.

However, as explained earlier, they also recognize that this "unicity" and "salvific universality" of Jesus are matters of the Christian faith and cannot be rationally and historically proved. Attempts at finding symbols and images in Asian cultures and religions that may have "deep resonances," as the FABC's document *The Spirit at Work in Asia Today* puts it, with what Christians believe about Jesus is not intended to *prove* that Jesus is the only one Savior, or that only he is the Sage, the Way, the Guru, the *Satyagrahi*, the Avatar, the Servant, the Compassionate, the Dancer, and the Pilgrim, and that the other religious figures, such as Confucius or the Buddha, are not, or that he is superior to all of them, singly or combined, or that he saves them all, or that Christianity is the only true and the highest religion. Such statements, as I have argued above, cannot in principle be proved on empirical evidence. Whether Christians can and should assert those statements as matters of *faith* in their encounter with people of other faiths is quite another matter, which I will take up in the chapter on church and mission.

An Interreligious Christology: A Possibility and a Desideratum?

In the final pages of this chapter, I would like to go beyond what Michael Amaladoss and other theologians have done and explore the possibility and even desirability of what I call an "interreligious/interfaith Christology." At first sight, "interfaith Christology" seems to be an oxymoron since by definition Christology is a faith-based reflection on the *Christian* confession in Jesus as the Christ. Yet, in a globalized age such as ours, and within the contemporary context of religious pluralism, it would seem that such theological reflection can no longer be done only confessionally. Hence, the question of the possibility and desirability of an "interfaith Christology." By this expression I do not mean simply a Christology undertaken by Christians on the basis of the Christian faith in dialogue with the beliefs of other religions; such Christology might be termed *dialogical Christology*. Rather, I would like to consider the possibility and desirability of a Christology constructed by Christians and non-Christians alike, ideally in collaboration with one another, on the common beliefs and practices of different religious traditions. Such a Christology replaces neither the classical Christology based solely on the Bible and the Christian tradition, which still retains its necessity and validity, nor the dialogical Christology that considers the Christian beliefs in Jesus as normative and seeks to enrich itself from the insights of non-Christian religions. What I am presenting here is more a programmatic manifesto for than a systematic elaboration of interfaith Christology.

Interfaith Christology:
Possibility, Limits, Desirability

The possibility of interfaith Christology by necessity rests on the kind of interreligious dialogue in which participants genuinely respect differences and try to understand religions other than one's own as they present themselves, on their own terms, and avoid interpreting them through the lens of one's categories and belief system. These differences do not of course preclude commonalities, or at least analogues, among religions, but they must not be papered over or minimized, much less homogenized as merely various ways of talking about absolute Spirit, God, or the ultimate, or the real.

Concerning the possibility of interfaith Christology, it will be objected at once that "Christology" is by definition a Christian category; and therefore calling the projected interreligious enterprise a "Christology" already violates the above hermeneutical principle. The point is well taken, but the objection can be obviated by the following considerations. First, "Christ," both as a term and a concept, is per se not restricted to Christianity; it is found in Judaism (the "messiah"), and the figure of Jesus is also present in the Qur'an. Consequently, at least as far as Judaism and Islam are concerned, an interfaith Christology is legitimate and not a prima facie impossibility.

Second, it is possible to speak of "Christology" without making the Christian claims about Christ, such as his divinity, resurrection, unique and universal role as Savior, and so forth, the starting point and norm of the interreligious discourse, even though these claims must not be dissimulated by the Christian partners-in-dialogue. In other words, it is possible to discuss the *meaning* of a statement (which concerns *understanding*) and thereby enriching our understanding of it without affirming its *truth* at the same time (which is an exercise of *judgment in faith*). In this kind of interfaith Christology as an exercise in understanding, the Christian claims about Christ are not denied a priori. They are theologically assumed but methodologically bracketed with the goal to arrive at a richer and pluralistic understanding of what constitutes the Christ on the basis of what Christianity and other religions say about the "Christ."

Third, strictly speaking, just as a Christian speaks of an interfaith Christology, a Buddhist can rightfully speak of an interfaith "Buddhology," a Hindu an interfaith "Krishnology," a Muslim an interfaith "Qur'anology" and perhaps "Muhammadology," a Sikh an interfaith "gurology," and so on. The point of interfaith Christology is not to demonstrate that the Christ of Christians is unique, universal, and superior to all other religious figures, or vice versa. It bears repeating that in principle a rational demonstration of such a claim is impossible since it is essentially an affirmation of faith. Rather it is to obtain as profound and diverse an understanding as possible of the Christ on the basis of the most varied and even contradictory affirmations of different religions on what makes a particular being (e.g., Siddhārtha Gautama, Jesus of Nazareth, or Muhammad) the "Christ."

Thus conceived, interfaith Christology no doubt has limitations. The most obvious one is that it is not a dogmatic Christology and hence would be judged by those seeking an orthodox Christology theologically inappropriate and even heterodox in light of, for instance, Chalcedonian Christology. Nor is it a "historical Christology," a "Christology from below," or an "ascending Christology" insofar as it is not based on the Gospels' account of Jesus's life and ministry, and is not designed to show that Jesus is the Word of God made flesh. In this respect it lacks the historical specificity characteristic of, for example, liberation Christology of various stripes (e.g., black, Latin American, Asian, feminist, ecological, etc.). Finally, it does not perform the apologetic function of a "transcendental Christology" such as that proposed by Karl Rahner, intended to explicate the conditions of possibility for the faith in Jesus as the Christ on the basis of a metaphysics of human knowledge and love.

Nevertheless, interfaith Christology, while distinct from the three above-mentioned Christologies, does not exclude them, but rather helps clarify some of their key concepts, one of which is of course the "Christ." Given the religiously pluralistic situation of our time and the urgent need for mutual understanding and collaboration among followers of different religions, such interfaith Christology arguably is a desideratum if not a pressing necessity for contemporary theology. Whether it is feasible cannot be settled a priori, nor should it be rejected simply because of potential errors and weaknesses. At least an outline of its general features may be attempted.

Contour of an Interfaith Christology

The central concept to be elaborated in interfaith Christology is of course the "Christ." Here an apparently unsurmountable challenge immediately surfaces. The term "Christ," and more crucially, the concept of "Christ"—at least as it is understood in Christianity—are not espoused by all religious traditions, and where the concept is used, it is far from univocal. Hence, a major task of an interfaith Christology is to determine the meaning of "Christ" and its place, if any, in a particular religion. In this conceptual elaboration of the "Christ," the Christian understanding of Jesus as the Christ, as pointed out above, can play a heuristic role but not a normative one. It must be correlated with concepts and images present in other religions that exhibit significant similarities or functional analogies with it. A new and enlarged understanding of the "Christ" may thus be construed out of these critically correlated concepts and images, and the result may be termed a "comparative" or "interfaith" Christology.

Which are, to begin with, the main features of the Christian concept of the Christ? A straightforward answer to this question is impossible since it is universally acknowledged that the Jesus of the Gospels fits no single description. He is, yet is not, in the usual sense of the words, a priest, a prophet, an apocalyptic seer, a rabbi, a teacher of wisdom, a miracle worker, a political leader. In the eyes of New Testament scholars, as Colin Greene notes, Jesus was variously a cynic, a mystic, a healer, a *hasid*, a prophet or the eschatological prophet, a reformer, a sage, personified wisdom, and a/the messiah.[11]

---

[11] Colin J. D. Greene, *Christology in Cultural Perspective: Marking Out the Horizons* (Grand Rapids, MI: Eerdmans, 2003), 6–15.

Until modernity, Christology, Greene goes on to show, emphasizes Jesus (1) as the eternal Logos made flesh (cosmological Christology), (2) as "Lord of lords and King of kings" (political Christology), and (3) as the New Adam (anthropological Christology).[12] Here, my interest is not to show how these three traditional Christologies have been challenged and emended in modernity and postmodernity,[13] but to use them as a launching pad for outlining an interfaith Christology.

Underlying these divergent Christologies, I suggest, is the notion that somehow in Jesus, however his historical role is interpreted, humans are given the possibility of fulfilling their nature and reaching their ultimate goal, referred to in theistic language as union with God and in nontheistic language as self-transcendence (e.g., liberation, enlightenment, salvation, redemption, transformation, etc.). This is central to the notion of the "Christ," apart from the concrete and historical way(s) in which such possibility of self-realization is realized. The basic question then is whether such a notion is found in religions other than Christianity (the answer to which is of course affirmative), and how they can be used to construct an interfaith Christology.

Concomitant with the notion of the Christ is that of a supernatural or superhuman power by which the Christ achieves his or her mission of bringing humans and the cosmos to fulfillment. The Christian faith confesses that this superhuman power is a gift of the risen Christ and that together with the Father and the Son, this personal power, who is named the "Holy Spirit," constitutes the Trinity, as I have shown in the previous chapter. Various symbols and images, such as breath, wind, fire, water, and dove, have been used to describe the Spirit's transformative power. Since the Spirit is the power by which both the Christ himself and all humans achieve their goals, it is theologically proper to preface interfaith Christology with pneumatology, as I have done so far. In fact, methodologically, from the Christian point of view, Christology, especially an interfaith one, makes more sense if we begin with the Spirit, then move to the Son, and end with the Father.

Since the Spirit is not embodied in any particular historical person, it is easier to find analogies—not identical entities—for the Christian concept of Spirit in non-Christian religions, such as *atman/brahman* in *advaita* Hinduism, *shakti* in classical Hinduism, *antaryamin* in *bhakti* Hinduism, *ch'i*

---

[12] Ibid., 30–71.

[13] On this, see Greene's study cited above.

in Daoism and Confucianism, the *yin* of the *yin-yang* polarity, and spirits in general, as the FABC's document *The Spirit at Work in the Asia Today* has done. Nor should an interfaith pneumatology limit itself to religious and philosophical sources. Since the Spirit is associated with freedom, it has often functioned as the source and inspiration for revolution and the struggle for personal and national independence.

Forerunners of Interfaith Christology

An interfaith Christology is essentially a Spirit or pneumatological Christology consisting in an elaboration on the work of Jesus as the Christ by virtue of the Spirit in bringing about humanity's union with God and/ or human self-realization. With pneumatology as its prolegomenon, inter-faith Christology can move forward to consider the many titles that have been ascribed to the Christ in the Christian tradition and inquire whether similar titles are also found in non-Christian religions, not to establish their conceptual equivalence, much less their truth, but in order to obtain a richer understanding of what the Christ means.

Mention has already been made of the figure of the Christ in Judaism and Islam, and studies on this theme are plentiful.[14] In addition, comparative studies between Jesus and Krishna, between Jesus and Confucius, between Jesus and other religious figures abound.[15]

An irony in the development of such interfaith "Christology" is that its most significant pioneers were not Christians but Hindus. The writings of Sri Ramakrishna, Swami Vivekananda, Keshub Chunder Sen, Mohandas Gandhi, Swami Akhiananda, and Sarvepalli Radhakrishnan are well known. Among Christian Indians, Manilal C. Parekh and Bhawami Charan Banerji (also known as Brahmabandhab Upadhyaya) were influential.[16] Among con-

---

[14] The literature is immense. On Jesus in Judaism, see the comprehensive articles by Susannah Heschel, "Jewish Views of Jesus" and Jacob Nuesner, "Why Jesus Has No Meaning to Judaism," in Barker, ed., *Jesus in the World's Faith*, 149–60 and 166–73, respectively. On Jesus in Islam, see Muhammad Ata ur-Rahim, *Jesus Prophet of Islam* (Elmhurst, NY: Tahrike Tarsile Qur'an, 1991); Tarif Khalidi, *The Muslim Jesus: Sayings and Stories in Islamic Literature* (Cambridge, MA: Harvard University Press, 2001).

[15] For an overview, see Clinton Bennet, *In Search of Jesus: Insider and Outsider Images* (New York: Continuum, 2001), 292–344.

[16] See the studies by M. M. Thomas, *The Acknowledged Christ of the Indian Renaissance* (Madras, India: Christian Literature Society, 1970); Stanley Samartha, *The Hindu Response to the Unbound Christ* (Bangalore, India: IISRS, 1974).

temporary Buddhist leaders, the works of the Dalai Lama and the Zen Vietnamese Buddhist monk Thich Nhat Hanh should be noted.[17]

Among contemporary Christian theologians M. M. Thomas,[18] Stanley Samartha,[19] George M. Soares-Prabhu,[20] Raimon Panikkar,[21] Samuel Rayan,[22] Michael Amaladoss,[23] Aloysius Pieris,[24] Roger Haight,[25] Thomas Thangaraj,[26] *Minjung* theologians, and Asian women theologians,[27] to cite only a few, have offered valuable insights into how an interfaith Christology can be constructed. Such a Christology is still in its infancy, but its future looks bright.

"From the beginning, the community of believers has recognized in Jesus a salvific value such that he alone, as Son of God made man, crucified and risen, by the mission received from the Father and in the power of the Holy Spirit, bestows revelation (cf. Mt 11:27) and divine life (cf. Jn 1:12; 5:25–26; 17:2) to all humanity and to every person. In this sense, one can and must say that Christ has a significance and value for the human race and its history, which are unique and singular, proper to him alone, exclusive, universal and absolute," so declares *DI* (no. 15). One cannot fail to notice the frenetic, almost frantic crescendo in the string of adjectives denoting the "unicity" and "salvific universality" of Jesus as Savior. A cynic,

---

[17] See The Dalai Lama, *The Good Heart: A Buddhist Perspective on the Teachings of Jesus* (Somerville, MA: Wisdom Publications, 1996); Thich Nhat Hanh, *Living Buddha, Living Christ* (New York: Riverhead Books, 1995); *Going Home: Jesus and Buddha as Brothers* (New York: Riverhead Books, 1999). See also Marcus Borg, *Jesus and Buddha: The Parallel Stories* (Berkeley, CA: Ulysses Press, 1997).

[18] See Thomas, *The Acknowledged Christ of the Indian Renaissance.*

[19] See Samartha, *The Hindu Response to the Unbound Christ.*

[20] See George M. Soares-Prabhu, *The Dharma of Jesus* (Maryknoll, NY: Orbis Books, 2003).

[21] Raimon Panikkar, *A Dwelling Place for Wisdom* (Louisville, KY: Westminster/John Knox, 1993).

[22] Samuel Rayan, *The Holy Spirit: Heart of the Gospel and Christian Hope* (Maryknoll, NY: Orbis Books, 1978).

[23] Michael Amaladoss, *The Asian Jesus* (Maryknoll, NY: Orbis Books, 2006).

[24] Aloysius Pieris, *Love Meets Wisdom: A Christian Experience of Buddhism* (Maryknoll, NY: Orbis Books, 1988).

[25] Roger Haight, *Jesus Symbol of God* (Maryknoll, NY: Orbis, 1999).

[26] Thomas Thangaraj, *The Crucified Guru: An Experiment in Cross-Cultural Christology* (Nashville, TN: Abingdon Press, 1994).

[27] See Muriel Orevillo-Montenegro, *The Jesus of Asian Women* (Maryknoll, NY: Orbis Books, 2006).

like the Queen in Shakespeare's *Hamlet,* would have said, "The lady doth
protest too much, methinks." I hope, however, that the foregoing reflections
will be of help in parsing the various expressions of the CDF's Declaration.
For one thing, as one venerable professor of church history of mine used
to warn with a twinkle in his eye, "From the beginning," when applied to
the life of the church, always raises a red flag. Secondly, one should carefully
exegete the four supporting New Testament passages adduced by *DI* to
see if they *really* and *exactly* say what it claims them to say, which is highly
debatable. Lastly, and most importantly, we can and should understand those
terms—*unique, singular, alone, exclusive, universal,* and *absolute*—in ways that
do not make them sound like they are making an empirically verifiable
statement, or denying the many and diverse ways in which Divine Spirit
can and does work in the world with its two hands, at times better with
one, at other times better with the other, always with both, in mutual collaboration, but not one in subjection to the other.

Like the Japanese American girl at the Narita International Airport,
Christians can certainly profess our faith in Jesus as our Savior. But, perhaps like her, we will avoid using words, albeit traditional and appropriate
in the past, that sound to exclude God's other ways, ways that are testified
by the anthropological observation: Japanese are born as Shinto, marry as
Christian, and die as Buddhist.

Perhaps the most fitting conclusion to this chapter is the witness of
Doug Venn, an American Maryknoll priest and a veteran missionary to
the Philippines and Bangladesh, whom I was blessed to know. I first met
him in Bangkok, Thailand, some twenty years ago, when I was lecturing
on mission to a group of Maryknoll missionaries. (I never felt more of a
fraud pontificating to this group of veteran missionaries to Asia on how
to be missionaries!). I was honored to be among those invited to celebrate
Doug's Fiftieth Jubilee of priestly ordination in 2009. His main "missionary" activities in Bangladesh consisted in working in the farm field with
other Muslim workers. One day, he heard his Muslim companions shout,
"Islam is the greatest! Islam is the greatest!" He said he did not know what
brought this on and just hanged his head in silence for a little while, and
then thought to himself: "Let Islam be the greatest. Jesus taught us to be
the least, the servant of all." Then he raised his head in confidence and "felt
at home with them all."

CHAPTER 5

Holy Pagans in Other Holy Religions

The Salvific Significance of Non-Christian Religions?

The title of this chapter contains a rather quaint term, *pagan*. It used to be the standard term for Christians to refer to the followers of other religions other than Judaism and Islam, at least up to Vatican II (1962–65). In the past, to declare someone a "pagan" (or "heathen") was tantamount to saying that he or she is destined to eternal damnation. At the General Council of Florence (1442) the Roman Catholic Church declared that it "firmly believes, professes and preaches that no one remaining outside the Catholic Church, not only pagans, but also Jews, heretics or schismatics, can become partakers of eternal life, but they will go to the eternal fire prepared for the devil and his angels unless before the end of their life they are received into it."[1]

Today this term is no longer officially used in the Catholic Church to refer to non-Christians. Even the term *non-Christian*, albeit unavoidable as a sociological category, sounds patronizing and disrespectful, from the religious point of view, to the people of other faiths, as though their religions can only be defined in relation to Christianity and not on their own terms. How would a Christian feel if his or her Christian identity is defined as "non-Hindu"? In this way, the "other" is only understood in terms of oneself, as different from and inferior to oneself, oneself being the norm by which the other is evaluated. It is well to remember throughout this chapter this distorting and potentially imperialistic theological bias that is built into our Christian discourse about other religions.

---

[1] See Joseph Neuner and Jacques Dupuis, eds., *The Christian Faith in the Doctrinal Documents of the Catholic Church* (New York: Alba House, 1982), 277–78.

Theologically, after Vatican II, it is no longer orthodox, at least for Catholics, to hold that Jews, Muslims, and other non-Christians will "go to the eternal fire prepared for the devil and his angels," unless before their death they join the Catholic Church, as the Council of Florence solemnly taught. How to reconcile this new-found truth with the solemn (and infallible?) teaching of the Council of Florence is a question for agile theological minds to resolve. However this vexing question is answered, at least since Vatican II, the question of the possibility of salvation for non-Christians is no longer in doubt. In its Dogmatic Constitution on the Church (*Lumen Gentium*), after listing the various groups of non-Christians (that is, Jews, Muslims, and "those who in shadows and images seek the unknown God"), the council declares, "Those who, through no fault of their own, but who nevertheless seek God with a sincere heart, and, moved by grace, try in their actions to do his will as they know it through the dictates of their conscience—these too may attain eternal salvation" (no. 16).

Granted that non-Christians may be saved, what and/or who is the cause of their salvation? For Vatican II, the source of all salvation is Jesus Christ, more precisely, it is God the Father who saves humankind in and through Christ and by the power of the Spirit. In addition, non-Christians are said to be "related" (*ordinantur*) in various ways to the People of God (*Lumen Gentium*, no. 16). But there still remains a question, which Vatican II declines to answer: even granted that a person's salvation is to be attributed to God who acts in and through Christ and by the power of the Spirit, what role if any is to be assigned to the religions to which the non-Christian persons who are supposedly saved belong? To put it concretely, if a Buddhist is saved, is he or she saved in and through Buddhism as a complex of beliefs and practices, or in spite of it? Does Buddhism play a role analogous—not identical—to that of Christianity in that person's salvation?

The subtitle of this chapter is borrowed from the second section of the United States Conference of Catholic Bishops' Committee on Doctrine (CD)'s critical statement on my book *Being Religious Interreligiously*. What is meant by the expression *salvific significance* and what the CD intends by "the salvific significance of non-Christian religions" will be elaborated in due course. Let it be noted here that my conjunctions of "holy" with "pagans" and of "holy pagans" with "holy religions" are deliberate. "Holy Pagans in Other Holy Religions" is a convenient shorthand for my current understanding of the role of religions in salvation that is the focus of this chapter.

A New Context for a Christian Theology of Religion

Allow me to tell you my experiences in Chiang Mai, Thailand, in June 2007 as the context of my reflections on non-Christian religions. This is not a self-indulgent trip down memory lane but a necessary and fruitful way of doing theology. Theology is unavoidably contextual. As has been pointed out in the second chapter, the context is not simply the venue in which theology is done but provides resources for theology as well as the lens through which the Christian doctrines are interpreted. Thus, the various sociopolitical, cultural, and religious contexts of Asia are the sources of new theological insights.

I was invited to deliver a lecture at a conference on "World Christianity" and its encounter with other religions at the University of Payap, a Church of Christ in Thailand institution, located in Chiang Mai, a city of enchanting beauty in mountainous northwest Thailand. As customary during academic conferences, there was a free day for sightseeing. Participants were given a tour of Wat Phrathat Doi Suthep, one of the most famous Buddhist pagodas in Thailand, built by King Keu Naone of the Lanna Kingdom in 1383 on a mountain at 1,676 meters above the city of Chiang Mai. Dominating the whole pagoda, which is reached by mounting 309 steps, is a monumental golden statue of a sitting Buddha in serene meditation.

Throngs of pilgrims, young and old, women and men, rich and poor, ritually circumambulated the statue in prayerful silence, hands clasped at their chests. Others stood in front of the Buddha, incense sticks in their hands, eyes closed, lips murmuring prayers. There was of course the usual number of tourists, but the vast majority were pious faithful worshiping in utter devotion. There was none of the hustling and chattering I have seen at Catholic pilgrimage centers and even in Saint Peter's Basilica in Rome. The atmosphere was suffused with an awe-inspiring aura of sacredness. I was told that on certain feasts, pilgrims would go on foot, sometimes on their knees, from the bottom of the mountain up to the monastery, a pilgrimage that would take days.

After the conference, I stayed another day to see the city of Chiang Mai. I hiked to one of the most famous pagodas mentioned in the tour guide, Wat U-Mong, just on the outskirts of the city. There were heavy, smoke-spewing traffic and ear-splitting din around the pagoda, but inside the pagoda enclosure, there was an eerie peace and tranquility. There were several small pagodas where people came in and out for prayer and a garden with

Buddhist proverbs in Thai and English on display on the trees to help the faithful meditate as they walk along the path. Deep silence reigned everywhere on this sacred ground; even birds seemed to cease twittering.

In the middle of the compound stood the main pagoda, majestic and magnificent. In it there were several statues of the Buddha and his disciples, with a huge golden Buddha placed at the center of a high stage near the back. On the left side there was an altar on which there was a sitting statue of Kwan Yin, commonly known as the Goddess of Mercy, whom many Asian Catholics regard as the equivalent of Mother Mary. As I walked toward it, I saw a young woman sitting in a lotus position a short distance in front of the statue, her head slightly bowed. Not to disturb her, I moved quietly to the back and sat on the floor about twenty feet behind her. Intrigued by this figure immersed in prayer, I decided to stay for a while. For nearly three-quarters of an hour, the young woman sat, wrapped in prayer and meditation, not a limb twitching, not a turning of the head, preternaturally still, like the unrippled water of an autumnal pond, under the loving gaze of the Buddha of Compassion, as people walked by. I was irresistibly moved to pray—to the Christian God *and* to Kwan Yin—by this Buddhist devotee. When I left, the young woman was still praying there, for how much longer I would never know.

On my way back to the hotel, as I walked the meandering streets of Chiang Mai, my mind was haunted by memories of the throngs of Buddhist devotees at Wat Phrathat Doi Suthep and of the praying young woman in Wat U-Mong. It was not the first time that I was blessed with opportunities to witness non-Christian worship and prayer. Several years earlier, I visited the Blue Mosque in Istanbul. It happened to be Ramadan and I was deeply moved by the sight of hundreds of Muslims on their knees, bowing to the ground in unison, as they expressed their total submission to Allah.

Also, years ago, during a conference on interreligious dialogue in New Delhi, India, I was sharing a room with a Nigerian imam. He woke up several times during the night to pray while I was enjoying my sweet slumber. At the airport, he rolled out his prayer mat and turned toward Mecca to pray, unostentatiously, while several Catholic hierarchs and I were enjoying drinks at the bar waiting for our flights. The imam had told me earlier that it would be impossible to lead an immoral life if one prays five times a day.

During the same conference in New Delhi, I visited a Sikh gurdwara and listened in awe as the Ādi Granth, the Sikh sacred Scripture, was continuously chanted, with a piety and devotion far surpassing anything I have ever experienced during biblical readings at Catholic liturgies. Near the entrance to the temple, food was distributed to visitors of all faiths, and both the rich and the poor partook of it, all sitting on the floor, as a sign of equality and solidarity, a powerful image of the Eucharist. Shortly afterward, a Sikh from Punjab, unasked, took off his turban and bracelet, symbols of Sikhism, and gave them to me to make me, in his words, an "honorary Sikh." On another day during the same trip, I was blessed to be present at a worship ritual of Krishna, where his devotees taught me through their example how to worship the Deity with utter joy and devotion.

I call all these opportunities, and countless others, "blessings" because I consider them to be God's gracious gifts, as precious as the gift of the Christian faith. I do not, however, claim to have any epistemological privilege or superior knowledge on account of these experiences. But I must confess that they have transformed me, for better or for worse, both spiritually and intellectually. They have taught me new ways of relating to the divine as well as stimulated me to examine anew traditional Catholic teachings on non-Christian religions. As a result, I have often wondered whether the magisterial authorities who make self-assured pronouncements on the "objective deficiencies" of "non-Christian" religions had ever had these life-changing "blessings," and whether, had they had them, they would not have come up with a different theology of religion.[2]

Beside these exceptional experiences, having lived as a religious minority in Vietnam and elsewhere, I have been blessed with many non-Christian friends and neighbors who have shamed me with their kindness and generosity, their deep commitment to justice and peace, their piety and prayerfulness, their fidelity to the teachings and practices of their religions, and above all, by their profound spirituality, even though some of them never mention God. Furthermore, they have never tried to turn me into a Buddhist or a Muslim or a Hindu. Never have they told me that I cannot be a good person (or be "saved," if a Christian term is permitted) without joining their religions, though they are willing to share with me their beliefs and practices and defend them with intellectual vigor and passion.

In a certain sense I do not "know" Hinduism, Buddhism, or Islam, though I may claim to have acquired some scholarly understanding of them. I only "know" Buddhists, Muslims, and Hindus, as friends, and they

---

[2] See *DI*, no. 22.

have blessed and graced me with their friendship. I love and respect them, and they respect and love me, and this friendship has made a profound theological difference to my reflections on what has been termed "the salvific significance of non-Christian religions" and to my elaboration of a theology of religion.

Again, I have often wondered whether the magisterial authorities who produce documents such as *Dominus Iesus* (*DI*) have ever been graced with genuine and loving friendships with Hindus, Buddhists, and Muslims, with whom they would share food and drink, joys and sorrows, hopes and fears, prayers and religious experiences—as *equals* and as *beloved friends*—and not just as "non-Christians" to be evangelized. Perhaps then they would not feel even the need to proclaim the "unicity and salvific universality" of Christ and the necessity of the church as the only and universal means of salvation, because they see with their own eyes how holy these non-Christians already are, not rarely holier than they themselves, precisely by *practicing their religions.* This of course does not mean that Christians should not bear witness to what Jesus did and taught and to what the church can offer in terms of salvation—indeed, they must. But they can do so most effectively not primarily by words but by living a holy life—as least as holy as their non-Christian friends. Ironically, however, often it is non-Christians who challenge Christians to practice the Gospel message more faithfully.

In light of this, instead of teaching non-Christians first, Christian evangelists would do well to let themselves be taught by non-Christians how to be persons of integrity and humility, kindness and generosity, forgiveness and reconciliation, peace and justice, prayer and devotion, self-denial and sacrifice, without obsessing about the necessity to proclaim the "unicity and salvific universality" of Jesus and the duty to join the church in order to be saved. These "pagans" may teach them all this, without fanfare and arrogance, without dismissing Christianity as "objectively deficient" in comparison with their religions, and without claiming, as Hindus, that whatever is true and good and holy in Christianity is derived from the Hindu sacred writings that are hundreds of years older than the Gospels, or as Buddhists, from the Buddha who lived hundreds of years before Jesus, or as Muslims, from the Qur'an, the Arabic text of which is professed to be literally the Word of God itself. Without doing any of this, these non-Christians are, however, no less effective "evangelizers" for their religions than Christians for theirs. Nor have they succumbed to the "dictatorship of relativism" simply because they acknowledge that there are many different ways to God or, if they do not speak of God at all, to reach one's ultimate destiny.

These troubling thoughts and many others churned in my mind as I was heading back to the hotel in Chiang Mai. My ruminations were made all the more poignant by the fact that I was walking in the land where Catholic Christianity, even after five hundred years of evangelization, makes up only 0.044 percent of the Thai population. I wondered why the Thais, and the vast majority of Asians—perhaps some 95 percent of them—have not rushed to join the church that proclaims itself to be "the unique and universal instrument of salvation"—to use the caption of the third section of the CD's statement. Are these Thais and other Asians so intellectually obtuse, morally corrupt, and spiritually evil that they are unable to reject their religions, accept the truth of the Gospel, and convert to the church? Why aren't they capable of recognizing that whatever "elements of truth and grace" of their religions are derived from Jesus and the church and that their religions are "preparations for the Gospel," destined to be "fulfilled" in Christianity? Why can't they recognize that their religions are "objectively deficient," as *DI* characterizes them, and that their religions have no "autonomous" contributions whatsoever to make to their followers' moral and spiritual life, guiding them toward truth and goodness and holiness, or to use the Christian language, to function for them as "ways of salvation"?

Meanwhile let us return to Chiang Mai. How do we speak of non-Christian religions in a way that truly honors and learns from the devotion of the circumambulating Buddhist devotees at Wat Phrathat Doi Suthep? How do we speak of the church in a way that we Christians can be taught by that perfect embodiment of the *ecclesia orans* (the praying church), or better still, of the *humanitas orans et meditans* (the praying and meditating humanity) at Wat U-Mong, sitting at her feet to learn about praying, just as she sat the feet of Kwan Yin?

More radically, how should we speak about Christ and the church in a way that recognizes—humbly and gratefully—that those Thai "holy pagans" as well as my Hindu, Buddhist, and Muslims friends have achieved a level of holiness higher than that of many Christians, both clerical and lay—certainly higher than mine—not in spite of their religions but *thanks to and because of them*? How do we speak of the value of non-Christian religions in a way that accurately reflects the actual impact of their teachings, rituals,

and moral practices on their adherents and not on the basis of our preconceived notions of what they *must* be in relation to Christ and Christianity
as "non-Christian" religions?

To answer these questions and related issues adequately, we must develop
a theology of religion in light of and for the new context of religious pluralism of Asia. As a preliminary step, I will consider the teaching of Vatican
II on non-Christian religions. My intention here is not to present a comprehensive exposition of Vatican II's teaching on non-Christian religions,
much less of the contemporary Catholic theology of religion, especially the
important contribution of Pope John Paul II.[3] Rather, while acknowledging
the enormous advance Vatican II and John Paul II have made in reshaping
the Catholic appreciation of non-Christian religions, one of the problems
that block our full appreciation of other religions, I submit, is the very
methodological approach of the council itself, and its negative impact is
abundantly borne out in *DI*.

Vatican II on "Non-Christian" Religions: A Thought Experiment

The year 2015 marked the fiftieth anniversary of the end of the Second Vatican Council (1962–65). It was an opportune moment to celebrate the enormous achievements of the council as well as to chart a
future path for the church into the twenty-first century, especially under
the leadership of Pope Francis. Whether one extolls Vatican II as a new
Pentecost bringing much-needed renewal to the church that was out of
step with the world or condemns it as a disastrous capitulation to the
spirit of the age—and there are plenty of people on both sides—there
is no denying that the council has truly changed, for good or for ill, the
face of the Catholic Church. With regard to the church's attitude toward
non-Christian religions, it is common knowledge that Vatican II marked
a significant evolution—I for one would argue, revolution. Summarizing
the changed attitude between "before Vatican II" and "after Vatican II,"
Jacques Dupuis uses the expression "From Confrontation to Dialogue"

---

[3] Among legions of books on these themes, I recommend Jacques Dupuis, *Christianity and the Religions: From Confrontation to Dialogue* (Maryknoll, NY: Orbis Books,
2002).

as the subtitle of his book on the recent Christian theology of religion.[4] Perhaps "From Condemnation to Dialogue" may be a more accurate description. Vatican II's teaching on other religions are found chiefly in three documents: the Dogmatic Constitution on the Church (*Lumen Gentium*), the Decree on the Missionary Activity of the Church (*Ad Gentes*), and most importantly, in the *Declaration on the Relation of the Church to Non-Christian Religions* (*Nostra Aetate [NA]*). In what follows I will focus mainly on the last document, which, in spite of the fact that it is only a "declaration" and not a "constitution' or a "decree" and the shortest, with only 1,114 words, in forty-one sentences, and five paragraphs, is arguably one of the most influential documents of the council.

Salvation of Non-Christian Individuals

It is important for our theme to distinguish between the council's teaching on non-Christians as individuals and its teaching on non-Christian religions as institutions. With regard to non-Christians, whom the council calls "those who have not yet received the Gospel," Vatican II first of all, as mentioned above, affirms that they are "oriented [*ordinantur*] in various ways to the People of God." The council goes on to list five groups of non-Christians, apparently in the descending order of relationship to the church: (1) Jews, (2) Muslims, (3) "those who in shadows and images seek the unknown God," (4) those who "seek God with a sincere heart," and (5) those who "have not yet reached an explicit knowledge of God." The council affirms the possibility of salvation for all these non-Christians, though always by the grace of Christ and in some kind of relationship to the church, and with various conditions (e.g., "invincible ignorance" and living a good moral life according to their conscience).[5]

It is to be noted that the pivotal paragraph 16 of *Lumen Gentium* focuses only on non-Christians as individuals, though of course in so doing it also refers, albeit obliquely, to their religions, especially with regard to Jews and Muslims. On non-Christian religions as such, *Lumen Gentium* merely says that through the church's missionary activities "what-

---

[4] Jacques Dupuis, *Christianity and the Religions: From Confrontation to Dialogue* (Maryknoll, NY: Orbis Books, 2002).

[5] See *Lumen Gentium*, no. 16. English translation of Vatican II's documents is taken from *Vatican II*, general editor Austin Flannery (Northport, NY: Costello, 1996).

ever good is found sown in people's hearts and minds, or in the rites and customs of peoples, is not only saved from destruction, but is purified, raised up, and perfected for the glory of God, the confusion of the devil, and the happiness of humanity."[6]

The same idea is repeated in the council's decree on mission, *Ad Gentes*:

> It [missionary activity] purges of evil associations those elements of truth and grace which are found among peoples, and which are, as it were, a secret presence of God, and it restores them to Christ their source who overthrows the rule of the devil and limits the manifold malice of evil. So whatever goodness is found in people's minds and hearts, or in the particular customs and cultures of peoples, far from being lost is purified, raised to a higher level and reaches its perfection, for the glory of God, the confusion of the demon, and the happiness of humankind. (no. 9)

Vatican II's fullest teaching on non-Christian religions qua religions is found in *NA*. The council begins by noting the unity of all humankind by virtue of its common origin and destiny, namely, God. It sees religions as diverse attempts at answering fundamental questions concerning the meaning of human existence. It goes on to expound briefly on different non-Christian religions, from the so-called primitive religions to world religions such as Hinduism, Buddhism, Islam, and Judaism. In this context, the council declares that

> the Catholic Church rejects nothing of what is true and holy in these religions. It has a high regard for the manner of life and conduct, the precepts and doctrines which, although differing in many ways from its own teaching, nevertheless often reflect a ray of that truth which enlightens all men and women.[7]

By "that truth which enlightens all men and women," the council refers to the Word of God made flesh in Jesus, and in this way affirms a connection between non-Christian religions and the Word of God. How such a connection is to be understood, the council does not explain.

---

[6] *Lumen Gentium*, no. 17.

[7] *NA*, no. 2.

In addition to sincere respect, Vatican II urges dialogue with non-Christians. It exhorts Catholics "to enter with prudence and charity into discussion and collaboration with members of other religions" and "while witnessing to their own faith and way of life, acknowledge, preserve and encourage the spiritual and moral truths found among non-Christians, together with their social life and culture."[8] How this dialogue should be done and, more to the concern of this chapter, which theological benefits, if any, it brings to Christianity, the council does not elaborate.

Reading NA in Reverse: A Thought Experiment

Reading *NA* fifty years after its promulgation, in a context deeply sensitive to religious diversity, and with a profound awareness of the necessity of seeing the other as *other* and not as a mirror of oneself, opens our eyes to the weaknesses of *NA*, despite its many great theological advancements. Those of us, church officials as well as theologians, who work all of our lives exclusively in majority-Christian milieus, might miss the offensive tone in the title of *NA: Declaration on the Church's Relations to Non-Christian Religions (Declaratio de ecclesiae habitudine ad religiones non-christianas)*. The use of "non" as a prefix to refer to others different from oneself is perhaps an unavoidable anthropological and sociological shorthand to distinguish "us" from "them." But the negative naming of the "other" loses its innocence as an identity marker when it is used by a group that has consistently claimed to be superior to all others in all aspects of life. The "non," when applied to others, implies the absence, or at least an imperfect presence, of all the things that make this group the norm and standard of perfection for all others. Thus, during the height of empire and colonialism, such sobriquets as "non-Greek," "non-Roman," "non-Persian," "non-Turkish," "non-British," "non-Russian," "non-Han" (Chinese), "non-American," just to cite a few that have been associated with empires, are powerful weapons in the imperial and colonialist arsenals to categorize other peoples as uncivilized and barbarian. These "others" therefore need to be brought into the fold by means of the *mission civilisatrice*, often by conquest and subjugation. Such negative designation of the "other" is by no means a neutral nomenclature but is part and parcel of the imperial politics of difference and power.

---

[8] Ibid.

In no way am I implying that the bishops at Vatican II in using the expression "non-Christian" to refer to religions other than Christianity were harboring imperialistic ambitions, religious and otherwise. Indeed, after using this negative umbrella term in the title of the document, they go on naming specific religions such as Hinduism and Buddhism, and specific groups of religious individuals such as Muslims (not Islam) and Jews (not Judaism). Nevertheless, there are too many commonalities between Christianity and empire—after all it was an imperial religion for nearly two millennia—to dismiss the concerns about religious domination and conquest as overheated conspiracy theorizing or trivial terminological nitpicking.[9]

On the contrary, what is at stake in this negative naming is, I submit, deeply theological. The thought experiment I am proposing serves to illustrate this point. Imagine you are a member of one of the so-called non-Christian religions mentioned by *NA*. How would you self-identify religiously, let's say, on the census form, under the section "Religious Preference"? Is there a box marked "Non-Christian Religion" in addition to, for instance, Hinduism, Buddhism, Judaism, and Islam, that you can tick off? Of course not, since there are no "non-Christian religions" as such anytime, anywhere. And if "non-Christian religions" is used as a collective moniker for all religions except Christianity, only the specificity of Christianity as a religion is officially and publicly recognized, whereas the other religions are lumped together in a generic and undefined heap of the *hoi polloi.*

Let's pursue the thought experiment further: Suppose you are a Christian living in Asia, in a country with a Hindu, or Buddhist, or Muslim majority, and are filling out a census form, and the form does not include the category "Christian" but only "non-Hindu," "non-Buddhist" or "non-Muslim" categories for Christians to self-identify. You would very likely reject this categorization as chauvinistic and are well within your rights to protest such classification as academically inaccurate at best and religiously discriminatory at worst. Indeed, whenever such negative appellation is used, for instance, when proponents of the nationalistic Hindutva ideology called Indian Christians "non-Hindu," it was done with the intent to impugn their civic status, question their patriotism, and discriminate against them.

---

[9] Careful readers will have noticed that in many places I have used the term *non-Christian* to refer to religions other than Christianity. I have used it for convenience's sake but with a clear conviction that it is theologically improper and offensive.

The crux of the problem is of course not merely lexicology. Rather, beneath this terminological infelicity lies a theological perspective that goes under the name of "fulfillment theology of religion" and was widespread at Vatican II. What is troublesome, especially for believers in other religions, is that Christianity is used as the measure and standard, as the *vera religio* ("true religion," the common designation used by Christian theologians to designate Christianity), to classify and evaluate other religions. Though *NA*'s focus is the relation between Christianity and other religions, these religions are described *from the vantage point of Christianity* to show how far they measure up to it. In fact, it seems that *NA* lists the various religions in the ascending order of the degree of their agreements with Christianity—from the so-called primal religion through Hinduism and Buddhism to Muslims and lastly to Jews. It is perhaps because of this approach that *NA* does not mention other Indian religions such as Jainism and Sikhism and the Chinese religious traditions such as Confucianism and Daoism, as these religions do not appear to bear significant similarities with Christianity. Be that as it may, clearly the relation between Christianity and non-Christian religions is not conceived of as *reciprocal* but only *unidrectional*, that is, how other religions are related to Christianity, and, as we will see, how they can be "fulfilled" in Christianity, *and not the other way round.*

Of course, it must be acknowledged that in *NA* the church made a complete volte-face in its understanding of its relation to other religions. Just to cite one example, for those who adopt Pope Benedict XVI's "hermeneutics of reform" and reject the "hermeneutics of discontinuity," it would be a herculean feat of mental prestidigitation to argue a theological continuity between what Pope Eugenius IV declared at the Council of Florence about the Jews on February 4, 1442, and what *NA* asserts in its paragraph 4. Similarly, what paragraph 2 of *NA* affirms about primal religions, Hinduism, and Buddhism is simply and utterly beyond the pre–Vatican II ecclesial imagination:

> The Catholic Church rejects nothing of what is true and holy in these religions. It has a high regard for the manner of life and conduct, the precepts and doctrines which, although differing many ways from its own teaching, nevertheless often reflect a ray of that truth which enlightens all men and women. . . . Let Christians, while witnessing to their own faith and way of life, acknowledge (*agnoscant*), preserve

(*servent*) and promote (*promoveant*) the spiritual and moral good things (*bona spiritualia et moralia*) as well as the socio-cultural values (*valores socio-culturales*) which are found among non-Christians.

Perhaps it was due to their justly enthusiastic appreciation for these radically positive changes in the attitude of the Catholic Church toward other religions, which is marked by genuine respect and readiness to dialogue, that church leaders and theologians did not notice the patronizing tone of *NA*'s negative naming of other religions. To remove this theological blight, it is not enough to tweak the title of the declaration and replace "non-Christian religions" with "*other* religions," though that would be a good place to start. The new title would signal a Copernican revolution in the way the relationship between the church and other religions is framed theologically. In brief, with the new title "Declaration of the Relations of the Church to Other Religions," Christianity relinquishes its claim to a privileged and superior status vis-á-vis other religions.

By contrast, Vatican II's theological framework for conceiving the relationship between the church and other religions is unidirectional, that is, it starts from the belief that there is only one true religion, namely, Christianity, and then proceeds to determine the truth and value of other religions by measuring the degree to which other religions possess the constituent elements that make Christianity the one true religion.

DI *on Non-Christian Religions*

This unidirectional method is applied rigorously by *DI* in matters regarding the true church (ecumenical unity) and the true religion (religious pluralism). Thus, with regard to the nature of the true church, *DI* posits that what makes the Catholic Church the only true church is the fact that it possesses, among other things, "apostolic succession" and seven sacraments, especially the Eucharist, which confer grace by virtue of the fact that they are performed validly. (The Latin formula for the validity of the sacrament is *ex opere operato* [from the work being done validly] as opposed to *ex opere operantis* [from the work of the person performing the sacrament].) Thus, if a particular Christian church, say the Baptist Church, does not have "apostolic succession" by virtue of a direct historical connection with an apostle through the "laying-on of hands," or does not have a valid Eucharist, it is judged by *DI* not to be "Church in the proper sense" (no. 17).

With regard to other religions, *DI* applies the same iron-clad logic. Though it recognizes that non-Christian religions contain and offer "religious elements which come from God," it states categorically that "some prayers and rituals of the other religions may assume a role of preparation for the Gospel, in that they are occasions or pedagogical helps in which the human heart is prompted to be open to the actions of God." Then, using the scholastic theology of the sacrament, it goes on to say, "One cannot attribute to these, however, a divine origin or an *ex opere operato* salvific efficacy, which is proper to the Christian sacraments." For good measure, the document adds, "Furthermore, it cannot be overlooked that other rituals, insofar as they depend on superstitions or other errors (cf. 1 Cor 10:20–21), constitute an obstacle to salvation" (no. 21).

Because the authors of *DI* operate in the rarified realm of deductive logic and rarely if ever are immersed in a dialogue of life, of collaboration for justice and peace, of theological exchange, and of shared religious experience with flesh-and-blood people of other faiths (and not just systems of religious ideas), they cannot recognize the authentic nature of the "prayers and rituals" of the holy pagans at Wat Phrathat Doi Suthep and of the Buddhist woman, the *humanitas orans et meditans* (the praying and meditating humanity), at Wat U-Mong, at whose feet they could sit and learn how to pray. Because they do not share in the religious experiences of these holy pagans, the latter's prayers are for them nothing more than "preparation for the Gospel" and "occasions or pedagogical helps in which the human heart is prompted to be open to the actions of God" and not already authentic prayers reaching the very heart of God, even though Buddhists do not speak of God. Because they theologize on the basis of the Catholic manualist theology of sacraments, they refuse to ascribe to these rituals "the *ex opere operato* salvific efficacy, which is proper to the Christian sacraments" and thus are blind to the sanctifying power *ex opere operantis* of the devotion and piety of the holy pagans.

To top it all off, the authors of *DI* cannot resist pointing out that these rituals "insofar as they depend on superstitions or other errors" constitute "an obstacle to salvation," as if Catholic devotions and sacramental celebrations themselves had not been tainted by "superstitions or other errors" down the centuries, and thus fail to acknowledge, with honesty and humility, that Christian piety has been purified and enriched by encounters with the "pagan" rites and rituals. Clearly, *DI* is unable to see other religions as *other*, on their own terms, but simply as *non-Christian*, and judges them as "objectively deficient" on allegedly Christian criteria. By the same token, were Buddhists to follow the same logic, they would be well within their rights to judge Christianity "objectively deficient" because, on Buddhist criteria, it fails to produce the kind of liberation that is the goal of Buddhism.

Again, starting from the idea that non-Christian religions have "a mysterious relationship to the Church" and *not also the other way round, DI* declares that "it would be contrary to the faith to consider the Church as *one way* of salvation alongside those constituted by the other religions, seen as complementary to the Church or substantially equivalent to her, even if these are said to be converging with the Church toward the eschatological kingdom of God" (no. 21). Incidentally, how the Congregation for the Doctrine of the Faith (CDF) knows about this relationship of non-Christian religions to Christianity is itself a mystery since this one-way relationship is deemed "mysterious"! By the same logic, cannot, say, Islam claim that Christianity has a "mysterious relationship" to it, and therefore Islam cannot be regarded as simply *one way* of salvation alongside others, and that Christianity cannot be seen as "complementary" or "equivalent" to it?

I do acknowledge that there is, particularly at the popular level, the idea that, just as there are different ways to reach the summit of the mountain, all religions are more or less the same, concerned as they all are to help their followers lead a good life. This view may give rise to a certain kind of dogmatic relativism that glosses over some real differences and even contradictions among religions. However, it also contains an important kernel of truth that it would be wrong to ignore, and that is, even if Christianity must be confessed *in faith*—and not rationally proved—to be the one way of salvation, it can and must learn from other religions how to live out fully its own teachings and ideals. *In this sense*, other religions can be said to be "complementary" to the church, just as Christianity is complementary to them, and thus, Christianity and all other religions, each in its own irreducible and autonomous way, contribute to the Kingdom of God.

In the theology of religion I am proposing, Christianity no longer considers itself the center around which other religions orbit, like multicolor-coated Joseph before whom the sun, the moon, and the eleven stars bow down (Genesis 37:9), nor does it view itself as the goal for which other religions are but stepping stones, as "preparation for the Gospel." Rather, the relation between Christianity and other religions is a genuinely *reciprocal* one, where all religions are equally willing to teach and to be taught by others, to complement others and to be complemented by them. Christianity's humble and honest acknowledgment of itself as simply one "religion" among many—not even as *primus inter pares* (first among equals)—entails a reversal of the two-thousand-year-old apologetics of Christianity as *sola vera religio*, not only as the sole *vera* but also as the sole *religio*, reserving this term exclusively for itself and dismissing other religions as *secta* or *superstitio*. This theology of religion, I will argue below, is in accord with the Christian belief in the self-emptying (*kenosis*) of the Word of God in Jesus as a human being among other human beings, more precisely, as their slave (Philippians 2:7).

Beyond the "Fulfillment Theology" of Non-Christian Religions

Before attempting a theology of religion that honors the intrinsic value of other religions in themselves as "ways of salvation," and not as a defective simulacrum of Christianity or at best its preparatory stepping stones, it would be helpful to take a close look at the theology of religion undergirding *NA* and *DI*. In the aftermath of Vatican II there has been a veritable avalanche throughout the globe of activities and writings, at both the official and grassroots levels, to promote interreligious dialogue in the fourfold forms of common living, collaboration for the common good, theological exchange, and spiritual sharing.

New theologies of religion have also been developed, using different paradigms comprising exclusivism, inclusivism, and pluralism. Exclusivism holds that only one religion (in this case, Christianity) is true. Inclusivism holds that only one religion (for example, Christianity) is true, but there are "elements of truth and grace" of this one true religion in other religions. Pluralism holds that all religions are valid paths leading, each in its own way, to salvation. These three paradigms have been expanded by Paul Knitter into four types or models, namely, "replacement" ("Only One True Religion"), "fulfillment" ("The One Fulfills the Many"), "mutuality" ("Many True Religions Called to Dialogue"), and "acceptance" ("Many True Religions: So Be It").[10]

It is safe to say that *NA*'s undergirding theology of religion hovers between "exclusivism" and "inclusivism," with a stronger nod toward the

---

[10] See Paul Knitter, *Introducing Theologies of Religions* (Maryknoll, NY: Orbis Books, 2002).

latter. More precisely, it is a "fulfillment" theology of religion (Knitter's second model), a combination of the exclusivist affirmation of the universality and uniqueness of the function of Jesus as the Savior and of the necessity of the church as the instrument of salvation (*extra ecclesiam nulla salus* [no salvation outside the church]) with the inclusivist acknowledgment of the presence of "elements of truth and grace," Karl Rahner's (1904–84) celebrated phrase, in other religions. This theology of religion has its roots in the writings of pre–Vatican II theologians such as Jean Daniélou (1905–74) and Henri de Lubac (1896–1991), and was developed further by Karl Rahner with his emphasis on the presence of the mystery of Christ (and later, he adds, the Holy Spirit) in all religions with his celebrated concept of "anonymous Christianity." This theology of the presence of Christ in all religions other than Christianity was elaborated in another direction by the Spanish-Indian priest Raimon Panikkar (1918–2010) who speaks of "Christ" as the "symbol" of the human-divine-cosmic ("cosmotheandric") mystery present in all religions, which is experienced in the one identical "faith" but expressed in different "beliefs."

It is Rahner's theology of the inclusive presence of Christ outside Christianity that shaped Vatican II's understanding of the relation of the church to other religions. This is obvious not so much in *NA* as in the Decree on the Church's Missionary Activity (*Ad Gentes*), as its paragraph 9 makes it abundantly clear:

> Through preaching and the celebration of the sacraments, of which the holy Eucharist is the center and summit, missionary activity makes Christ present, who is the author of salvation. It purges of evil associations those elements of truth and grace which are found among people, and which are, as it were, a secret presence of God, and it restores them to Christ their source who overthrows the rule of the devil and limits the manifold malice of evil. So, whatever goodness is found in people's minds and hearts, or in the particular customs and cultures of peoples, far from being lost is purified, raised to a higher level and reaches its perfection, for the glory of God, the confusion of the demon, and the happiness of humankind.

That this text is an unambiguous and resounding affirmation of the fulfillment theology of religion leaves no doubt. Phrases such as *elements of truth and grace, a secret presence of God, is purified, raised to a higher level, and reaches its perfection* are the shibboleths of the fulfillment theology of religion. While it no doubt constitutes an enormous advance over the purely exclusivist theology of religion of ages past, it leads to the kind of unilateral, unidirectional, patronizing, and arrogant view of "non-Christian" religions I described above. In spite of its genuine admiration and respect for other religions, *NA*, and to a much larger extent *DI*, seems to be incapable of appreciating the value of other religions except insofar as they contain "elements of truth and grace" that are said to belong by right to Christ (and, by extension, to the church). Outside both Christ and the church, they are said to suffer from "the rule of the devil" and "the manifold malice of evil."

In "restoring" these "elements of truth and grace" to Christ as "their source" by means of the church's "missionary activity," Vatican II declares that "whatever goodness is found in people's minds and hearts, or in the particular customs and cultures of peoples, far from being lost is purified, raised to a higher level and reaches its perfection." This affirmation sounds at first generous and benevolent toward other religions, but in fact, at least to the ears of believers of other religions, the wall separating this task of purifying, raising to a higher level, and bringing to perfection the "elements of truth and grace" found in other religions, on the one hand, and an outright supersession by which they are eliminated, on the other, is menacingly thin and porous. Among contemporary Catholic theologians of religion, James Fredericks has made a scathing critique of this type of fulfillment theology. In his judgment, it is a Christians-talking-to-Christians, in-house discourse; it distorts other religions for Christian purposes; it domesticates differences; and it lessens the urgency of interreligious dialogue and undermines its value.[11]

It is to be noted that what *NA* says so far about other religions applies only to the so-called primal religions, Hinduism, and Buddhism (paragraphs 1 and 2). (*NA* speaks of Islam and Judaism only in paragraphs 3 and 4, respectively.) Though the declaration does not mention other Indian religions such as Jainism and Sikhism and Chinese religious traditions such as Confucianism and Daoism, and other living religions, it is safe to assume that *NA*'s fulfillment theology applies to them as well. In general, it must

---

[11] See James Fredericks, *Buddhists and Christians: Through Comparative Theology to Solidarity* (Maryknoll, NY: Orbis Books, 2004), 14–21. Fredericks's critique of fulfillment theology of religion is well-taken. The question of course is whether all theologies of religion are but iterations of fulfillment theology, or whether there is a form of theology of religion that is genuinely Christian but does not espouse the main tenets of fulfillment theology. This is the direction I attempt to take in this essay

be recognized that *NA*'s apparently favorable attitude toward these religions is likely to be seen as a Trojan horse that Asian religions receive at their own risk of self-destruction. When *NA*'s assertion about the need for the "elements of truth and grace" of these religions to be purified, raised and perfected in Christianity is coupled with the rhetoric of the Decree on the Church's Missionary Activity about the "rule of the devil" and the "malice of evil" from which these religions must be delivered through Christ and the church's mission, and when the later Declaration of the Congregation for the Doctrine of the Faith *DI* asserts that these religions do not contain divine revelation, that "inspiration" cannot be ascribed to their sacred Scriptures and that their followers do not have "faith" but only "belief," it comes as no surprise that Vatican II's fulfillment theology of religion leaves the believers of Asian religions cold, to put it mildly.

Toward a Kenotic Theology of the Relations among Religions

To move beyond Vatican II's fulfillment theology of religion and to develop an alternative theology that helps effectively to implement *NA*'s exhortation that Christians "acknowledge," "preserve," and "promote" the truths and values of other religions, it would be necessary to adopt a reversal of the council's perspective on other religions, one that may be termed a *kenotic theology of religion*, in the mold of Christ's *kenosis* (self-emptying) affirmed in Philippians 2:7 which says that Christ Jesus,

> Though in the form of God,
> did not regard equality with God
> as something to be exploited,
> but emptied himself,
> taking the form of a slave,
> being born in human likeness.
> And being found in human form, he humbled himself
> and became obedient to the point of death—
> even death on the cross.

In such a theology of religion, like Jesus who did not exploit his equality with God for his own gains, Christianity humbly renounces its claim of "unicity" and superiority over other religions and sets itself among other religions as one of them, just like Jesus who lives as a human being among his fellow human beings. Such a theology may be called "kenotic," in the self-emptying (*kenosis*) way of Jesus.

I will attempt to outline the contour of such a theology of religion by drawing on the Jewish–Christian dialogue in the last fifty years. The reason for choosing the Jewish–Christian dialogue as resource is that by any standard, it is arguably the most theologically advanced and institutionally successful form of interfaith dialogue in the aftermaths of Vatican II. This comes as no surprise given the intimate historical and theological connections between Judaism and Christianity, the complex and not rarely tragic relations between them for two millennia, the fact that *NA* began as a document about the Jews (*De Judaeis*), the significant contributions of Pope John Paul II to the Christian–Jewish dialogue, the many official statements on Jewish–Christian relations, and not least, the immense scholarly and institutional resources that both partners-in-dialogue have at their disposal.

One possible objection against the use of the Jewish–Christian dialogue as a model for interreligious dialogue in general is that the relation of Christianity to Judaism is said to be unique and therefore cannot be extended to other types of interreligious dialogue. Of course, there is no denying the "unique" character—theological and historical—of the relation between Judaism and Christianity. Judaism, to use John Paul II's expressions, is not "extrinsic" but in a certain way "intrinsic" to Christianity. But whether the uniqueness of this relationship prohibits the applicability of its theology of religion to other religions should not be decided a priori and *in globo*, that is, on the ground that it is unique. Rather its analogical applicability must be assessed in each particular aspect of this theology of religion.

Let it be noted in passing that the intimate bond between Judaism and Christianity does not make the understanding of the precise relation between them any easier. On the contrary, it has been made much harder, especially in light of the Christian "teaching of contempt" and the Christian responsibility for the Shoah. Fortunately, the enormous progress that has been accomplished in the last fifty years in both the religious relations between Jews and Christians and the theology of Jewish–Christian dialogue can, in my judgment, form a most helpful basis for constructing a general theology of religion that promotes a reading of *NA* in reverse.

1. One of the most important elements of the contemporary theology of Jewish–Christian dialogue is the unequivocal rejection of what is termed

supersessionism, the belief that God's covenant with Israel has been "fulfilled" by Jesus and therefore abolished. That covenant is declared "old" and has been replaced by the "new" and "better" covenant that God has made in his Son Jesus. As the result, Israel has been superseded by the church, the new and true People of God, the *verus Israel* (true Israel). Over against supersessionism, it is now widely acknowledged that God's covenant with Israel has not been revoked; rather it remains eternally valid. Hence, the fulfillment theology of religion as expounded above does not apply to Judaism. However "fulfillment" is understood, it cannot mean abolition or replacement.

How does this antisupersessionist theology of Judaism apply to other religions? In terms of covenant, it has been shown that for St. Irenaeus, God has made four covenants with humanity, namely, in Adam, in Noah, in Abraham, and in Jesus, and that none of the three covenants preceding the one made in Jesus was abolished by the fourth.[12] If God's covenant with Abraham, and in him with his descendants, has not been abolished, not even *aufgehoben* (raised up and subsumed) in the Hegelian sense, the same must be said of the other covenants God made with all peoples, especially in Adam and Noah.

In particular, God's covenant with Noah, that is, the Noachic covenant, has never been revoked but remains eternally valid and is realized primarily in peoples' religions. Therefore, the fulfillment theology of religion cannot and must not be applied to them. They have been neither abolished nor replaced by Christianity. In this context it is important to recall the danger I alluded to above, namely, that the line separating the rhetoric of purification, elevation, and perfection as applied by *NA* and *Ad Gentes* to Asian religions, on the one hand, and their actual supersession, on the other, is perilously thin, and the tendency to cross the line is well-nigh irresistible, and *DI* is Exhibit A for it.

2. Another positive achievement of the Jewish–Christian theology is the overcoming of what the French Jew Jules Isaac (1877–1963) calls the "teaching of contempt," part of which is the representation of Judaism at the time of Jesus as a legalistic and ritualistic religion without a soul, and as a result incapable of accepting Jesus's message, and as a sterile religious tradition lacking spiritual substance and vitality. Thanks to recent biblical

---

[12] For a helpful exposition of St. Irenaeus's theology of the fourfold covenant, see Jacques Dupuis, *Toward a Christian Theology of Religious Pluralism* (Maryknoll, NY: Orbis Books, 1997), 60–66.

and historical scholarship on Second Temple Judaism and on early Christianity, we can now interpret the invectives present in the Gospels against the Pharisees and the "Jews" (*hoi iudaioi*), Paul's contrast between faith and works, and the Letter to the Hebrews's statement on Jesus's high priesthood in opposition to the priesthood of ancient Israel not as implying God's rejection of his covenant with Israel because of its alleged defects. Rather they should be understood in the context of the dispute between rabbinic Judaism and the Jewish followers of Jesus, at times vitriolic, regarding the correct interpretation of the Torah and the obligatory character of certain Jewish laws such as circumcision, the Sabbath, and kosher foods. Furthermore, we now understand Judaism not just as the "Old Testament" but as a living, vibrant, historically evolving religion that provides its followers sure guidance in the practice of the way of the covenant.

Similarly, with regard to Asian religions, we have rejected the "teaching of contempt" that Catholic and Protestant missionaries have propagated against them, depicting them as rank superstition, witchcraft, idolatry, immorality, and works of the devil, a faint echo of which resounds, as we have seen, in *DI*. This kind of scurrilous attack filled the pages of early missionaries' descriptions of the religions they encountered in Asia, Africa, and Latin America. To cite just an infamous example, in the so-called Chinese Rites Controversy, ancestor veneration in Asia was severely condemned by various popes, and Catholic missionaries were obligated to take an oath under pain of excommunication to prohibit the converts from practicing it. Of course, some enlightened missionaries have taken a more benign view of this practice not as a religious cult but as acts of purely civil and political import and deemed it acceptable. A more enlightened theology may even discern "elements of truth and grace" in these rites and other practices of other religions, to be purified, perfected and elevated by Christianity. However, under the veneer of missionary and theological accommodation, there lies a thick layer of the "teaching of contempt" not very different from that directed against Judaism.

Fortunately, in recent decades, many Christians who live among the followers of other religions, especially those with the so-called double religious belonging, have come to appreciate, learn from, and be spiritually nourished by their sacred scriptures, their doctrinal teachings, their moral practices, their monastic and ascetic traditions. Furthermore, we have also come to appreciate Asian religions not as outmoded relics of technologically backward cultures, a view promoted by Enlightenment historians of religion with an antireligious bias, but as living, vibrant, evolving religious practices of billions of people struggling to find meaning and God in the midst of poverty, oppression, and suffering.

3. Within this theology of the relation between Christianity and Judaism and between Christianity and other religions, such as Islam and Asian religious traditions, the role of Christ as unique and universal Savior and of the church as a community of salvation have of course to be understood differently. As I have argued in the earlier chapters, the role of Christ as unique and universal Savior can no longer be interpreted apart from the equally unique and universal role of the Spirit, who are, in Irenaeus's felicitous expression, "the two hands" with which God works out God's one plan of salvation in the world, not independently from, much less in opposition to, each other, but, by the same token, not in an identical, uniform manner everywhere and at all times. Thus, both God's Logos and Pneuma can and do function salvifically in history not as parallel agents (since both are agents of God's one economy of salvation) but before, after, with, and outside each other. In this way, all religions, in which God's Logos and Pneuma are actively present, can legitimately be said to be "ways of salvation" together with Christianity, one religion among other religions.

4. Finally, a few words in response to the charges of the CDF and the Committee on Doctrine (CD) against *Being Religious Interreligiously* (*BRI*). The theology of religion expounded in my book can claim some foundation in St. John Paul II's teaching, though admittedly it also goes beyond it. No doubt, of all popes, John Paul II has contributed the most to interreligious dialogue, through his richly symbolic actions and his theology of religion, especially his theology of the Spirit (pneumatology). Yet, in spite of the fact that he regards non-Christian religions as "participated forms of mediation of different kinds and degrees" in the mediation of Christ and that he sees a "common soteriological root" in all religions—both teachings do go beyond Vatican II—John Paul never asserts that non-Christian religions are salvific or function as ways or means of salvation for their adherents, either in connection with Christ and the church or independently of them.[13]

Furthermore, John Paul affirms that the Holy Spirit (and hence, not mere human religiousness) is "at the very source of man's existential and religious questioning," especially in prayer, and that "the Spirit's presence

---

[13] *Redemptoris Missio*, no. 5.

and activity affect not only individuals but also society and history, peoples, cultures and *religions.*"[14] From this teaching that the Spirit is actively present in non-Christian religions, and not just in individuals, it follows that when non-Christians respond positively to the Spirit's activities, they do so by faith and not simply by belief, and consequently, faith must be associated with non-Christian religions. Again, if non-Christians are saved (and they may be, according to Vatican II), they must have faith and not merely belief, since "without faith it is impossible to please God" (Hebrews 11:6).

Of course, the pope hastens to add that the Holy Spirit is "not an alternative to Christ, nor does he fill a sort of void which is sometimes suggested as existing between Christ and the Logos."[15] Furthermore, the Spirit's activity, the pope insists, is "not to be separated from his particular activity within the Body of Christ, which is the Church."[16] The question then is how to account for the reality of faith in non-Christian religions, which therefore do have a role *of their own* to play in the salvation of their followers without separating the Spirit from Jesus Christ, making the Spirit an "alternative" to Christ or filling "a sort of a void" between the Logos-still-to-be incarnated and the Logos incarnated in Jesus of Nazareth, and without separating the Spirit's activity from the church.

Both the CDF's and the CD's statements about *BRI* have charged that the book contains ambiguities and even errors in its affirmation about the "salvific significance" of non-Christian religions. Their accusations would have been well founded had I maintained anything close to what they say I do. To be clear, I have never affirmed that non-Christian religions are "ways of salvation" that are *parallel* or *equal* "alternatives" to Christ and Christianity in the sense that they are "complementary to the Church or substantially equivalent to her" (*DI*, no. 21). Such judgment would require a set of common and measurable criteria on which Christianity and other religions are assessed, which of course does not exist, unless of course one assumes a priori, as *DI* does, a set of *Christian* criteria and proceed to rank other religions as more or less "*non*-Christian."

I do not affirm that there two "economies," namely, that of Christ and that of the Holy Spirit, the former realized in Christianity, the latter in other religions. Rather I affirm that there is only *one* plan of salvation, which is

---

[14] *Redemptoris Missio*, no. 28, emphasis added.
[15] *Redemptoris Missio*, no. 29.
[16] Ibid.

that of Divine Spirit and is carried out by his two hands, to use St. Irenaeus's metaphor. As a person can perform a single task well, sometimes using both hands at the same time and equally, at other times, better with one hand than with the other, and still at other times, one rather than the other, so analogously the Holy Spirit and the Son, God the Father's two hands, can operate in similar ways in carrying out his single plan of salvation, in Christianity as well as in other religions. As a consequence, Christianity and other religions are *mutually* "complementary," not in the sense that one is not fully what it is without the other, but in the sense that in order to realize its potential to the full, one needs to learn from the other in reciprocal exchanges since as historical realities they all are imperfect and incomplete.

There is another simpler way to understand how non-Christian religions can help the church understand and practice better the teaching of Jesus and in that precise sense "complement" the church. It has been asserted that the church contains the fullness of divine revelation. But to possess something in full is not the same thing as understanding and living it fully. Only an idealistic or blinkered reading of church history, including the history of the Roman Catholic Church, would deny this. It is a historical fact that throughout its history the church has corrected its errors and changed its immoral behaviors. How did it do this, always without the help of insights and good examples and at times fierce criticism from outside the church, from non-Christian believers, secular society, and even nonbelievers?

When St. John Paul II asks for forgiveness for the church's behavior in anti-Judaism, racism, sexism, the Inquisition, the crusades, and a host of other sins and evil structures, can one say with a straight face that the church has come to recognize these corporate failings just simply and exclusively by meditating on the Bible and magisterial teachings? Pope John Paul II has explicitly confessed that the spiritual practices of non-Christian believers have sometimes put Christians to shame. But there is no need of a solemn declaration from the lips of the Supreme Pontiff to know this. Just to have the blessing of contemplating the praying Buddhist woman in Wat U-Mong would suffice.

The CD's statement argues that "the affirmation [which it says I have made] of a process of complementation and correction implies the existence of someone above the Christian faith who is able to judge that such a process has in fact occurred." In light of this, it also says that *BRI's* "basic perspective is not specifically Christian but a more universal 'religious' perspective, one that is somehow higher than that of any particular religion." These are two of the many strange charges that have been leveled against *BRI*. For the CDF and the CD, to recognize that there has been a mutual correction and enrichment between Christianity and other religions requires a third party "above the Christian faith" to make a judgment "that such a process has in fact occurred."

But why is such a third party, supposedly of superior intellectual and religious authority, required for such an act of recognition? In everyday life, can I not recognize that I have learned from, or have been intellectually and spiritually enriched, or have been corrected by someone, without needing someone in higher authority to tell me so? Just a moment of self-reflection, discernment, humility, and honesty suffices. Without a higher authority to tell me so, must I not acknowledge my own limitations and admit that I do not know everything, that I am not perfect in every respect, and that someone has something I do not have, or has something I have but in a more perfect degree? Similarly, for the church to be able to recognize that it has been corrected, enriched, and taught by other religions, all that the church needs is intellectual honesty, humble acknowledgment of its deficiencies and sins, and openness of mind and heart.

As to the second charge that methodologically speaking, the perspective of *BRI* is a generally "religious" rather than a specifically Christian one, perhaps the CDF and the CD have been misled by its title of "being *religious*." But any fair reading of the book will recognize that its theological reflections do not start from a generic concept of religion and then apply it to Christianity and other religions, even though such a concept is not impossible in the context of comparative religion. Rather its perspective is distinctly Christian (and even more narrowly, Roman Catholic), but it asks whether such a perspective can be enlarged, enriched, and corrected by the perspectives of other religions. Rather being "universal" from the start and becoming gradually particular through a process of deduction, the perspective of *BRI* is from the beginning Christian and grows more universal through the process of dialogue of mutual enrichment with cultures and other religions.

Furthermore, I have never suggested that there exists a "sort of void"—to use John Paul II's expression—between the Logos and Jesus that is filled by the Spirit. My attempt was to do justice to the reality of faith, grace, and salvation in not only non-Christian individuals but also in "non-Christian" religions as such. It does not seem contrary to the faith to suggest that non-Christian religions can function as "ways of salvation" to their adherents in the sense that if and when non-Christians are saved, and this possibility has been affirmed by Vatican II, they are saved *through* and *by means of* their religions, not *in spite of* them. In other words, non-Christian religions do have a positive role to play in or a positive contribution to make to the salvation of their followers. It is only in *this* sense that I have argued that non-Christian religions have an "autonomous" salvific significance, that is, intrinsic to them, or of their own, even though I have maintained that this salvific efficacy is due to the work of the Spirit who acts not in opposition to or apart from Jesus, but also not in total dependence on Christ (hence "autonomously").

This theologoumenon (theological opinion) has been suggested, somewhat indirectly, by a 1991 joint document of the Pontifical Council for Interreligious Dialogue and the Congregation for Evangelization of People, *Dialogue and Proclamation*:

> Concretely, it will be in the sincere practice of what is good in their own religious traditions and by following the dictates of their conscience that the members of other religions respond positively to God's invitation and receive salvation in Jesus Christ, even while they do not recognize or acknowledge him as their Savior.[17]

The salvific value of non-Christian religions is affirmed, more clearly albeit elliptically, some might say convolutedly, by a 1997 statement of the International Theological Commission entitled *Christianity and the World Religions*. Appealing to John Paul's pneumatological theology of religions, it says,

> Given this explicit recognition of the presence of the Spirit of Christ in the religions, one cannot exclude the possibility that they exercise as such a certain salvific function, that is, despite their ambiguity, they help men achieve their ultimate end. In the religions is explicitly thematized the relationship of man with the Absolute, his transcendental dimension. It would be difficult to think that what the Holy Spirit works in the hearts of men taken as individuals would have salvific value and not think that what the Holy Spirit works in the religions

---

[17] *Dialogue and Proclamation*, no. 29.

and cultures would not have such value. The recent magisterium does not seem to authorize such a drastic distinction. (no. 64)[18]

Perhaps the strongest support for my position comes from the Catholic Bishops' Conference of India, which leaves no doubt as to the salvific role of non-Christian religions:

> In the light of the universal salvific will and design of God, so emphatically affirmed in the New Testament witness, the Indian Christological approach seeks to avoid negative and exclusivistic expressions. Christ is the sacrament, the definitive symbol of God's salvation for all humanity. This is what the salvific uniqueness and universality of Christ means in the Indian context. That, however, does not mean there cannot be other symbols, *valid in their own ways*, which the Christian sees as related to the definitive symbol, Jesus Christ. The implication of all this is that for hundreds of millions of our fellow human beings, salvation is seen as being channeled to them not in spite of but *through and in* their various sociocultural and *religious* traditions (emphasis added).[19]

Both the CDF's and CD's statement will very probably judge this statement by the Catholic Bishops' Conference of India "confused" and "confusing" because they think in terms of either-or: either non-Christian religions function autonomously and independently of Christ, or they have no salvific significance whatsoever. For them the first alternative is false, and therefore the second, and only the second, is true. Any mediating position that does not repeat exactly the formulas of *DI* is automatically condemned as confused, confusing, and contrary to the Christian faith.

On the other hand, I have attempted to think in terms of both-and: I try to remain faithful to the Christian teaching on Christ and the church and at the same time I want to honor "the facts on the ground," that is, I want to acknowledge and learn from the holy lives of my non-Christian friends, the Buddhist pilgrims at Wat Phrathat Doi Suthep, and the icon of

---

[18] For the text of the International Theological Commission, *Christianity and the World Religions*, see *Origins* 27 (August 14, 1997), 149–66.

[19] *The Asian Synod: Texts and Commentaries*, ed. Peter C. Phan (Maryknoll, NY: Orbis Books, 2002), 22.

the *humanitas orans* at Wat U-Mong, who lead a life marked by holiness, not rarely higher than that of Christians (certainly mine), precisely insofar as they believe in and put into practice the teachings of their religions, most of the time in total ignorance of Christianity and at times rejecting what Christianity is represented to them though the teachings and practices of Christians.

"Holy Pagans" in other "Holy Religions": There can be no denying that there are holy people outside Christianity—and sometimes *in spite of* Christianity, as history sadly shows. They are holy not in spite of their religions but *thanks to* and *because of* their faithful and devout practices of what their religions teach them to believe and do. By what power they become holy is not an issue most of them care or worry about. Rather it is a question that Christians have to confront because of their exclusivistic claims about Jesus and their church.

In *BRI* and the preceding pages, I have attempted to formulate a way to understand the power of other religions to "sanctify" their "faithful" (with "faith" and not just "belief") that both preserves the Christian doctrines about Christ and the church, and at the same time honors—and gives thanks to—our fellow believers in other religions for teaching us Christians how to be human and religious, not least the Buddhist pilgrims circumambulating the statue of the Buddha at the Wat Phrathat Doi Suthep, and the female icon of the *humanitas orans* at Wat U-Mong,

CHAPTER 6

Church and Mission

Walking Together with Other Religions
toward the Kingdom of God?

I have noted in Chapter 4 that the Congregation for the Doctrine of the Faith (CDF)'s Declaration *Dominus Iesus* (*DI*) claims "unicity" and "universal salvific mediation" not only for Jesus but also for the church (no. 4). That the same expressions, that is, "unicity" and "universal salvific mediation" (or "salvific universality"), are used for both Christ and the church is prima facie misleading, since it is obvious that, whatever the truth of the two claims, we are dealing with two radically different realities. *DI* apparently deduces the unicity and universality of the church from the unicity and universality of Christ as though the former is a logical consequence of the latter. But of course no such logic obtains, since whatever is true of Christ is not necessarily true of the church, and almost always is not, at least to the same degree. The temptation of idolatry in identifying the human with the divine is ever lurking, one that is very hard to detect and resist, especially when it is camouflaged as a defense of the church. It is important for our discussion of church and mission to note that strictly speaking, from a logical point of view, it is possible to follow the teaching of Jesus, thus accepting his "salvific universality," as Gandhi and countless other Asians have done without joining the church and accepting its "universal salvific mediation." The implications of this fact for Christian mission will be discussed below.

I have touched on the "unicity" and "universal salvific mediation" of the church in the previous chapter, where the relationship between Christianity and other religions and vice versa is discussed. The kenotic theology of religion, which I tentatively put forward, insists on the *reciprocal* relation between Christianity and other religions. While preserving the "unicity" and "universal salvific mediation" of Christianity, such a theology of religion recognizes the positive role that other religions play in fostering the spiritual welfare of their followers—call them "ways of salvation" if you will—and demands that all religions, as historical institutions made of sinful beings, learn from, correct, and enrich each other, or to use the taboo term, be *complemented* by others. If a Hindu or a Buddhist can say, and there have been notable Hindus and Buddhists who have done so, that he or she has learned from Christ and his church how to be a better human person and a more devout Hindu or Buddhist, so, too, a Christian can say, with sincerity and gratitude, that he or she has become a better human person and a more practicing Christian thanks to what they have learned from other religions. Such confessions from Christians who practice multiple religious traditions are becoming more common, to quote the arresting title of a recent book by Paul Knitter, *Without Buddha I Could Not Be a Christian*.[1]

As is well known, Vatican II is the first ecumenical council to make the church the central focus of its agenda, completing Vatican I's task of self-examination that was interrupted by the Franco-Prussian War in 1870. Indeed, its sixteen documents can be divided into two groups, the first dealing with the internal life of the church (*ad intra*), the most important document of which is the Dogmatic Constitution on the Church (*Lumen Gentium*), and the second dealing with the relation of the church to the world (*ad extra*), the most influential document of which is the Pastoral Constitution on the Church in the Modern World (*Gaudium et Spes*). In the post–Vatican II era, arguably no theological theme has received more scholarly and popular attention than ecclesiology. The purpose of this chapter, however, is not to present a survey of contemporary theology of the church. Rather its overriding intent is to examine what the CDF and the Committee on Doctrine (CD) have said about the connection between the church and the reign of God and about the church's mission, the two areas in which *Being Religious Interreligiously* (*BRI*) has been judged confused and confusing. I will first consider the relationship between the church and the kingdom of God and its implications for the mission of the church. Next I

---

[1] Paul Knitter, *Without Buddha I Could Not Be a Christian*, 2nd ed. (London: Oneworld Publications, 2013).

will elaborate a theology of mission in which Christians and the faithful of other religions can and should work together for the reign of God. I end with some reflections on Pope Francis's theology of the church and mission.

Church and Kingdom of God:
Toward an Asian Ecclesiology

Google "Asian ecclesiology" and you will not find many webpages, a tell-tale sign that ecclesiology, as a theological treatise on the institutional and hierarchical structures of the church, such as those discussed in Chapter 3 of *Lumen Gentium*, entitled "The Hierarchical Constitution of the Church and in Particular the Episcopacy," does not occupy in Asian theology the lion's share as it does in the theology of, say, the West. However, it would be wrong to infer from this paucity of bibliographical references that "church" is not a major concern for Asian Christians. On the contrary, a "new way of being church," to use a popular slogan among Asian theologians, arguably lies at the heart of the Asian churches' efforts to become churches *in* and *of* Asia.[2] Christianity, though born in Asia, is still regarded by many Asians as a foreign religion, and this new "way of being church" aims at erasing that perception by rooting the Christian faith in the Asian soil and creating a Christianity with an authentically Asian face while remaining true to the mission and teaching of Jesus. In a nutshell, this new way of being church consists in decentering the church from itself and recentering its mission on serving the reign of God.

A Kingdom-centered Church

Before elaborating an Asian ecclesiology, it is important to note that much to its credit *Dominus Iesus* (*DI*), following the teaching of *Lumen Gentium* (no. 5) and especially of Pope John Paul II's encyclical *Redemptoris Mis-*

---

2 Given the importance of the Federation of Asian Bishops' Conferences (FABC) and the abundance of the theological literature emanating from it, my focus will be on the ecclesiology of Asian Roman Catholicism. This concentration on Roman Catholic ecclesiology, albeit dictated by my theological expertise, is not narrowly denominational as it may at first appear. Of course, it has distinctly Roman Catholic accents (such as the focus on sacramental life and collaboration between the hierarchy and the laity). However, to the extent that it emphasizes the centrality of the kingdom of God, mission as dialogue, and the importance of the laity, this Roman Catholic Asian ecclesiology resonates with the concerns and approaches of other Christian churches in Asia.

sio (nos.12–20), insists that "the Church is not an end unto herself, since she is ordered toward the kingdom of God, of which she is the seed, sign and instrument" (no. 18). The document goes on to state that "the kingdom of God—even if considered in its historical phase—is not identified with the Church in her visible and social reality" (no. 19). Furthermore, it recognizes the legitimacy of a "kingdom-centered" or "regnocentric" ecclesiology that stresses "the image of the Church which is not concerned about herself, but which is totally concerned with bearing witness to and serving the kingdom" (no. 19). However, the document hastens to warn against three errors in this "kingdom-centered" ecclesiology: First, it speaks of the kingdom of *God* and remains silent about the kingdom of *Christ*; second, it puts great stress on the mystery of creation and keeps silent about the mystery of redemption; and third, it speaks so much about the reign of God and leaves little room for the church or undervalues the role of the church because of the alleged past "ecclesiocentrism." In conclusion, it states peremptorily, "These theses are contrary to Catholic faith because they deny the unicity of the relationship which Christ and the Church have with the kingdom of God" (no. 19). I will come back to these charges made by *DI*.

For the moment, let us note that one of the most curious features in Asian magisterial documents and theological writings on the church is the conspicuous absence of issues that have occupied much of the attention of European and American Catholics. One hardly finds therein an extensive discussion of staple ecclesiological topics such as papal primacy and infallibility, episcopal collegiality, the Roman Curia, the ordination of women, mandatory clerical celibacy, institutional and canonical reforms, and the like. This lack of interest in intraecclesiastical issues is not dictated by merely pragmatic considerations but is derived, I suggest, from what might be called "ecclesiological kenosis," a moving away from the church *ad intra* to the church *ad extra*, from self-absorption to mission. The resulting "kenotic ecclesiology," like its cognate "kenotic theology of religion," anticipates Pope Francis's theology of the church and mission as expressed in his Apostolic Exhortation *Evangelii Gaudium* (The Joy of the Gospel):

> I prefer a Church which is bruised, hurting and dirty because it has been out on the streets, rather than a Church which is unhealthy from being confined and from clinging to its own security. I do not

want a Church concerned with being at the center and then ends
by being caught up in a web of obsessions and procedures. (no. 49)[3]

This ecclesiological kenosis is predicated upon the theological conviction that at the heart of the Christian faith and practice, there lies not the
church and all its institutional elements but the reign of the Triune God. It
is only by bearing witness to and serving the reign of God among the Asian
peoples, and not by expanding its membership and sociopolitical influence,
that the church will truly become Asian. To be truly church, the Asian
church, paradoxically, must cease to be "church," that is, it must "empty"
itself and cease to exist for its own sake for the service of a higher reality,
namely, the kingdom of God. What the church is, is determined by what
it must do; its essence is defined by its function. Ecclesiology, in the Asian
perspective, must be essentially pastoral theology. It should not be given
pride of place in theological discourse; it does not occupy a high position
in "the hierarchy of truths," to use an expression of Vatican II.

Recent Asian theology has vigorously urged this "ecclesiological kenosis." In his book *Pentecost in Asia* Thomas C. Fox describes well the evolution
of the Asian Catholic Churches from their church-centered way of being
church to a regnocentric or kingdom-centered ecclesiology. This collective
conversion to the kingdom of God took place over three decades, from
the foundation of the Federation of Asian Bishops' Conferences (FABC) in
1972 to the Special Assembly of the Synod of Bishops for Asia (the "Asian
Synod") which met in Rome from April 19 through May 14, 1998.[4]

In this kingdom-centered ecclesiology, no longer is the church considered to be the pinnacle or the center of Christian life. Rather it is moved
from the center to the periphery and from the top to the bottom. Like
the sun around which the earth and the other planets move, the reign of
God is the center around which everything in the church revolves and to
which everything is subordinated. In the place of the church, the reign of
God is now installed as the ultimate goal of all the activities within and
without the church. Now both what the church is and what it does are

---

[3] Pope Francis, *The Joy of the Gospel: Post-Synodal Apostolic Exhortation* (Città del
Vaticano: Libreria Editrice Vaticana, 2013).

[4] Thomas Fox, *Pentecost in Asia: A New Way of Being Church* (Maryknoll, NY: Orbis
Books, 2002).

defined by the reign of God and not the other way round. The only reason for the church to exist is to serve the reign of God, that is, to help bring about what has been commonly referred to as the "kingdom values." It is these values that the church must promote and not its self-aggrandizement, or reputation, or institutional survival. Every law and policy of the church must pass the litmus test of whether they promote the reign of God.

The point of regnocentric ecclesiology is not to devalue the role of the church but to determine it correctly with regard to the kingdom of God. Needless to say, there is an intrinsic connection between the reign of God and the church, as is well expressed by Pope John Paul II in his apostolic exhortation *Ecclesia in Asia* (*EA*) promulgated after the Asian Synod:

> Empowered by the Spirit to accomplish Christ's salvation on earth, the Church is the seed of the Kingdom of God and she looks eagerly for its final coming. Her identity and mission are inseparable from the Kingdom of God which Jesus announced and inaugurated in all that he said and did, above all in his death and resurrection. The Spirit reminds the Church that she is not an end unto herself: in all that she is and all that she does, she exists to serve Christ and the salvation of the world.[5]

There is therefore no intrinsic incompatibility between serving the kingdom of God and expanding church membership and influence—often euphemistically referred to as "church growth" in missiological literature. Indeed, the two activities of Christian mission must go hand in hand. The issue is rather one of theoretical and practical priority. Real life does not always allow an easy choice between church and reign of God, and not every decision in favor of the church promotes the reign of God. When push comes to shove, what is to be favored, the reign of God or the church? When, for instance, the choice is between standing in solidarity with the poor and the oppressed and forfeiting the church's privileges and favors among the powerful and the wealthy, which in theory could be used for the benefit of the poor, what option must the church make?

The same problem can be framed in terms of the relationship between the reign of God and the church. Clearly, the church is not identical with

---

[5] *EA*, no. 17. For the English text of *EA*, see Peter C. Phan, ed., *The Asian Synod: Texts and Commentaries* (Maryknoll, NY: Orbis Books, 2002), 286–340.

the kingdom of God, nor is the kingdom of God confined to the church. The church is only, as Vatican II puts it, "the seed and the beginning of that kingdom."[6] Its constitution is defined by the kingdom of God, which acts as its goal and future, and not the other way round. The church is not an end unto itself; its *raison d'être* is to serve the kingdom of God. It is a means to an end. When this relationship is reversed, with the church turned into the goal of one's ministry, the possibility of moral corruption, especially by means of power, is enormous. Worse, one is tempted to protect one's personal advantages and interests under the pretext of defending the church! Asian theologians are particularly sensitive to this temptation, given past connections between Catholic missions and colonialism in their countries.

The Way to the Kingdom of God:
A Triple Dialogue

A regnocentric church is by nature a missionary church, committed to promoting the "kingdom values" preached by Jesus. But what are these? Or, more concisely, what does the kingdom of God stand for? Despite Jesus's frequent use of the symbol of the reign of God, he did not give it a clear definition. What is meant by the reign of God and the values that it proclaims are implicit in Jesus's parables, miracles, and above all in his death and resurrection. After all, the kingdom of God has come in and with Jesus who himself is the *auto-basileia*, the very embodiment of the kingdom. In a nutshell, the reign of God is nothing less than God's saving presence and action in God's two hands, the Word of God made flesh in Jesus of Nazareth and the Holy Spirit, a presence that brings about forgiveness and reconciliation and restores universal justice and peace between God and humanity, among humans themselves, and between humanity and the cosmos.

In the Asian economic, cultural, and religious contexts, Asian bishops and theologians propose that the church's mission of realizing the kingdom values take the form of a triple dialogue. The reason for this dialogical modality is the presence in Asia of the many living religions and rich cultures, among whom Christians are but a tiny minority and therefore must, even on the purely human level, enter into dialogue with other believers, in an attitude of respect and friendship, for survival. But, more than pragmatic considerations, there is the theological doctrine today, at least in the

---

[6] *Lumen Gentium*, no. 5.

Roman Catholic Church, that, as John Paul II says, "the Spirit's presence and activity affect not only individuals but also society and history, peoples, cultures and religions. Indeed, the Spirit is at the origin of the noble ideals and undertakings which benefit humanity on its journey through history."[7]

Given this religious pluralism, it is only natural that dialogue is the preferred mode of proclamation. As Michael Amaladoss puts it,

> As soon as one no longer sees the relationship of Christianity to other religions as presence/absence or superior/inferior or full/partial, dialogue becomes the context in which proclamation has to take place. For even when proclaiming the Good News with assurance, one should do it with great respect for the freedom of God who is acting, the freedom of the other who is responding and the Church's own limitations as a witness. It is quite proper then that the Asian Bishops characterized evangelization itself as a dialogue with various Asian realities—cultures, religions and the poor.[8]

It is important to note also that dialogue as a mode of being church in Asia does not refer primarily to the intellectual exchange among experts of various religions, as is often done in the West. Rather, it involves a fourfold presence:

> a. The *dialogue of life*, where people strive to live in an open and neighborly spirit, sharing their joys and sorrows, their human problems and preoccupations. b. The *dialogue of action*, in which Christians and others collaborate for the integral development and liberation of people. c. The *dialogue of theological exchange*, where specialists seek to deepen their understanding of their respective religious heritages, and to appreciate each other's spiritual values. d. The *dialogue of religious experience*, where persons, rooted in their own religious traditions, share their spiritual riches, for instance, with regard to prayer and contemplation, faith and ways of searching for God or the Absolute.[9]

---

[7] John Paul II, *Redemptoris Missio* (*RM*), no. 28. For the English translation of *RM*, see William Burrows, ed., *Redemption and Dialogue: Reading* Redemptoris Missio *and* Dialogue and Proclamation (Maryknoll, NY: Orbis Books, 1993), 3–55.

[8] Michael Amaladoss, *Making All Things New: Dialogue, Pluralism, and Evangelization in Asia* (Maryknoll, NY: Orbis Books, 1990), 59.

[9] The Pontifical Council for Interreligious Dialogue and the Congregation for the Evangelization of Peoples, *Dialogue and Proclamation*, 42 (May 19, 1991). See also *FAPA*, I, 21–26.

In terms of areas in which dialogue must be carried out, the FABC suggests three: dialogue with the Asian people, especially the poor; with their cultures; and with their religions.[10] In other words, the three essential tasks of the Asian churches are liberation, inculturation, and interreligious dialogue.[11] It is vital to note that for the FABC, these are not three distinct and separate activities of the church; rather they are three intertwined dimensions of the church's one mission of evangelization.[12] As the FABC's Seventh Plenary Assembly puts it concisely,

> These issues are not separate topics to be discussed, but aspects of an integrated approach to our Mission of Love and Service. We need to feel and act "integrally." As we face the needs of the 21st century, we do so with Asian hearts, in solidarity with the poor and the marginalized, in union with all our Christian brothers and sisters and by joining hands with all men and women of Asia of many different faiths. Inculturation, dialogue, justice and option for the poor are aspects of whatever we do.[13]

A Local Church Built on Communion and Equality

To be a kingdom-centered church, that is, an efficacious sign of the reign of God anywhere, the church must also be a truly local church built on communion and equality everywhere. And to achieve this goal, the church, according to the FABC, must be characterized by the following features.

1. First, the church, both at the local and universal levels, is seen primarily as "a *communion of communities*, where laity, Religious and clergy recognize and accept each other as sisters and brothers."[14] At the heart of

---

[10] See *FAPA*, I, 14–16, 22–23, 34–35, 107, 135, 141–43, 281–82, 307–12, 328–34, 344; *FAPA*, II, 196–203.

[11] As Archbishop Oscar V. Cruz, secretary general of the FABC, said at the Seventh Plenary Assembly: "The triple dialogue with the poor, with cultures, and with peoples of other religions, envisioned by FABC as a mode of evangelization, viz., human liberation, inculturation, interreligious dialogue." See *A Renewed Church in Asia: Pastoral Directions for a New Decade*. FABC Papers, no. 95 (Hong Kong: FABC, 2000), 17.

[12] For reflections on the connection between evangelization and liberation according to the FABC, see Peter C. Phan, "Human Development and Evangelization: The First to the Sixth Plenary Assembly of the Federation of Asian Bishops' Conferences," *Studia Missionalia* 47 (1998), 205–27.

[13] *FAPA*, III, 8.

[14] *FAPA*, II, 287. The FABC applies this vision of church as "communion of com-

the mystery of the church is the bond of communion uniting God with humanity and humans with one another, of which the Eucharist is the sign and instrument par excellence.

2. Moreover, in this ecclesiology there is an explicit and effective recognition of the *fundamental equality* among all the members of the local church as disciples of Jesus and among all the local churches insofar as they are communities of Jesus's disciples and whose communion constitutes the universal church. The communion (*koinonia*) which constitutes the church, both at the local and universal levels, and from which flows the fundamental equality of all Christians, is rooted at its deepest level in the life of the Trinity in whom there is a perfect communion of equals. This fundamental equality among all Christians, which is affirmed by Vatican II,[15] annuls neither the existence of the hierarchy in the church nor the papal primacy. Rather it indicates the modality in which papal primacy and hierarchical authority should be exercised in the church, that is, in collegiality, coresponsibility, and accountability to all the members of the church. Unless this fundamental equality of all Christians with its implications for church governance is acknowledged and put into practice through concrete policies and actions, the church will not become a communion of communities.

This vision of church as communion of communities and its corollary, namely, fundamental equality, are the sine qua non condition for the fulfillment of the church's mission. Without being a communion, the church cannot fulfill its mission, since the church is, as indicated above, nothing but the bond of communion between God and humanity and among humans themselves. As *EA* puts it tersely, "communion and mission go hand in hand."[16]

---

munities" to the church both at the local and universal levels: "It [the church] is a community not closed in on itself and its particular concerns, but *linked* with many bonds *to other communities of faith* (concretely, the parishes and dioceses around them) and to the one and universal communion, *catholica unitas*, of the holy Church of the Lord" (*FAPA*, I, 56). In other words, not only the diocese but also the church universal are a communion of communities. The universal church is not a church above the other dioceses and of which the local churches are constitutive "parts" with the pope as its universal bishop. Rather, it is a communion in faith, hope and love of all the local churches (among which there is the Church of Rome of which the pope is the bishop), a communion in which the pope functions as the instrument of unity in collegiality and co-responsibility with other bishops.

[15] See *Lumen Gentium*, no. 32: "All the faithful enjoy a true equality with regard to the dignity and the activity which they share in the building up of the body of Christ."

[16] *EA*, no. 24.

3. This pastoral "discipleship of equals" leads to the third characteristic of the new way of being church in Asia, that is, the participatory and collaborative nature of all the ministries in the church: "It is a *participatory* Church where the gifts that the Holy Spirit gives to all the faithful—lay, Religious, and cleric alike—are recognized and activated, so that the church may be built up and its mission realized."[17] This participatory nature of the church must be lived out not only in the local church but also among all the local churches, including the Church of Rome, of course, with due recognition of the papal primacy. In this context it is encouraging to read in *EA* the following affirmation:

> It is in fact within the perspective of ecclesial communion that the universal authority of the successor of Peter shines forth more clearly, not primarily as juridical power over the local churches, but above all as a pastoral primacy at the service of the unity of faith and life of the whole people of God.[18]

A "pastoral primacy" must do everything possible to foster coresponsibility and participation of all the local churches in the triple ministry of teaching, sanctification, and service in the church, and must be held accountable to this task so that these words do not remain at the level of pious rhetoric but are productive of concrete structures and actions.

4. The fourth characteristic of the new way of being church in Asia is the *dialogical* spirit: "Built in the hearts of people, it is a Church that faithfully and lovingly witnesses to the Risen Lord and reaches out to people of other faiths and persuasions in a dialogue of life towards the integral liberation of all."[19] Ever since its first plenary assembly in Taipei, Taiwan,

---

[17] *FAPA*, I, 287. See also ibid., 56: "It [the Church] is a community of authentic *participation and co-responsibility*, where genuine sharing of gifts and responsibilities obtains, where the talents and charisms of each one are accepted and exercised in diverse ministries, and where all are schooled to the attitudes and practices of mutual listening and dialogue, common discernment of the Spirit, common witness and collaborative action." "The Exhortation also recognizes this participatory character of the Church but emphasizes the fact that each person must live his or her 'proper vocation' and perform his or her 'proper role'" (*EA*, no. 25). There is here a concern to maintain a clear distinction of roles in ministry, whereas the FABC is concerned that all people with their varied gifts have the opportunity to participate in the ministry of the Church.

[18] *EA*, no. 25.

[19] *FAPA*, I, 287–88.

1974, the FABC has repeatedly insisted that the primary task of the Asian Churches is the proclamation of the Gospel. But it has also maintained no less frequently that the way to fulfill this task in Asia, as pointed out above, is by way of dialogue, indeed a triple dialogue, with Asian cultures, Asian religions, and the Asians themselves, especially the poor.[20]

5. The fifth and last feature of the new way of being church in Asia is *prophecy*: The church is "a leaven of transformation in this world and serves as a *prophetic sign* daring to point beyond this world to the ineffable Kingdom that is yet fully to come."[21] As far as Asia is concerned, in being "a leaven of transformation in this world," the church must now understand its mission of "making disciples of all nations" not in terms of converting as many Asians as possible to the church (which is a very unlikely possibility) and in the process increasing its influence as a social institution. Rather, being a "small remnant" and likely to remain so for the foreseeable future, Christians must journey with the followers of other Asian religions and together with them—not instead of, or worse, against them—work for the coming of the kingdom of God.

This necessity to be local churches living in communion with each other was reiterated by the FABC's Seventh Plenary Assembly (Samphran, Thailand, January 3–12, 2000). Coming right after the Asian Synod and the promulgation of the Apostolic Exhortation *EA* and celebrating the Great Jubilee, with the general theme of "A Renewed Church in Asia: A Mission of Love and Service," this assembly is of particular significance because it highlights the kind of ecclesiology operative in the Asian churches. In the first place, the FABC takes a retrospective glance over a quarter of a century of its life and activities and summarizes its "Asian Vision of a Renewed Church." It sees it as composed of eight movements that constitute a sort of Asian ecclesiology. Given its central importance, the text deserves to be quoted in full:

> 1. A movement towards a Church of the Poor and a Church of the Young. "If we are to place ourselves at the side of the multitudes in our continent, we must in our way of life share something of their poverty," "speak out for the rights of the disadvantaged and power-

---

[20] For the intrinsic connection between the proclamation of the Gospel and dialogue in its triple form, see *FAPA*, I, 13–16.

[21] *FAPA*, III, 288.

less, against all forms of injustice." In this continent of the young, we must become "in them and for them, the Church of the young" (Meeting of Asian Bishops, Manila, Philippines, 1970).

2. A movement toward a "truly local Church," toward a Church "incarnate in a people, a Church indigenous and inculturated" (2 FABC Plenary Assembly, Calcutta, 1978).

3. A movement toward deep interiority so that the Church becomes a "deeply praying community whose contemplation is inserted in the context of our time and the cultures of our peoples today. Integrated into everyday life, "authentic prayer has to engender in Christians a clear witness of service and love" (2 FABC Plenary Assembly, Calcutta, 1978).

4. A movement toward an authentic community of faith. Fully rooted in the life of the Trinity, the Church in Asia has to be a communion of communities of authentic participation and co-responsibility, one with its pastors, and linked "to other communities of faith and to the one and universal communion" of the holy Church of the Lord. The movement in Asia toward Basic Ecclesial Communities expresses the deep desire to be such a community of faith, love and service and to be truly a "community of communities" and open to building up Basic Human Communities (3 FABC Plenary Assembly, Bangkok, 1982).

5. A movement toward active integral evangelization, toward a new sense of mission (5 FABC Plenary Assembly, Bandung, Indonesia, 1990). We evangelize because we believe Jesus is the Lord and Savior, "the goal of human history . . ., the joy of all hearts, and the fulfillment of all aspirations" (GS, 45). In this mission, the Church has to be a compassionate companion and partner of all Asians, a servant of the Lord and of all Asian peoples in the journey toward full life in God's Kingdom.

6. A movement toward empowerment of men and women. We must evolve participative church structures in order to use the personal talents and skills of lay women and men. Empowered by the Spirit and through the sacraments, lay men and women should be involved

in the life and mission of the Church by bringing the Good News of Jesus to bear upon the fields of business and politics, of education and health, of mass media and the world of work. This requires a spirituality of discipleship enabling both the clergy and laity to work together in their own specific roles in the common mission of the Church (4 FABC Plenary Assembly, Tokyo, 1986). The Church cannot be a sign of the Kingdom and of the eschatological community if the fruits of the Spirit to women are not given due recognition, and if women do not share in the "freedom of the children of God" (4 FABC Plenary Assembly, Tokyo, 1986).

7. A movement toward active involvement in generating and serving life. The Church has to respond to the death-dealing forces in Asia. By authentic discipleship, it has to share its vision of full life as promised by Jesus. It is a vision of life with integrity and dignity, with compassion and sensitive care of the earth; a vision of participation and mutuality, with a reverential sense of the sacred, of peace, harmony, and solidarity (6 FABC Plenary Assembly, Manila, Philippines, 1995).

8. A movement toward the triple dialogue with other faiths, with the poor and with the cultures, a Church "in dialogue with the great religious traditions of our peoples," in fact, a dialogue with all people, especially the poor.[22]

This eightfold movement describes in a nutshell the new way of being church in Asia. Essentially, it aims at transforming the churches *in* Asia into the churches *of* Asia. Inculturation, understood in its widest sense, is the way to achieve this goal of becoming local churches. This need for inculturation in the church's mission of "love and service," according to the FABC's Seventh Plenary Assembly, has grown even more insistent in light of the challenges facing Christianity in Asia in the next millennium such as the increasing marginalization and exclusion of many people by globalization, widespread fundamentalism, dictatorship and corruption in government,

[22] *A Renewed Church in Asia: A Mission of Love and Service: The Final Statement of the Seventh Plenary Assembly of the Federation of Asian Bishops' Conferences. Samphran, Thailand, January 3–12, 2000*, 3–4. For the Final Statement of the Seventh FABC Plenary Assembly, see *FAPA*, III, 1–16.

ecological destruction, and growing militarization. The FABC sees these challenges affecting special groups of people in a particular way, namely, youth, women, the family, indigenous people, and sea-based and land-based migrants and refugees.[23] To meet these challenges fully, the FABC believes that it is urgent to promote the "Asianness" of the church, which it sees as "a special gift the world is waiting for": "This means that the Church has to be an embodiment of the Asian vision and values of life, especially interiority, harmony, a holistic and inclusive approach to every area of life."[24]

In sum, this Asian way of being church places the highest priority on communion and collegiality at all the levels of church life and activities. At the vertical level, communion is realized with the Trinitarian God whose *perichoresis* the church is commissioned to reflect in history. On the horizontal level, communion is achieved with other local churches, and within each local church, communion is realized through collegiality, by which all members, especially laywomen and men, are truly and effectively empowered to use of their gifts to make the church an authentically local church.

At this point it is helpful to return to the three warnings of the CDF about kingdom-centered ecclesiology, namely, silence about the kingdom of Christ, silence about the mystery of redemption, and undervaluing of the role of the church. Any fair reading of the FABC's theology of the church—which I call "dialogical ecclesiology" and to which I fully subscribe—will agree that it totally eschews these three dangers. There is in it no silence about the kingdom of Christ, nor about redemption, nor about the role of the church, even though it does not use *DI*'s favorite expressions "unicity" and "universal salvific mediation." With regard to Christ, the Sixth FABC Plenary Assembly (January 1995) offers one of the most comprehensive and moving portraits of Christ: "The image of Jesus—man of the creative Spirit, friend of God, person of interiority, bringer of harmony, lover of the poor, healer and liberator, bold prophet, suffering companion, victor over death, sharer of his Spirit—resonates with the Asian peoples' vision of life."[25]

With regard to redemption, the FABC insists on not only the salvation of individuals from sin but also the removal of what it calls "death-dealing forces": "whatever threatens, weakens, diminishes and destroys the life of individuals, groups or peoples; whatever devalues human beings, conceived,

---

[23] See *FAPA*, III, 6–12.

[24] *FAPA*, III, 265.

[25] *FAPA*, II, 7.

born, infant, old; whatever socio-cultural, religious, political, economic, or environmental factor that threatens or destroys life in our countries."[26]

With regard to the role of the church, the FABC's Seventh Plenary Assembly (2000) took as its theme "A Renewed Church in Asia: A Mission of Love and Service," an incontrovertible evidence that "church" is not swept aside in Asian theology. But what the FABC has in mind when seeking church renewal in Asia might not be what *DI* is concerned about when it condemns kingdom-centered ecclesiology for "either leaving little room for the Church or undervaluing the Church in reaction to a presumed 'ecclesiocentrism' of the past and because they [proponents of kingdom-centered ecclesiology] consider the Church herself only a sign, for that matter a sign not without ambiguity" (no. 19). First of all, note the strikingly palpable defensive tone of the quoted passage. It refers to "presumed"(!) ecclesiocentrism when this feature is readily acknowledged by anyone passably familiar with the Roman Catholic ecclesiology since Vatican I, which is not only "ecclesiocentric" but also "Roman-Curia-centric." The expression "contrary to Catholic faith" is liberally sprinkled throughout the document to characterize opinions that differ from its own. Furthermore, it laments the fact that regnocentric theologians view the church as "a sign not without ambiguity" even while it was dealing behind closed doors with clergy sex-abuse scandals and episcopal cover-up. Contrast this self-exculpatory tone with the FABC's honest admission of the church's mistakes in its attitude toward other religions:

> This basic negative attitude of the Church and Christian theology towards other Asian cultures and religions accounts for much of the failure of the Christian mission to strike roots in Asia and come to a genuine encounter with the religious traditions of Buddhism, Confucianism, Hinduism, Islam and the many other Asian religions.[27]

With regard to church structures, the FABC is blunt when describing the church renewal it tries to promote: "A renewal that does not count merely on numbers and crowded churches, nor on the numerous services we render. What counts inestimably more is our identity and the quality of our witness as servants and disciples of Jesus and the Kingdom of God for the peoples of Asia."[28]

---

[26] *FAPA*, II, 3.

[27] *FAPA*, II, 240.

[28] *FAPA*, III, 5.

Clearly, Asian dialogical ecclesiology, which is expounded in *BRI*, has little to do with either the kingdom-centered ecclesiology condemned by *DI* or that espoused by *DI* itself, in both substance and tone. Perhaps the radical difference between the FABC and the CDF's *DI* lies in what the former calls "the Asian soul." Instead of insisting on the "unicity" of Christ, and much less that of the church, dialogical ecclesiology emphasizes, to use the much-dreaded word in *DI*'s theology of the relation between Christianity and other religions, namely, "complementarity." Citing the authority of no less than St. John Paul's Apostolic Exhortation *EA* (no. 6), the Sixth FABC Plenary Assembly (January 1995) declares that it believes in

> the innate spiritual insight and moral wisdom in the Asian soul; and it is the core around which a growing sense of "being Asian" is built. This "being Asian" is best discovered and affirmed not in confrontation and opposition, but in the spirit of *complementary and harmony.* In this framework of *complementarity and harmony,* the Church can communicate the Gospel in a way which is faithful both to her own Tradition and to the Asian soul.[29]

Later, in April of the same year, the FABC's Theological Advisory Commission, later known as the Office of Theological Concern, issued a seventy-page document entitled *Asian Christian Perspectives on Harmony*, in which the relation between the church and Asian cultures and religions is amply discussed.[30] After reviewing the various challenges to harmony in Asia and the different attempts at promoting harmony, the document explains what it means by "harmony": "Harmony is neither a compromising with conflictual realities, nor a complacency about the existing order. Harmony demands a transformative attitude and action to bring about a change in contemporary society. This can be provided only by a prophetic spirituality which exercises charitable but courageous criticism of the situation."[31]

To develop an Asian theology of harmony, the document goes on to say, over against the "method proper to Catholic theology" imposed by the United States Conference of Catholic Bishops' Committee on Doctrine and in line with the theological approach I propose in Chapter 2, it

---

[29] *FAPA*, III, 9, emphasis added.
[30] See *FAPA*, III, 229–98.
[31] *FAPA*, II, 290.

cannot be formed solely within the categories of a traditional Christian theology, by reading Christian revelation and applying its principles to the conflictual situation in Asia. It has to be a reading and reflection of the realities themselves, along with other religions and cultural revelations, as well as of the messages continually emerging from the conflicts themselves.[32]

From such a theology of harmony a new Christology will emerge, which the FABC's Theological Advisory Committee calls "a Cosmic Christology of Harmony" and a "Cosmic Ecclesiology." In words that anticipate Pope Francis's *The Joy of the Gospel,* the committee boldly declares: "We must evolve a Cosmic Christology of Harmony. Only by basing itself on such a Christology will the theology of the Church go beyond its institutional concerns to understand the Church essentially as a centrifugal Church, open to the whole universe and present in and for the universe (Cosmic Ecclesiology)."[33] The "centrifugal Church" is by nature missionary, but how mission is to be understood and carried out in Asia is something requiring a quite different missiology from the one implicit in *DI.*

Mission *Inter Gentes Asiae*

Contemporary Theologies and Practices of Mission in Asia

Christian mission to non-Christians used to be called, and still is in the documents of the papal magisterium, *missio ad gentes.*[34] Note the theological force of the preposition *ad* (to). The *gentes,* that is, those who have not yet accepted the good news and are still to be incorporated into the church through baptism, were once termed *pagans* or *heathens,* and were regarded as the object or target of evangelization and conversion.

Though proselytism, that is, conversion of the *gentes* by physical force, psychological pressure, or material enticements, is frowned upon, the *gentes* are still thought to be those *to* whom the Gospel is "proclaimed" and

---

[32] *FAPA,* II, 291–92.

[33] *FAPA,* II, 294.

[34] See, for instance, Pope John Paul II's encyclical on mission *Redemptoris Missio* (1990). The pope laments the waning of *missio ad gentes* and devotes a whole chapter of his encyclical to it (Chapter IV: "The Vast Horizons of the Mission *Ad Gentes*").

"preached." In *missio ad gentes*, the missionaries preach, the *gentes* listen; the missionaries teach, the *gentes* learn; the missionaries bestow the means of sanctification, the *gentes* receive them; the missionaries lead, the *gentes* follow; the missionaries command, the *gentes* obey.[35] In other words, the *gentes* are the beneficiaries of the threefold ministry—prophetic, priestly, and kingly—of the missionaries. In contrast to *ad*, the preposition *inter* abolishes this one-way direction from the missionaries to the *gentes* in which the former enjoy superiority and dominance over the latter in all aspects of life and radically reframes their relationships. It establishes fundamental interdependence and equal relationship between the two groups. Mission is not something done by one group, that is, Christian missionaries, *to* and *for* another, that is, Asian non-Christians, but rather something carried by *both* groups to and for each other. Thus, instead of *missio ad gentes*, contemporary missiology speaks of *missio inter gentes* (mission among the peoples). Furthermore, mission in Asia is a collaborative work carried out by Christians and non-Christians *together* for a common cause so that *missio inter gentes Asiae* (mission among the peoples of Asia) must also be *missio cum gentibus Asiae* (mission with the peoples of Asia). In contrast to the traditional understanding of mission as *missio ad gentes*, which undergirds *DI*, I will present this new double understanding of Christian mission, *missio inter gentes* and *missio cum gentibus*, especially in Asia.[36] I begin with a description of the religious situation of Asians as *gentes*.

---

[35] I am not asserting that this is how all missionaries who adopt the *missio ad gentes* model actually behave; in fact, many don't. I am only claiming that the *missio ad gentes* model of mission conceives, at least implicitly, the relation between the missionary and the *gentes* in this way.

[36] Among the plethora of contemporary works on mission the following deserve mentioned: David Bosch, *Transforming Mission: Paradigm Shifts in Theology of Mission*, 20th Anniversary Edition (Maryknoll, NY: Orbis Books, 2011); J. Andrew Kirk, *What Is Mission? Theological Explorations* (Minneapolis: Fortress Press, 2000); Stephen B. Bevans and Roger P. Schroeder, *Constants in Context: A Theology of Mission for Today* (Maryknoll, NY: Orbis Books, 2004); Stephen Bevans and Roger Schroeder, eds., *Mission for the Twenty-first Century* (Chicago: CCGM Publications, 2001); Roger Schroeder, *What Is the Mission of the Church? A Guide for Catholics* (Maryknoll, NY: Orbis Books, 2008); Wilbert R. Shenk, *Changing Frontiers of Mission* (Maryknoll, NY: Orbis Books, 1999); Andrew Walls and Cathy Ross, eds., *Mission in the 21st Century: Exploring the Five Marks of Global Mission* (Maryknoll, NY: Orbis Books, 2008); Robert J. Schreiter, ed., *Mission in the Third Millennium* (Maryknoll, NY: Orbis Books, 2001); Francis Anekwe Oborji, *Concepts of Mission: The Evolution of Contemporary Missiology* (Maryknoll, NY: Orbis Books, 2006); Dana Robert, *Christian Mission: How Christianity Became a World Religion* (Oxford: Wiley-Blackwell, 2009); Charles E. Van Engen, Darrell Whiteman, and

I then expound the concept of *missio inter gentes* and *missio sum gentibus* and their missiological implications. Lastly, I explore the practices of mission in light of *missio inter gentes* and *missio cum gentibus*.[37]

The Context for Christian Mission in Asia:
Who Are the *Gentes* of Asia?

The first context is paradoxical since in a true theological sense Asians are not the *gentes* in the old meaning of this term, that is, *pagans* or *heathens*. The term *gens/gentes* has a long and complex history. It has its roots in the Hebrew *goy/goyim*, which was used to designate the "nations," that is, those peoples who, in Israel's view, have not been chosen to be in covenant with Yahweh, the non-Jews, the uncircumcised, and the impure. The Hebrew *goy/goyim* was translated with the Greek *ethne* (with the adjective *ethnikos*, meaning "belonging to the nations"); in turn, *ethne/ethnikos* was translated with the Latin *gentes/gentiles*. Finally, the Latin *gentes/gentiles* is often rendered in English as pagan or heathen. Pagan comes from the Latin *paganus*, literally, villager, often in the pejorative sense of uncultured, as opposed to sophisticated city-dweller or urban.

From the third century, *paganus* was equated with non-Christian, since the majority of Christians were city-dwellers. Soon, it acquired the connotation of idolatry and superstition and was applied to Hellenistic and Roman religions, which were regarded as rife with doctrinal errors, moral depravities, and idolatrous worship. After the discovery of the Americas and Asia, the term designates the indigenous religions of these continents, and their inhabitants are called the *gentes* (or *pagani*) and are considered as the primary target of Christian missions, the *missio ad gentes*.

In the aftermath of Vatican II, the Catholic Church's perception of the *gentes* and their religions has undergone a radical change. *Nostra Aetate*'s statement regarding non-Christian religions illustrates this theological shift well:

J. Dudley Woodberry, eds., *Paradigm Shifts in Christian Witness: Insights from Anthropology, Communications, and Spiritual Power* (Maryknoll, NY: Orbis Books, 2008); and Robert L. Gallagher and Paul Hertig, eds., *Landmark Essays in Mission and World Christianity* (Maryknoll, NY: Orbis Books, 2009).

[37] For a survey of contemporary Asian Christianity, see Peter C. Phan, ed., *Christianities in Asia* (Oxford: Wiley-Blackwell, 2010).

The Catholic Church rejects nothing of what is true and holy in these religions. It has a high regard for the manner of life and conduct, the precepts and doctrines which, although differing in many ways form its own teaching, nevertheless often reflect a ray of that truth which enlightens all men and women. (no. 2)[38]

Compared with the older concept of *gentes*, Vatican II's description of the *gentes* and of the relation between them and the church represents, as it were, a Copernican revolution, and this sea change must be taken into account when we refer to Asians as *gentes* in either *missio ad gentes* or *missio inter gentes*. Clearly, we can no longer view Asians as people living in spiritual darkness and sin who cannot be saved except through conversion to Christianity, nor can we condemn their religions as human inventions corrupted by superstitions and vices.

Second, the political situation of a huge number—well over one billion—of the *gentes Asiae* massively complicates the work of Christian missionaries, and that is, the continuing domination of the Socialist–Communist system, mainly in China and Vietnam. As is well known, the relation between the Vatican and the Chinese government, as well as between the "official" or "patriotic" church and the "unregistered" or "underground" Church in China, and the fraught *modus vivendi* of Christianity in Vietnam present enormous challenges to how Christian mission is to be carried out. While both China and Vietnam are increasingly adopting the free market economy, their Communist governments still regard Christianity, and especially the Catholic Church with its Vatican City State, as a threat, if not an enemy, to their survival. The *gentes Asiae* are thus a complex religious and political species among whom missionaries must dwell, and their work of evangelization is profoundly affected by these two aspects of Asian religions and politics.

Third, there is a stubborn fact that despite centuries of Christian mission, Christianity in Asia still remains a very small minority. Except in the Philippines, Timor-Leste, South Korea, and Vietnam, Christians make up only a tiny percentage of the population, especially in the three most populous countries, namely, China, India, and Indonesia. Though there are

---

[38] The English translation is taken from Austin Flannery, ed., *Vatican II: Constitutions Decrees Declarations* (Northport, NY: Costello, 2007). For a comprehensive overview of Catholic theology of religion, see Karl J. Becker and Ilana Morali, eds., *Catholic Engagement with World Religions: A Comprehensive Study* (Maryknoll, NY: Orbis Books, 2010).

breathless reports about a vast number of conversions, especially in the Evangelical/Pentecostal Churches in China, mass conversions of Asians to Christianity are, barring an act of divine intervention, extremely unlikely. In other words, the *gentes Asiae* will most likely remain *gentes*, even if there were to be a massive evangelization in the future, and the main reason for this state of affairs, as Aloysius Pieris has pointed out, is that Asians already have their well-established religions.[39] This prognosis must not of course discourage mission work nor dampen missionary zeal, but it is important to take note of it so that missionaries will not entertain unrealistic expectations, and the lack of conversion and baptism will not be taken as evidence of the failure of Christian mission.[40]

Objectives and Tasks of Missio inter Gentes Asiae

In this complex and multifaceted situation of the *gentes Asiae*, what must be the tasks and objectives of Christian mission in Asia? Of course, the answer depends largely on how certain key New Testament texts regarding the so-called missionary mandate are selected and interpreted, such as Matthew 28:19–10, Mark 16:15–18, Luke 24:47–48. Another possible approach is to examine both the teaching and the practice of the paradigmatic missionary, namely, the apostle Paul, as described in his letters and the Book of Acts.[41] While acknowledging the fruitfulness of these two ways, I propose a third, that is, examining the *missionary practice* of Jesus himself, and not only his words, during his public ministry as a whole. It is in the light of Jesus's practice of his mission that the above-cited biblical texts, as well as Paul's teaching and practice, can be correctly understood. Subsequently we will ask how Jesus's missionary practice can be a model for mission *inter gentes* and *cum gentibus Asiae*.

---

[39] See Aloysius Pieris, *An Asian Theology of Liberation* (Maryknoll, NY: Orbis Books, 1988).

[40] On the relation between mission and conversion, see Peter C. Phan, *In Our Own Tongues: Perspectives from Asia on Mission and Inculturation* (Maryknoll, NY: Orbis, 2004), 45–61.

[41] There is no point in citing works on mission in the New Testament here since there are literally legions of them. For a massive, two-volume study, totaling three thousand pages (quite a few of them with very small print!), see Eckhard J. Schnanel, *Early Christian Mission* vol. 1 *Jesus and the Twelve* and vol. 2 *Paul and the Early Church* (Downers Grove, IL: InterVarsity Press, 2004).

Missio inter Gentes as Bridge-Building

Before exploring the tasks and objectives of Christian mission *inter gentes Asiae* in the light of Jesus's missionary practice, I would like to examine mission as bridging the divides that separate groups of people. Demographically, according to Pio Estepa, there are today in Asia three divides: urban dwellers vs. rural people, nationals vs. migrants, and the educated vs. the illiterates.[42] Joining the two sides of these three divides together through bridge-building constitutes the primary task of Christian mission in Asia today. This crossing must be a mutual movement, a two-way traffic, so as to enable all the groups to communicate with each other and to live and work together for the common good, enjoying equal rights and dignity. The ultimate goal of this crossing over and mutual encounter is the removal of all factors contributing to mutual hatred and reconciliation of the various groups living on the opposite sides of the three divides, in both society and church.[43] The hoped-for result is new human and ecclesial communities marked by justice, forgiveness, peace, and love. Needless to say, missionaries have an important role to play in promoting this bridge-building process and reconciliation.

Of course, bridge-building and reconciliation do not require forgetting, much less ignoring, past and current injustices committed by those having the power and means to control the crossing of the industrial, migrational, and informational divides and, in order to maintain their hegemony, bar others from coming over into their domains. On the contrary, genuine and long-lasting reconciliation is impossible without remembering the past truthfully, by victimizers and victims, the former to acknowledge their guilt, and the latter to regain their human dignity in spite of their dehumanizing sufferings. Only from this truthful memory can both victims and victimizers work together to build a new society with legal and political structures promoting justice, equality, and reconciliation. Furthermore, this task of bridge-building does not in any way invalidate the "option for the poor"

---

[42] See Pio Estepa, "The Asian Landscape of Mission in the 21st Century," Lecture given at SEDOS Residential Seminar, May 17–21, 2011.

[43] On the reconciliation as part of mission, see the numerous works of Robert Schreiter. See also Peter C. Phan, "Peace Building and Reconciliation: Interreligious Dialogue and Catholic Spirituality," in *Peacebuilding: Catholic Theology, Ethics, and Praxis*, ed. Robert J. Schreiter, R. Scott Appleby, and Gerard Powers (Maryknoll, NY: Orbis Books, 2010), 332–65.

that was the hallmark of Jesus's ministry and has been repeatedly advocated by the FABC.

In addition to understanding *missio inter gentes* as bridge-building *between* the two sides of the three divides, I suggest that we take the preposition *inter* in the phrase *missio inter gentes* to mean *among* or *in the midst of*, so that *missio inter gentes* means *reciprocal* mission between the missionaries and the *gentes Asiae*. In other words, mission is not a one-way activity, done by the missionaries to the *gentes*, but rather a two-way activity done by the *gentes* to the missionaries and by the missionaries to the *gentes*. It is therefore a *mutual* mission: both the missionaries and the *gentes* "do mission" (as agents) and "are missioned" (as recipients). Furthermore, in addition to reciprocity between missionaries and the *gentes*, mission in Asia is performed *together*, so that *missio inter gentes* is also *missio cum gentibus,* which implies that there is a common cause to which both the missionaries and the *gentes* are committed and for which they labor together. I now explore these two aspects of *missio inter gentes* and *cum gentibus Asiae* in some detail.

Missio inter Gentes as Mutual Evangelization

Perhaps a story in the life of Chrys McVey (1933–2009), the American Dominican veteran missionary in Pakistan, serves as the best illustration of what follows. Once he was asked how many converts he had made during his four decades of mission; he replied, "One, myself."[44] It is a widely common experience of mission in Asia (and of course also elsewhere) that in evangelizing the *gentes*, missionaries themselves are evangelized by them, and indeed, that the effectiveness of their mission work depends on the extent to which they are open to being evangelized by the *gentes*. By this, I do not refer to the banal fact that there are *gentes* who are much wiser and holier, even by Christian standards, than the missionaries themselves, or that there are certain official actions by the church as an institution that the *gentes* deem immoral and therefore find no compelling reasons to join the church. I refer rather to the fact that in not a few areas of Christian life, there are teachings and practices of the religions and cultures of the *gentes* that missionaries would do well to learn and practice in order to be better Christians and missionaries. Examples abound in areas such as sacred

---

[44] See Prakash Lohale and Kevin Toomey, eds., *Dialogue as Mission: Remembering Chrys McVey* (Chicago: New Priory Press, 2014).

books, ethics, prayer, spirituality, and monasticism. This fact was recognized by luminaries such as Matteo Ricci in China, Roberto de Nobili in India, Alexandre de Rhodes in Vietnam, and countless other, lesser-known but no less effective, missionaries, both women and men, in the distant past as well as in the present.[45]

Recognizing and celebrating the goodness and holiness of people outside one's religious tradition and culture—the *goyim* or *gentes*—is not an invention of progressive missionaries. It was practiced by Jesus himself. Jesus praises the Samaritan leper who alone among the ten lepers whom he has cured comes back to thank him (Luke 17:17–18). He also holds up a Samaritan as the model of love of neighbor (Luke 10:33–35). Jesus is said to have been astonished or amazed by "such great faith" of the Roman centurion (Matthew 8:10). That Jesus was—and did not pretend to be—"astonished" (*ethaumasen*) implies that the existence of such faith in a *goy* was something he did not expect or know. Thus, in a real sense, the Roman centurion's faith-filled behavior revealed to Jesus how universal God's saving grace is. Even more tellingly, the "great faith" (Matthew 15:28) and the perseverance of the Canaanite woman, in spite of Jesus's curt, even insulting, refusal to grant her request for her daughter's healing, and her humble retort that even "the dogs [a Jewish term of abuse for the *goyim*, which Jesus himself used] eat the crumbs that fall under their masters' table" (Matthew 15:27) succeeded in changing Jesus's earlier understanding that he was sent only to the lost sheep of Israel. Here, it is Jesus's ethnocentric understanding of his ministry that was changed and enlarged by a Gentile, and a woman to boot!

In their work, in light of Jesus's own practice, missionaries in Asia must be willing and able to open their minds and hearts to be changed intellectually and transformed spiritually by the "reverse mission" of the *gentes Asiae* to them. Admittedly, they are severely hampered in this by the fact that the traditional descriptions of mission as "teaching," "proclamation," "evangelization," and "conversion" that form part of the theology of *missio ad gentes* do not dispose missionaries to adopting a posture of listening and humility.[46] Indeed, if one comes to a foreign place with the conviction that

---

[45] In this context it is vitally important, even a matter of sheer justice and historical accuracy, to recognize the role of lay women and women religious in mission. On this, see the pioneering works of Dana Robert.

[46] On the relationship among proclamation and mission, see Phan, *In Our Own Tongues*, 32–44.

one or one's church already possesses exclusively all the truths in all their fullness; that one's primary task is to "proclaim" these truths, as if standing at a pulpit or behind a lectern, with a megaphone in hand, and "teach" them like an all-knowing professor; and that the objective of one's mission is to "convert" the *gentes*, would it come as a surprise that the *gentes* are seen as nothing but targets of one's mission (as implied by the preposition *ad*) and that success in mission is measured by the number of baptisms, just as victory in a war is demonstrated by the number of casualties and cities destroyed or occupied? Would it be strange that the *gentes Asiae* will look upon Christian mission as a neocolonialist attempt to conquer and destroy their religions? How can we plausibly defend ourselves against this charge if in fact the goal of our mission is to "convert" the followers of other religions to Christianity?

In contrast, as a thought experiment, suppose we no longer use terms that imply superior knowledge and moral excellence, such as *evangelize, convert, teach,* and *proclaim* to describe the objectives and tasks of Christian mission, so prevalent in magisterial documents and used by theological watchdogs as a litmus test for orthodoxy. What would missionaries do and how would they act if they come to Asia not as proclaimers and teachers and converters and evangelizers but as guests—and uninvited, and even unwanted, guests at that—who totally depend for their physical and spiritual survival on the kindness and generosity of the *gentes* as hosts? What if we bring our Christian faith not as something to be proclaimed and taught in order to evangelize and convert the Asian *gentes* but as a humble gift, as a token of our gratitude for their hospitality, which our hosts have the perfect right to accept or refuse, use or not use? What if, as befitting grateful guests, we do not insist that they abandon their beliefs and adopt ours, reject their moral norms and follow ours, condemn their rituals and practice ours, disown their religions and be baptized into ours? Suppose, with a sincere and humble heart, we let ourselves be "taught," "proclaimed," "evangelized," and "converted" by our hosts' beliefs, moral values, modes of worship, and religious affiliations because in fact there are things that are of great, or even greater, truth and value in these than in ours.[47]

Perhaps, someday, after we have known and trusted each other as friends, we can play host in our turn and invite the *gentes* as honored guests into our spiritual home, which we call "church." Then we can proudly display its

---

[47] On the concept of the missionary as guest, see the insightful writings of the Catholic anthropologist and missiologist Anthony Gittins.

splendor and *gemütlichkeit*, its welcoming atmosphere and warm hospitality. Then we can talk about our beliefs and practices; tell them our family history, from the ancient Hebrews to Jesus to us as Jesus's disciples, with warts and all; and invite them to create with us a larger religious family made up of theirs and ours. But then we must reckon with the likelihood that as guests, they too will bring us their own gifts of faith, which may very well be of great use to us, or which we even may find that we are in need of very badly. In this way, our mission is no longer *ad gentes* but *inter gentes*. The "evangelizers" become "evangelized" and the "evangelized" become "evangelizers," in mutual respect and appreciation, in open honesty and genuine friendship, correcting one another when necessary, and always reaching out to greater truth and goodness. In such dialogical mode of mission, is there any need to insist on the "unicity" and "salvific universality" of Jesus and the church?

Missio cum Gentibus:
The "Reign of God" as Our Shared Goal and Destiny

The above reflections on *missio inter gentes Asiae* may appear to some to deny the possibility and necessity of mission (as *BRI* has been accused of doing). In fact, however, what is denied is only that conversion, baptism, and incorporation into the church should be conceived *simply and exclusively* as the goal and fulfillment of mission. In other words, what is denied is not the possibility and necessity of mission as such. Rather it is denied that mission should be undertaken simply as *missio ad gentes,* and not primarily as *missio inter gentes.* What mission should intend to do is not simply making the *gentes* into members of our presently existing church, which, with all its current beliefs, practices, and institutions, is still too small and narrow in structural design, too limited and provincial (i.e., Western and Roman) in theological outlook, too imperfect and even sinful in institutional leadership to offer the *gentes* a livable home.

In fact, before we invite our guests into our home, even for a short visit, let alone for a permanent stay, must we not, as good hosts, clean and spruce it up, even remodel and rebuild it, to meet their special needs and to make them feel welcome and comfortable? So, too, must we do with the church and with the help with the *gentes.* It is also a common practice for the host to ask the guests in advance what kinds of food and drink they cannot eat and which they favor. So also must we do when we invite the *gentes* to come to (or into) the church, our spiritual home: are there, we must ask ourselves, anything they find objectionable or harmful, and anything to be modified and improved? In this way, our church will truly become the "house of God for all peoples." Only in this way, I submit, the very goals of *missio ad gentes*, which are alleged to be denied by the above considerations, will be achieved, and even more effectively, by *missio inter gentes*. Of course, it is not guaranteed that the *number* of conversions will become thereby bigger, but no doubt the quality, that is, the depth and genuineness of faith will grow, and not least, the church itself will become more conformable to what God intends it to be.

Implicit in this theology of mission is the notion that mission is a collaborative enterprise in which both Christian missionaries and the *gentes Asiae* are engaged and that they help each other carry out. It may be objected that it is naive to expect the *gentes Asiae* to contribute to Christian mission. The point is well taken only if mission is conceived as *missio ad gentes*. Obviously the Asian *gentes* can hardly be expected to help missionaries expand their own church. Nor should they be blamed for their suspicion and rejection of Christian mission if it is geared toward what they perceive as a destruction of their religions by converting them to Christianity, notwithstanding the Catholic Church's official rhetoric about respecting the "elements of truth and grace" that may be found in their religions. (The Catholic Church would no doubt do as much if, say, Hindus, or Buddhists or Muslims, try to "steal its sheep," even though they may acknowledge "elements of truth and grace" in Catholicism!)

The situation would be completely different if mission is undertaken as *missio inter gentes*, since in this case the ultimate goal of mission and the final destiny of humanity are not the expansion of the church but the realization of the kingdom of God, however this reality is understood and named in various religious traditions.[48] To make the kingdom (or reign or rule) of God (or Heaven)—and not the church—the ultimate goal of mission is no theological innovation. On the contrary, it represents fidelity to Jesus since there is no doubt that Jesus himself made the reign of God the center of his life and ministry. It is this total commitment to the reign of God that allowed Jesus to recognize that a man who drove out demons in his name, even though he was not one of his disciples ("not one of us," said John), was not against him but for him and should not be stopped from doing

---

[48] On the symbol of the kingdom of God in mission, see Peter C. Phan, *Christianity with an Asian Face* (Maryknoll, NY: Orbis Books, 2003), 75–97.

it, since driving out demons was part of working for the kingdom of God (Mark 9:38–40). Interestingly, there is no record that the exorcizing man ever knew Jesus personally, or that Jesus ever attempted to make him his disciple, or required him to be one. It is thus possible (and indeed is a fact) that a person can do something "in the name of Jesus" without knowing him or being his follower.

There is another reason why in Asia *missio inter gentes* must also be *missio cum gentibus*. I mentioned above both the tiny percentage of Christians among the Asian population and the unlikelihood of mass conversion of the Asian *gentes* to Christianity. This means that from a practical point of view, Christians in Asia will never be able to effectively work for God's reign of justice, peace, and reconciliation without the collaboration of the *gentes*. They simply cannot "go it alone." This is especially true in Socialist–Communist countries and in countries with a Muslim majority, where Christianity lacks the necessary resources and encounters severe restrictions to its mission. Thus, while the *gentes* cannot and must not be expected to work for the expansion of the church, they can be encouraged to work with Christians for the reign of God—however this reality is named, since Buddhists, for instance, do not even mention God—by promoting justice and peace, reconciliation and love. Indeed, in many places of Asia, they have in fact already done so. Once again, it is to be noted that in *missio inter gentes* and *cum gentibus*, the goals of Christian mission can be amply fulfilled, without the *gentes* being converted, baptized, and made members of the church. Of course, there is no opposition between church and the reign of God. In fact, the former is a sign and instrument, or sacrament, or symbol of the latter. But it would be idolatrous to identify the church with the reign of God. It is the difference between the two that enables the *gentes Asiae* to work for the kingdom of God and yet not belonging to the church, either *reapse* (in fact) or *in voto* (in desire).

Mission as Action:
Doing Things "In the Name of Jesus"

It has often been said that the church's pastoral ministry can be fulfilled only if the church follows the threefold pattern of "see–judge–act." It must see accurately, judge truthfully, and act effectively. Thus, Christian mission presupposes seeing accurately the situation in which it is carried out and judging truthfully its objectives and goals. However, these are only conditions for acting effectively in mission. Mission itself requires doing concrete things, and not just preaching and proclaiming and teaching, even though these do constitute mission, provided that they are done in the way of *missio inter gentes et cum gentibus* as proposed above. But mission must involve much more than *verbal* activities, important though they may be. No doubt the Western churches heavily favor the use of words and speeches and books, and, not to fall behind the times, social media such as Facebook and Twitter. Witness the tsunami of documents and pronouncements of all kinds emanating from the Roman magisterium, not to mention papal autobiographies and theological tracts, inundating churches that hardly have the time and ability to read and understand them, written as they often are in a theological idiom well-nigh incomprehensible to the average people. Sadly, some think that in issuing these documents, the magisterium is fulfilling its "prophetic" or teaching mission.

Mission as *action* involves of course much more than producing this deluge of words. Mission demands, at least in Asia, as much if not more, nonverbal actions. Silence, profound and contemplative, that follows speaking, still remains the most effective communication among believers. In addition, mission includes actions for liberation and development, human rights, social justice, peace and reconciliation, education, and health care, just to mention a few areas in which missionaries in Asia, both Catholic and Protestant, have labored long and well, sometimes at the risk of losing their own lives.

The question inevitably arises as to how to distinguish these activities as part of Christian mission from those of social activists and nongovernmental organizations of various kinds. Beneath this question is the anxiety, especially among church authorities, that missionaries have become mere secular social activists and have lost what is called the vertical dimension of Christian mission. In response, let it be noted first of all that *from a sociological point of view*, there are no differences between the activities of missionaries and those of social activists in these areas. The former are not nobler, holier, or more effective than the latter simply because they are done by the church, nor should they be played against each other. Instead of competition for resources and influence, there should be collaboration between church agencies and secular groups.

Second, these social activities must not be viewed simply as—to use a common expression of the recent past—*preevangelization* (to be done by the laity, mostly), that is, a prelude to or means for "real" evangelization through preaching, sacramental celebrations, and pastoral leadership which are the reserved province of the ordained. Rather, they are a constitutive and integral part of mission in which the *gentes* can fully participate.

Third, the difference between church mission and social activism is not between the alleged "verticality" of the former and the "horizontality" of the latter or between the former's concern for salvation of the soul and the latter's concern for the welfare of the body. In fact, one cannot be obtained in its fullness without the other. Rather the distinctiveness of Christian mission lies in the fact that it is performed "in the name of Jesus." This, as we have seen above, does not mean with an explicit knowledge of Jesus or membership in his circle of disciples. Much less does it mean with the official authorization or "mandatum" by the church hierarchy, or with the powers associated with the sacrament of orders, or with the spiritual sacrifices of religious vows. Rather, mission done "in the name of Jesus" means mission carried out in the way Jesus did and for the cause for which he lived and was killed, that is, the reign of God. Thus, the distinction between mission and social activism does not lie in *what* is being done and in the alleged spiritual superiority of the former over latter, but in *how* mission is done (i.e., in Jesus's way of self-emptying and powerlessness) and *why* it is done (i.e., for the sake of the reign of God).

In summary, to carry out their mission, Christians must *see* accurately, *judge* truthfully, and *act* effectively. Mission in Asia requires that we know who the *gentes Asiae* are in their contemporary sociopolitical and religious contexts; that we do mission among them (*inter gentes*) and with them (*cum gentibus*); and that we work together for the reign of God. Because the goal and destiny of mission is the kingdom of God, mission is neither ours nor the church's. Rather, it is the mission of the Trinitarian God (*missio Dei*), for the sake of reconciling all things in God and a sharing in God's eternal life. All humanity—including the *goyim/ethne/gentes/pagans*—is called to participate in this mission, and the church is but a sacrament of the *missio Dei*, and we the unworthy servants.

Pope Francis and the *Joy of the Gospel*

Ever since he was elected to the see of Peter on March 13, 2013, Jorge Bergoglio, like his immediate predecessors, has, to the delight of Catholic publishers, caused a veritable publication cottage industry on all things papal. I do not intend to jump on the bandwagon with this brief epilogue to this chapter on church and mission. But Francis's Apostolic Exhortation *The Joy of the Gospel* (JG), following the XIII Ordinary General Assembly of the Synod of Bishops on the New Evangelization (October 7–28, 2012), is so relevant to the theme of my book that it is hard to resist the temptation to reflect on how Pope Francis has given voice to some of the ideas espoused by the FABC. Indeed, I have often noted how the FABC has anticipated by nearly twenty years, sometimes almost verbatim, what Pope Francis says in *JG* about church and mission.

My purpose here is of course not to expound or to summarize the pope's document, which together with his encyclical on ecology *On the Care of Our Common Home,* has been justly described as Pope Francis's manifesto and the magna carta of church reform under Francis's pontificate. I will focus only on Chapter 1 ("The Church's Missionary Transformation") and Chapter 4 ("The Social Dimension of Evangelization"). The one expression that epitomizes Francis's ecclesiology is "Go forth." Citing the final document of the Fifth General Conference of the Latin American and Caribbean Bishops at Aparecida, Brazil (June 2017), Francis urges the church to be "permanently in a state of mission" (*JG*, no. 25). Like Dr. Martin Luther King Jr., Francis has a dream:

> I dream of a "missionary option," that is, a missionary impulse capable of transforming everything, so that the Church's customs, ways of doing things, times and schedules, language and structures can be suitably channeled for the evangelization of today's world rather than for her self-preservation. The renewal of structures demanded by pastoral conversion can only be understood in this light: as part of an effort to make them more mission-oriented, to make ordinary pastoral activity on every level more inclusive and open, to inspire in pastoral workers a constant desire to go forth and in this way elicit a positive response from all those whom Jesus summons to friendship with him. (*JG*, no. 27)

This missionary "going forth," Francis insists, must be the defining characteristic of parishes, basic communities, dioceses, episcopal conferences, and even the papacy (*JG*, nos. 28–33). (Pope Francis says that he must practice what he preaches and so imposes upon himself the "conversion of the papacy."). Again, with indefatigable insistence, Francis urges, "I invite everyone to be bold and creative in the task of rethinking the goals, structures, styles and methods of evangelization in their respective communities" (*JG*, no. 33).

But missionary renewal is not restricted to church structures and organization. Even doctrines and formulations of doctrines must fall under the missionary impulse. In words that no doubt raise eyebrows at the CDF's offices, the pope says: "Pastoral ministry in a missionary style is not obsessed with the disjointed transmission of a multitude of doctrines to be insistently imposed" (*JG*, no. 35). Without naming names, the pope goes on,

> Within the Church countless issues are being studied and reflected upon with great freedom. Differing currents of thought in philosophy, theology and pastoral practice, if open to being reconciled by the Spirit in respect and love, can enable the Church to grow, since all of them help to express more clearly the immense riches of God's word. For those who long for a monolithic body of doctrines guarded by all and leaving no room for nuances, this might appear as undesirable and leading to *confusion*. But in fact such variety serves to bring out and develop different facets of the inexhaustible riches of the Gospel. (*JG*, no. 40, emphasis added)

In the footnote to this quotation (note 41), St. Thomas is invoked to defend the necessity of multiplicity and variety in doctrinal expressions that Pope Francis advocates. The note concludes: "We need to listen to and *complement* one another in our partial reception of reality and the Gospel" (*JG*, note 41, emphasis added). In one fell swoop, Francis uses two of the CDF's taboo words: "confusion" and "complement"!

Francis goes on to discuss two of the central aspects of evangelization as proposed by the FABC, namely, option for the poor and interreligious dialogue. He highlights the "social dimension" of evangelization and its intrinsic connection with service and "mercy" (Francis's favorite word) to the poor:

> I want a Church which is poor and for the poor. They have much to teach us. Not only do they share in the *sensus fidei*, but in their difficulties they know the suffering Christ. The new evangelization is an invitation to acknowledge the saving power at work in their lives and to put them at the center of the Church's pilgrim way. We are called to find Christ in them, to lend our voice to their causes, but also to be their friends, to listen to them, to speak for them and

to embrace the mysterious wisdom which God wishes to share with us through them. (*JG*, no. 198)

For Francis, the "poor" are not restricted to the economically poor; they include the people that the FABC never tires of referring to: "I think of the homeless, the addicted, refugees, indigenous peoples, the elderly... migrants... victims of various kinds of human trafficking...the unborn" (*JG*, nos. 210–213). Quoting the bishops of the Philippines, the pope also includes among the "poor" the destroyed earth and the endangered species (*JG*, no. 215).

With regard to interreligious dialogue, Francis turns first to Judaism and acknowledges "a rich complementarity" (again, the dreaded word!) between it and Christianity (*JG*, no. 249). Then, speaking of interreligious dialogue in general, the pope commends "an attitude of openness in truth and in love" (*JG*, no. 250). Citing the bishops of India, the pope indirectly refers to the fourfold area of dialogue and says that interreligious dialogue involves first living together and sharing joys and sorrows, then working for justice and peace, and theological conversation in which "by mutual listening, *both parts can be purified and enriched*" (*JG*, no. 250, emphasis added). Finally, Francis writes,

> Non-Christians, by God's gracious initiative, when they are faithful to their own conscience, can live "justified by the grace of God," and thus be "associated to the paschal mystery of Jesus Christ." But due to the sacramental dimension of sanctifying grace, God's working in them tends to produce signs and rites, sacred expressions which in turn bring others to a communitarian experience of journeying toward God. While these lack the meaning and efficacy of the sacraments instituted by Christ, they can be channels which the Holy Spirit raises up in order to liberate non-Christians from atheistic immanentism or from purely individual religious experiences. The same Spirit everywhere brings forth various forms of practical wisdom which help people to bear suffering and to live in greater peace and harmony. As Christians, we can also benefit from these treasures built up over many centuries, which can help us better to live our own faith. (*JG*, no. 254)

How far removed we are in this passage from the theological world of the CDF's *DI* perhaps need no extensive demonstration, in both tone and substance. Though recognizing that the "signs and rites, sacred expressions" of other religions lack "the meaning and efficacy of the sacraments instituted by Christ," an idea that is expressed in *DI* with the concept of *ex opere operato*, the pope explicitly states that they are the results of "God's working" in these religions. If so, then they operate not simply by human work but by God's grace—another type of *ex opere operato*! Consequently, "non-Christians" must be said to have *faith* and not mere *belief*. There is no condescending declaration that "it is also certain that *objectively speaking* they [the followers of other religions] are in a gravely deficient situation in comparison with those who in the Church have the fullness of the means of salvation" (*DI*, no. 22). Most importantly, the pope acknowledges that these "signs and rites, sacred expressions" can be "channels which the holy Spirit raises up to liberate non-Christians from atheistic immanentism or purely individual religious experiences"—is this (not) a clever circumlocution to avoid the much-abused expression "ways of salvation"? Finally, the pope recognizes the existence of "various forms of practical wisdom," which the Spirit brings forth, in other religions, and which, if we Christians accept and practice them, will "help us better to live our own faith." In my wickeder moments, I have wondered if *JG*, had it been penned by a mere theologian, would not have been condemned by the CDF as "confused," "confusing," and even "erroneous."

It would not be amiss to end not only this chapter but this whole little book with a story in the life of the American Maryknoll missionary to Bangladesh Douglas Venn, whom we have already met at the end of Chapter 4. As you recall, Doug's main "missionary" work was praying and doing manual labor in the farm field with Muslims. Doug writes,

> One of my earliest experiences in interreligious dialogue happened when I was weeding some crops in a field that belonged to the father of the head Imam. He saw me in the squat position, weeding alone. He approached me and asked, "Are you a Jesuit?" Being an educated person, he probably had seen Jesuit missionaries in Kolkata earlier in his life.
>
> "No," I answered, "but I am something like a Jesuit."
>
> He quickly continued, "Are you here to convert our people?"
>
> I had not followed the advice in the Letter of St. Peter to always be ready with an answer for your life, but the Lord Holy Spirit provided, "Our Prophet Isa [Jesus] asked us to go and help the poor, and I have chosen to do that among the poor of Bangladesh. If anyone

comes closer to Allah because I have come, I will be happy." The Imam nodded his head, "I can accept that."[49]

Compared to those words, this book, and all that I have written, are but straw and long-winded blabber.

---

[49] John C. Sivalon, *God's Mission and Postmodern Culture: The Gift of Uncertainty* (Maryknoll, NY: Orbis Books, 2012), 104.

The Joy of Religious Pluralism

Cynics would smirk at the title of this epilogue as well as that of this book as a blatant attempt at mimicking Pope Francis's eye-catching proclivity to make "Joy" part of the titles of his writings: *The Joy of the Gospel* (*Evangelii Gaudium*) and *The Joy of Love* (*Amoris Laetitia*). Of course, before Francis, there were *The Joy of Cooking* and *The Joy of Sex*. Certainly the Gospel, love, cooking, and sex may bring joy, but religious pluralism? If anything, in the recent past, writing on religious pluralism in the Roman Catholic Church is like waving a red flag in front of the charging ecclesiastical bull, and the outcome is anything but joy.

Yet, it may be argued that under the pontificate of Francis, there has been in the Catholic Church a movement, however imperceptible, from sadness to joy as an appropriate response to religious diversity. Perhaps the more accurate word is not sadness but fear or suspicion. Sadness is the opposite of joy, of course, but the centuries-long attitude of Christianity toward religious pluralism is marked more by fear and suspicion than by sadness at the prospect of the eternal damnation of billions of non-Christian souls. Fear and suspicion are natural reactions against the "Other" that is perceived as a threat to one's survival and self-identity. This posture was directed first against Judaism, then the "pagan" religions of the Roman Empire, next Islam, and finally the various "superstitions" and "sects" in Latin America, Asia, and Africa. Such an attitude was not of course limited to hateful emotional outbursts and vicious apologetical tracts, the latter being plentiful against Jews and Muslims. On the contrary, when power and weapons were available, oppression, violence, and even large-scale war were carried out against individual believers and religious groups, as the Crusades and the Holocaust, just to cite two of the most horrendous events, are sad reminders.

Conversion from Fear to Joy

To change from fear and hatred to joy and gladness—*gaudium* and *laetitia*—toward the Religious Other is a radical and massive conversion of heart and mind, one that cannot happen all of a sudden and in the twinkle of an eye. Nor is it the result of deep theological lucubration at an interreligious conference or in a university classroom. Rather it starts from the experiences of daily and protracted sharing of life and continuous work with people of faiths other than one's own for the welfare of all, especially the poor and the marginalized. By living with them as friends (sometimes even as family members) and by working together for the common good, we come to see the Religious Other not as a person of an opposite faith to be converted to our own but as a fellow traveler on a spiritual journey toward the same goal, though on a different route and with different means of transportation, and with sometimes very different and apparently opposite conceptions of what that goal is, whether it is God or gods, salvation from sin or liberation from suffering, total submission to Allah or loving union with the Divine.

These theological differences, honestly acknowledged as radically different and not homogenized as merely various ways of speaking about the same thing, can and should be brought to the table in interreligious dialogues so that persons of one faith can learn from other faiths what is missing in their understanding and living of their own faith, to correct the defects and deficiencies of their own religion, and to share with others their religious insights and practices as humble gifts in deep gratitude for the generous hospitality that the Religious Other offers them.

Finally, out of this intimate sharing of life, peaceful collaboration for the common good, and enriching theological exchange, we can come to worship *together*, and not simply to gather together to worship, each in his or her own tradition. The difference between being together to pray and praying together is well illustrated by the difference between the Day of Prayer for World Peace convoked by Pope John Paul II in 1986 and the shared worship that is practiced in some interfaith circles. For fear of promoting religious syncretism, strongly objected to by then-Cardinal Ratzinger, Prefect of the Congregation for the Doctrine of the Faith, during the Assisi meeting invited leaders of various religious traditions gathered in one and the same location but prayed silently, or separately with their own communities. In contrast, in his encyclical on ecology *Laudato Si': On Care for Our Common Home* (May 24, 2015), Pope Francis, for the first time ever in a papal document, ends with *two* prayers: "I propose that we offer two prayers. The first we can share with all who believe in a God who is the all-powerful Creator, while in the other we Christians ask for inspiration to take up the commitment to creation set before us by the Gospel of Jesus" (246).

What is most significant is that in contrast to his predecessor's fear and suspicion of the possibility of religious syncretism, Pope Francis invites those who believe in God the Creator, among whom Jews, Muslims, and Hindus figure predominantly, to pray *together*, and with a prayer of his own composition to boot! With this invitation, Francis lays to rest the official disapproval of interreligious prayer, which is deemed to lead to religious syncretism or promiscuity.

Moreover, with Francis opening the door, I would suggest that the invitation to pray for the protection of the earth can and should be extended to believers in religious traditions which do not profess faith in God the Creator, such as Buddhism, Confucianism, and Daoism, and even to non-believers, since "to protect life and beauty," "to rescue the abandoned and forgotten of this earth," to "struggle for justice, love and peace," to "protect the world and not prey upon it," and to "sow beauty, not pollution and destruction" (no. 246 "A prayer for our earth") are incumbent upon us all, and in this Sisyphean task, we could use help from any source, whether it is named God, or gods, or not named at all.

Of course, Pope Francis does not come to a positive regard for other religions all by himself. Between his "joy" and the older "sadness" at religious pluralism lie centuries of the church's struggle to make sense of the presence of the Religious Other. Any decent book on religious pluralism and interreligious dialogue, among which the works of the Jesuit Jacques Dupuis stand out, would provide a narrative of the church's journey from the exclusive principle "Outside the Church there is no salvation" (*extra ecclesiam nulla salus*) to an inclusive affirmation of the presence and activity of the Spirit in all religions and of God's offer of grace to all, always and everywhere, as stated officially by Vatican II. It was a very long, arduous and tortuous journey, with twists and turns, forward and backward, but its trajectory toward openness and humility toward other religions is clearly discernible and irreversible.

My Journey from Exclusivism to Religious Pluralism

The subtitle of this book, *A Personal Journey*, hints at my own pilgrimage toward interreligious coexistence. It is not a journey I could foresee in my early days of theological studies in Rome where even the expression "religious pluralism" did not exist. But life, as always, has its surprises, even academic life. As I began to take part in interfaith dialogue in the early 1980s and later as I was researching Christian missions in Asia, I was struck by the pervasive reality of religious diversity on the continent, not as something to overcome through missionary efforts at converting pagans to Christianity, but as God's gift to the world to be thankful for and to celebrate. Even when an Asian converts to Christianity, gallons of baptismal water would not wash away his or her original religious DNA. To the question "Do you reject Satan and all his works?" in the baptism ritual, Asian catechumens will firmly answer affirmatively, but for them "Satan and all his works" does not include all the good things that their religions teach and enjoin and that will continue to nourish their spiritual lives, along with Christian teachings, sacraments, and practices. The oft-cited *bon mot* that the Japanese is born as a Shinto, marries as a Christian, and dies as a Buddhist is a bit of an exaggeration, but it illustrates well the reality of "multiple religious belonging" of most Asians. Religious diversity and pluralism are a common fact of life, not a rarified theological problem.

This discovery spurred me on to reexamine fundamental Christian beliefs in the context of religious pluralism: Who is God? Is Jesus the universal and unique Savior? Where is the Spirit present? Is there divine revelation outside Judaism and Christianity? What is the theological status of the holy books other than the Bible? Can they be said to be "inspired"? Is there no salvation outside the church? Is Christianity the only way to God? Are other religions merely human inventions that happen to help their followers lead a good life, or are they intended and revealed by God as ways of salvation? If so, what is the relation between them and Christianity? What is the value of the prayers, rituals, moral teachings, monastic traditions, and spiritual practices of "non-Christian" religions? Are these destined to disappear once Christianity has appeared on the scene? If they continue to flourish, at times and in places better than Christianity, what is the nature or purpose of Christian mission? Is it something Christians do *to* peoples of other faiths, or something they do *among* and *with* other believers, in collaboration and reciprocity? How can believers of different faiths live together in harmony and peace, collaborate together for justice and the common good, converse with each other in honesty and humility about their beliefs and with the genuine desire to learn from each other, and share in common prayer and worship? Can the "kingdom of God," or equivalent expressions that do not even mention God, and the values they stand for, be taken as the symbol for what all religions endeavor to achieve and the meaning of history itself?

These questions are but a sample of the issues I have tried to interrogate in my writings, some of which have attracted the disapproving gaze of ecclesiastical authorities. But where is the *joy* of religious pluralism? Well, it is not as easy to describe it as detailing the pleasures of food and sex. But *gaudium* and *laetitia* there certainly are in dealing with religious pluralism. Ask anyone who has found an answer to a hard and vital question after a long and intense intellectual struggle how she or he feels, and they will shout the joyful *Eureka*! Far be it for me to suggest that finding an answer to a theological problem is equivalent to Archimedes's discovery of the method of determining the purity of gold, who may have jumped up and down, waving arms in the air and dancing at his discovery, but the joy and delight in theological reflection, albeit quieter, is no less profound and satisfying.

Christian Faith in the Midst of Religious Pluralism

In addition to the joy of discovery, engaging religious pluralism seriously will open up insights about God and everything connected with God that will bring joy. One of the insights discovered in exploring religious pluralism that infinitely gladdens our hearts is that "God is greater than our hearts" (1 John 3:20). This biblical truth was brought home to me in a most unexpected way. In April 2010, when I was delivering the Edward Cadbury Lectures (funded by the famous and much-loved British chocolate-making company, now owned by Kraft) at the University of Birmingham (UK), an eighty-three-year-old woman asked to meet with me for tea. She was born in China, she said, of British Baptist missionary parents, became a Buddhist when she married a Chinese, and now is a Quaker. During our conversation about religious pluralism and her spiritual journey, she declared at one point, to quote her verbatim, "Our concept of God is ridiculously small!" That nugget of theological wisdom sent me right back to Meister Eckhart, the fourteenth-century Dominican mystic, some of whose views were condemned in 1329 by Pope John XXII as heretical and misleading.

Both Mary (that is her name) and Meister Eckhart provide the richest foundation for religious pluralism that I know. In our theology about God, Christ, Spirit, revelation, salvation, church, worship, and spirituality—our talk about God and anything related to God—we have hemmed ourselves within the narrow confines (*prison* might be a better term) of our finite (and sinful) hearts and minds, which we judge larger than and capable of containing God. We have set up conceptual boundaries beyond which we dare not roam unfettered for fear of getting lost. With regard to religion, we have concocted clear and distinct ideas about who God is; where God, Christ, and the Holy Spirit are actively present; where salvation can exclusively be found; which religion is the only true one; which kinds of prayer will be heard by God; and which religious and mystical experiences can reach God. Our religious self-identity is defined by these ideas, and we use them as criteria to evaluate the Religious Other. Where this Religious Other is different from us, we condemn it as erroneous and superstitious; where it agrees with us, we either judge it as inferior or claim that it is "included" in and "fulfilled" by Christ and the church. Pressed to explain how this inclusion and fulfillment of the Religious Other can take place if it has preexisted Jesus by centuries, we resort to a "mystery" that somehow connects this Religious Other with Jesus the unique and universal Savior and the church.

Instead of this fear and suspicion of the Religious Other and rather than trying to twist it to conform to our preconceived criteria of what counts as true, we should recognize, with joy and gladness, the Religious Other as *other*, as a different but truthful and valuable manifestation of God, from which we should humbly and gratefully learn, because "God is greater than our hearts" and because "our concept of God is ridiculously small." What *gaudium* and *laetitia* will fill our hearts when our minds are freed from their self-constructed prison, and with freedom comes joy. Joy is the fruit of seeing the truth, for it is only in truth that there is genuine joy.

This recognition of difference is no license for relativism and indifferentism, according to which "all the religions are the same." On the contrary, in spite of family resemblances, all religions are different, some radically so. However, religious differences and even contradictions need not and must not lead us to despair of our search for truth. But truth, much less the Truth (another name for God), is not the exclusive possession of any one religion. All religions, Christianity included, are subject to ignorance and error as well as to moral failures and sins: "If we say that we have no sin, we deceive ourselves, and the truth is not in us. . . . If we say we have not sinned, we make him [God] a liar, and his word is not in us" (1 John 1:8–10). It is only when all religions and their believers come together and together search for the Truth, learning from and teaching one another, that the Truth can be fully understood and lived. Only by recognizing their past errors and sins, and helping one another to do so by kindly pointing them out, can religions, Christianity among them, repent and move nearer to the Truth. Truth is not something that can be possessed with pride of ownership by any religion; rather it is a reality that can only be approached asymptotically, while bits and pieces of it are grasped and formulated along the way.

In the Gospel of John, Jesus told his disciples that there were many things he could say to them, but they were not able to bear them then. But "when the Spirit of truth comes, he will guide you into all the truth" (John 16:13). John goes on to say that what the Spirit will say will be taken from what is of Jesus: "He will take what is mine and declare it to you" (John 16:14). But it is not stated that the Spirit will say the same things, in the same place, and in the same manner as Jesus did; otherwise, the Spirit would be redundant. Hence, we must expect from the Spirit new things, different places, and diverse manners. Do not "non-Christian" religions offer the new things, different places, and diverse manners by which the Spirit speaks to us today? If so, dialogue among religions in which there is *mutual* learning and teaching, *reciprocal* listening and speaking, is the indispensable and only way for *all* believers, including Christians, to know and walk in the truths to reach the Truth.

It is important to recall that Jesus does foretell that his followers will "weep and mourn" during his temporary absence ("a little while"). But he assures them that their "pain will turn into joy" (John 16:20). He compares the disciples' pain to that of a woman in labor who will forget her pain because of "the joy of having brought a human being into the world." In a similar way when the disciples see Jesus again, their "hearts will rejoice, and no one can take your joy from you" (John 16:21–22).

And so it is with the search for the Truth in the midst of religious pluralism. There will be pain when our former certainties are shaken to the core, when the walls and boundaries we have so carefully and laboriously built to protect ourselves from the perceived threat of the Religious Other tumble down, and when we wander confused and seemingly lost in the unfamiliar "lands of the Gentiles" (Psalms 105:44). But when we discover that God the Spirit has been actively present in these lands long before we enter them to bring the good news, that not a few of the Gentiles ("heathens" or "pagans") lead a holier life than many Christians, and that they do so thanks to (and not in spite of!) their religions, we shout joyful hallelujahs. Our sadness is turned into joy, and our fear into love: "There is no fear in love, but perfect love casts out fear; for fear has to do with punishment, and whoever fears has not reached perfection in love" (1 John 4:18). I invite you to take up this journey of religious pluralism from fear and sadness to perfect love and unalloyed joy.

APPENDIX

Correspondence Regarding
Being Religious Interreligiously

**From Most Rev. Charles V. Grahmann, Bishop of Dallas
to Rev. Peter Phan**
August 30, 2005

Dear Father Phan:

Msgr. Milam Joseph has called your home and office and left several messages. We had hoped to reach you personally regarding the enclosed letter I received from the Office of the Apostolic Nunciature.

As you will see from the *Observations* sent from the Congregation for the Doctrine of the Faith, there appear to be concerns and doctrinal problems with your recent book, *Being Religious Interreligiously: Asian Perspectives on Interfaith Dialogue.*

May I kindly ask you to complete the directives stated in the letter from CDF within the appropriate time frame. Should you wish to discuss this matter further with me in person, I would be happy to meet with you.

I look forward to hearing from you soon.

Assuring you of my unity and prayers, I am

Sincerely yours in Christ,
Most Reverend Charles V. Grahmann, D.D.
Bishop of Dallas

From Angelo Amato, Titular Secretary
of the Congregation for the Doctrine of the Faith
to Bishop Grahmann
July 20, 2005

Your Excellency:

Recently, a book by the Rev. Peter Phan of the Diocese of Dallas, entitled *Being Religious Interreligiously: Asian Perspectives on Interfaith Dialogue* (Orbis Books: New York, 2004) was brought to the attention of this Dicastery.

As is evident from the enclosed *Observations*, an initial examination of the text has indicated serious ambiguities and doctrinal problems. The Congregation would be grateful, therefore, if you would ask the author to correct the problematic points by means of an article, which, after first being submitted to this Dicastery within the next six months, would then be published in an appropriate theological journal.

This Dicastery also asks your Excellency to direct Father Phan to inform his publisher that this book is not to be reprinted.

With kind regards and prayerful best wishes, I am

Sincerely yours in Christ,
Angelo Amato, S.D.B.
Titular Archbishop of Sila
Secretary, Congregazione per la Dottrina della Fede
enclosure

CONGREGATION FOR THE DOCTRINE OF THE FAITH
Some observations on the book by Rev. Peter C. Phan
Being Religious Interreligiously:
Asian Perspectives on Interfaith Dialogue
(Orbis Books: New York, 2004)

This text is notably confused on a number of points of Catholic doctrine and also contains serious ambiguities. Taken as whole, it is in open contrast with almost all the teachings of the Declaration *Dominus Iesus*.

I.   On the salvific value of non–Christian religions

1. The author states quite explicitly that non-Christian religions are in themselves "ways of salvation" and that, therefore, religious pluralism is positively willed in God's providential plan. He writes:

> "In spite of its positive evaluation of non-Christian religions in general and of Judaism in particular, Vatican II self-consciously refrains from affirming that these religions as such function as ways of salvation in a manner analogous, let alone parallel, to Christianity. In the last three decades, however, extensive reflections have been done on the relationship between Christianity, and by implication, Jesus Christ, on the one hand, and non-Christian religions, especially Judaism, on the other. A new theology of religions has reassessed the role of Christ as the unique and universal savior and the function of non-Christian religions themselves within God's plan of salvation. Several theologians—myself included—have argued that these religions may be said to be ways of salvation and that religious pluralism is part of God's providential plan" (p. xxiii).

2. The author quotes Dominus Iesus 22 and states that the Declaration condemns the idea that other religions are ways of salvation solely when such religions are viewed as "complementary" to the Church. He holds that one can affirm that they are ways of salvation without affirming their "complementarity" (p. 239, footnote 74). In fact, however, in an earlier chapter, Father Phan states that, while in Christ there is the fullness of revelation, there is,

between the Church and the other religions, a relationship of reciprocal complementarity in understanding revelation and in living according to it:

> "Not only are the non–Christian religions complemented by Christianity, but Christianity also is complemented by other religions. In other words, the process of complementarity, enrichment, and even correction is two-way or reciprocal. This reciprocity in no way endangers the Christian confession that the church has received from Christ the fullness of revelation, since it is one thing to receive the definitive gift of God's self-revelation in Jesus and quite another to *understand* it fully and to *live* it completely" (p. 144).

3. The author states that pluralism is a reality not only *de facto*, but also *de iure*:

> ". . . religious pluralism, then, is not just a matter of fact but also a matter of principle. That is to say, Judaism and other non-Christian religions should be seen as part of the plan of divine providence and endowed with a particular role in the history of salvation. They are not merely a 'preparation' for, 'stepping stones' toward, or 'seeds' of Christianity and destined to be 'fulfilled' by it. Rather, they have their own autonomy and their proper role as ways of salvation, at least for their adherents" (p. 143).

It is surprising that the author holds that this thesis does not contradict *Dominus Iesus:*

> "It is to be noted that the expression 'matter of fact' (*de facto*) and 'matter of principle' (*de iure*) are not used in the sense rejected by *DI*, no. 4. Here by 'matter of principle' is meant simply the intrinsic value of non-Christian religions as ways of salvation in the one plan of God. It does not question any of the Christian claims listed in *DI*, no. 4" (p. 65, note 16).

4. Father Phan denies that the value of non-Christian religions can be limited to the presence of elements which prepare for the Gospel: *"Furthermore, because non-Christian religions possess an autonomous function in the history of salvation, different from that of Christianity, they cannot be reduced to Christianity in terms of preparation and fulfillment"* (p. 144). This contradicts

what was stated in 2001 by the Congregation for the Doctrine of the Faith in the *Notification* on the book by Father Jacques Dupuis *Toward a Christian Theology of Religious Pluralism:* "In accordance with Catholic doctrine, it must be held that 'whatever the Spirit brings about in human hearts and in the history of peoples, in cultures and religions, serves as a preparation for the Gospel' (cf. Dogmatic Constitution *Lumen gentium*, 16)".

5. According to the author, it would make little sense to try to convert nonChristians to Christianity:

> "Such a theologoumenon [the notion that non-Christian religions are ways of salvation and that religious pluralism is part of God's providential plan] brings with it far-reaching and radical consequences for the practice of Christian mission and raises thorny questions regarding conversion and baptism as the primary goals of evangelization. Indeed, if religious pluralism belongs to divine providence and is not just the fruit of human sinfulness, then it may not and must not be abolished by converting all the followers of non-Christian religions, at least during our common journey in history" (p. xxiii, cf. also pp. 139–140).

6. Father Phan explains what he believes to be the theological note of this thesis: "the theory that non-Christian religions are 'ways of salvation' cannot be taught as Christian doctrine, but it is at least a *sententia communis* and *theologice certa*, and certainly not *temeraria* and *scandalosa*" (p. 64, note 13).

II. On the uniqueness and universality of Jesus Christ

1. The author interprets the uniqueness, absoluteness and universality of Jesus Christ in keeping with the interpretation of Father Jacques Dupuis as "non exclusive," but "constitutive" and "relational." The salvific uniqueness of Christ would consist in being "a most effective" way—though not exclusive—in which God accomplishes in Christ salvation for all humanity. The author writes:

> "Christ's uniqueness, absoluteness, and universality are not exclusive, eliminative, and abrogative but, to use Jacques Dupuis's expressions, 'constitutive' and 'relational.' That is to say, because the Christ-event, according to the Christian faith, belongs to and is the definitive real-

ization of God's plan of salvation, Christ is 'constitutive' of salvation in a very special manner. In him God has brought about salvation for all humanity in a most effective and powerful manner" (p. 144).

The revelation and the salvation accomplished in Jesus Christ would be complemented by God's self-revelation and redemption manifested in "other saving figures":

". . . though Jesus Christ is confessed by Christians to be the fullness of revelation and the definitive savior, there is also a reciprocal relationship between him and other 'saving figures,' since Jesus' uniqueness—should this word still be used—or more appropriately, definitiveness, is not absolute but relational. In this sense Jesus' revelation and salvation are also complemented by God's self-revelation and redemption manifested in other saving figures" (ibid.).

2. Father Phan believes that it would be better to avoid the use of the terms "unique," "absolute" and "universal" for the salvific role of Christ:

". . . one may question the usefulness of words such as *unique, absolute,* and even *universal* to describe the role of Jesus as savior today. (. . .) They are not the most effective means to convey Christ's message of humble service and compassionate love, especially to victims of political, economic, and religious persecution. In particular, in the post-Holocaust era, these expressions, I suggest, have outlived their usefulness and should be jettisoned and replaced by other, theologically more adequate equivalents" (pp. 143–144).

The author had earlier revealed his perplexity regarding the use of the word "exclusive" in the Declaration *Dominus Iesus*, n. 15:

"*DI* makes a confusing statement that on the one hand recognizes the inclusiveness of Christ's saving work and on the other hand affirms that 'Jesus Christ has a significance and a value for the human race and its history, which are unique and singular, proper to him alone, *exclusive,* universal, and absolute (no. 15, emphasis added). How can Jesus' significance and value be inclusive and exclusive at the same time?" (p. 66, note 17).

III. On the relationship between Jesus, the Logos and the Holy Spirit

1. The author states—again in contradiction to the teaching of *Dominus Iesus*—that there is a saving action of the Logos which is wider than that of Jesus of Nazareth, because Jesus, as the Logos incarnate, is necessarily limited. For example:

> "However, the Logos was not, and could not be, exhaustively embodied in Jesus of Nazareth, since Jesus was spatially and temporally limited and hence could not exhaustively express the divine, infinite saving power in his human words and deeds. This is part of what is meant by saying that the Logos 'emptied himself' in the man Jesus and was subjected to human limitations (though not to sin). There is therefore a 'distinction-in-identity' or 'identity-in-distinction' between the eternal, 'unincarnate' Logos and the Jew Jesus in whom the Logos became flesh in time and with whom he is personally identified. Hence, the activities of the Logos, though inseparable from those of Jesus, are also distinct from and go beyond Jesus' activities, before, during, and after the incarnation" (pp. 142–143).

2. In addition, Father Phan maintains that the Holy Spirit operates in a salvific way independently of the Logos and that what the Spirit and the Logos accomplish in non-Christian religions can be truly different from what Jesus and the Spirit effect in Christianity:

> ". . . the Holy Spirit, though intimately united with the Logos, is distinct from him and operates in a saving manner outside and beyond him, before, during, and after Jesus' ministry . . . Thus, God's saving presence through Word and Spirit is not limited to the Christian covenant but was active and continues to be active in the history of Israel and, one might add, is extended to the whole human history, especially in the sacred books, rituals, moral teachings, and spiritual practices of all religions.
>
> In this way, what the Holy Spirit says and does is truly different from, though not contradictory to, what the Logos says and does, and what the Logos and the Spirit do and say in Israel and in non-Christian

religions may be truly different from, though not contradictory to, what Jesus and the Spirit do in Christianity. Needless to say, these activities of the Logos and the Spirit do not mean that the human responses that constitute part of Judaism and other non-Christian religions as religious institutions are always free from sin and error, but, of course the same thing must be said of Christians as well" (p. 143).

These statements are contrary to the teaching of the Declaration *Dominus Iesus*, 9–12.

IV. On the uniqueness and salvific universality of the Church

1. The author explicitly denies that the notions of "uniqueness" and "salvific universality" can be applied to the Church, while at the same time affirming a certain possible application of these concepts to Jesus (cf. above; section II). He presents a vision of the Church as "a religious institution" like others, to be judged by its work:

"If Jesus and the church cannot be identified with each other, whatever is claimed for one needs not and cannot be *ipso facto* claimed for the other. In particular, the claim of uniqueness and universality, if claimed at all for either, must be understood differently. From the historical point of view, in my judgment, it is the claim of uniqueness and universality of the Christian church that is most problematic, and not the claim of uniqueness and universality for Jesus . . .

. . . what arouses much skepticism and even outrage is that a human institution such as the Christian church, with a history of light and darkness, a mixture of good and evil, claims to be the exclusive vessel of divine grace while there is plenty of evidence that other religious institutions, no less than the church, have been instrumental in achieving good (and, of course, evil as well)" (p. 95; cf. p. 100).

2. According to Father Phan, the Second Vatican Council modified the traditional doctrine on the Church by introducing a distinction between the "Church of Christ" and "the Catholic Church".

"Vatican II modified Pius XII's teaching [in the Encyclical *Mystici Corporis*] by introducing a distinction between the church of Christ and the Catholic church and taught that the church of Christ, 'constituted and organized as a society in the present world, subsists in the Catholic church, which is governed by the successor of Peter and by the bishops in communion with him'" (p. 46).

In other words, Father Phan states *"Vatican II's refusal to identify the Catholic church with the church of Christ"* (p. 50).

The author's thought is ambiguous in this point since he does not seem to accept the correct interpretation of *Lumen Gentium 8* regarding the one subsistence of the Church of Christ in the Catholic Church, as this was clarified in *Dominus Iesus*, n. 16 and note 56.

V.   On the relationship between Christianity and Judaism

1. The notion that it does not make much sense to seek the conversion of non-Christians (cf. above; Section I, n. 5) receives more elaboration in reference to the Jews. In fact, Father Phan is quite explicit in setting forth the thesis that Christians are not called to convert the Jews:

> ". . . intimately connected with the issue of Judaism as a revealed living religion is the question of Christian mission to the Jews. Preaching and catechesis must squarely face the problem of whether Christians are called to carry out their mission to the Jews. The *Catechism* deals with mission in detail (nos. 849–56) but does not have anything specific to say about mission to the Jews. It is universally agreed today that all forms of proselytism must be rejected in the pejorative sense of the term, that is, the attempt to win converts by means of cajolery, pressure or intimidation, or other improper methods. But is it not possible to acknowledge further that Jews are already in a covenantal relationship with God and therefore that Christians are not called to convert Jews to their faith? Rather, the mission of both Jews and Christians is to be understood as dialogue, mutual witness, and service to the world" (pp. 159–160).

In this passage, in the form of a rhetorical question, the possibility is presented of recognizing the covenant between the Jewish people and God as still in existence and salvific, without reference to Christ. The author seeks to present a version of Christianity in which God's covenant with the Jewish people does not find its completion in Jesus Christ; the author writes:

> "The challenge for Roman Catholic theologians, then, is to articu-
> late a coherent and credible Christology and soteriology (theology
> of salvation) that honors the Christian belief in Jesus as the savior
> of all humankind and at the same time includes the affirmation that
> Judaism is and remains eternally a 'saving covenant with God'. In
> other words, what is needed is what has been called a non- or post-
> supersessionist Christology, or more generally, an inclusivist-pluralist
> Christology" (p. 141; cf. also p. 138, note 4; p. 145).

In the following pages, Father Phan develops this "post-supersessionist Christology" by maintaining that the Logos and the Holy Spirit "operate distinctly and diversely from each other" and that these two, in turn, operate "beyond" the person of Christ (noted above; cf. Section III).

2. The position of the author on the relationship between Jesus and the Messiah still awaited by the Jewish people is erroneous. In particular, he asserts that the document of the Pontifical Biblical Commission states that when the Messiah of the Jews appears, he will have "*some* of the traits" of Jesus Christ: "*The Pontifical Biblical Commission's important document The Jewish People and Their Sacred Scriptures in the Christian Bible asserts that when the Jewish messiah appears, he will have some of the traits of Christ and that Christians will recognize the traits of Jesus in him*" (p. 145). In fact, the document of the PBC states that we too, like the Jews, are waiting for the coming of the Messiah, but we know that he who is to come at the Parousia is he who has already come once: Jesus Christ.

Father Phan even states that presenting the text of the *Catechism of the Catholic Church* without comment will lead to a misunderstanding of the Gospel and to hostility against the Jews:

> "It is obvious that if the Catechism's uncritical retelling of the passion
> narratives is transmitted in catechesis and preaching without a careful
> attempt at contextualizing passages describing the conflicts between
> Jesus and various Jewish groups, it will lead to a misunderstanding of
> the nature of the Gospels' account of Jesus' trial and death and even
> to anti-Jewish hostility, as history has shown all too well" (p. 157).

He concludes therefore that the *Catechism* must be corrected (cf. p. 160).

VI. Other erroneous or confused statements

1. In addition to the book's principal topics, as noted in the preceding paragraphs, there are others on which the author's statements are also erroneous or quite confused. Some of these are of a methodological nature; for example, the value given to Holy Scripture and the texts of the Church's Magisterium as well as their interpretation. Others relate to doctrinal points like the mystery of the Holy Trinity.

2. It appears that the author's desire to give theological justification to his positions on religious pluralism leads him to make statements about the Triune God which are seriously confused. Concretely, he puts forth the idea that the unity of God does not consist in a unity of nature or substance:

"Divine unity does not consist in the one *nature* or *substance* but in the unity of the eternal threefold relations" (p. xxi).

"Furthermore, God's *unity* is seen to consist in the unification of the relationships among the three divine persons or their communion in love rather than in the abstract oneness of a single divine substance" (p. 39).

3. The author also presents a mistaken conception of the nature and authority of the Church's Magisterium and in fact does not give it the proper consideration. He writes instead that the determination of which doctrines are "necessary" needs to be undertaken in consultation with non-Catholics and non-Christians:

"The question then turns to how the church goes about determining what is necessary and essential. . . . At any rate, however this determination is carried out, clearly it cannot be done by the Magisterium alone or by the theologians alone or the laity alone. It must be a common and concerted effort by the church as a whole, in which all voices and experiences, even those of non-Catholics and non-Christians, are respectfully and carefully listened to and evaluated, in which the *ecclesia docens* is also the *ecclesie discens* and vice versa" (p. 250).

4. The author does not refrain from explicit criticism of the interventions of the Congregation for the Doctrine of the Faith (the Declaration

Dominus Iesus and the *Notification* on the book by Father Jacques Dupuis: cf. pp. xxiii–iv, 79).

5. Finally, the book is silent regarding the reality of sin, forgiveness, and the redemption of the sinner. If the author rejects a kind of gnostic syncretism as incompatible with the Christian faith, there is nonetheless a gnostic tenor running through his book. For example, he speaks about a "new Church", in which the essential element would be witnessing to the truth about God's love:

> "Not a church proclaiming itself as the exclusive channel of God's grace and asserting its superiority over the religions of the 'pagans' whom it comes to save from spiritual darkness and moral depravity, but a church humbly walking side by side with other seekers of God and God's reign, witnessing to them its faith in Jesus as God's gift of all-inclusive love to humanity and recognizing the presence of God's spirit among them and learning from them ways of being more faithful to God's call" (p. xxvii).

From Peter Phan
To Most Rev. Charles V. Grahmann, Bishop of Dallas
September 19, 2005

Your Excellency:

Your letter dated August 30, 2005, reached me today, September 19, 2005. Enclosed in the envelope is the text of the Congregation of the Doctrine of the Faith containing observations on my book Being Religious Interreligiously: Asian Perspectives on Interfaith Dialogue (Orbis Books, 2004). The text lists a series of "serious ambiguities and doctrinal problems" allegedly proposed in my book.

The Congregation requires that I "correct the problematic points by means of an article" which will have to be submitted to the Congregation "within the next six months" and be "published in an appropriate journal."

The letter of the Congregation is dated July 20, 2005. If the six months deadline is applied, then I would have to comply with the request of the Congregation before January 20, 2006. However, since the text reached me only on September 19, 2005, I will not have sufficient time to comply with the request of the Congregation, given my many teaching, writing, and lecturing responsibilities.

I would therefore respectfully request that the deadline be extended to March 20, 2006.

Sincerely yours,
Peter C. Phan, S.T.D., Ph.D., D.D.
Ignacio Ellacuría Chair of Catholic Social Thought
Georgetown University

From Peter Phan
to His Emminence Cardinal William Levada,
Prefect of the Congregazione Della Dottrina Della Fede
April 4, 2006

Your Eminence:

A letter dated July 20, 2005 and signed by Archbishop Angelo Amato, S.D.B., Secretary of the Congregation, reached me at my office at Georgetown University on September 19, 2005 through the office of Bishop Charles Grahmann. Enclosed with the letter is a text containing nineteen observations listed under six headings on my book *Being Religious Interreligiously: Asian Perspectives on Interfaith Dialogue.* The text also states that my book "is notably confused on a number of points of Catholic doctrine and also contains serious ambiguities. Taken as a whole, it is in open contrast with almost all the teachings of the Declaration *Dominus Iesus.*"

Because of these alleged "serious ambiguities and doctrinal problems," the letter asks me (1) "to correct the problematic points by means of an article, which, after being submitted to this Dicastery within the next six months, would then be published in an appropriate journal"; and (2) "to inform [his] publisher that this book is not to be reprinted."

Because the letter reached me only in the middle of September, the deadline of "within six months" could not be met and accordingly I asked for an extension until March 2006.

Allow me now to respond, albeit briefly, to the letter of the Congregation and to express my own concerns. I will begin with the second request.

I.   Prohibition of the Reprint of My Book

I am astounded by the injustice of the procedure of the Congregation. Before I even have the chance to explain and defend my positions, I am already forbidden to have my book reprinted. That such a prohibition might be imposed *after* my explanation and defense is judged unsatisfactory is within the rights of the Congregation, but I believe that your Eminence understands the injustice of "shoot first and ask after." Even in my home country, which is communist and where religious freedom is sometimes infringed upon, the accused always has the right to due process before being convicted and condemned, even when a verdict has been predetermined. I expect at least that much from a self-proclaimed champion of human rights such as the church. Furthermore, to my knowledge, even authors whose works have been censured and even condemned by the Congregation have not been prohibited from reprinting them, albeit with a notation from the Congregation. Why am I the exception, and before due process?

In spite of this injustice, I have informed my publisher (Orbis Books) of the Congregation's prohibition to reprint my book. I did this, not because I agree with the directive of the Congregation but because the people at Orbis Books are my friends and I want to spare them of any problem with the Congregation.

However, I retain the rights guaranteed by Georgetown University to its faculty, commonly known as "academic freedom," which the Faculty Handbook defines as "free inquiry, free expression, intellectual honesty, respect for the academic rights of others, and openness to change." The Handbook further states: "A Faculty member has rights and responsibilities common to all citizens, free from institutional censorship" (p. 17 of the 1999 Faculty Handbook).

In view of the procedural injustice and of my rights as a Georgetown University faculty member I hereby request that the Congregation withdraw the prohibition to reprint my book.

II. Requiring an Article to Be Published in an "Appropriate Theological Journal"

1. The nature of the article demanded by the Congregation is unclear. Its stated purpose is "to correct the problematic points" allegedly present in my book. I will come back to these alleged "problematic points" presently. Here I want to raise questions regarding the nature and scope of the article. As you well know, an article must have a central theme and a well-defined focus. But the "problematic points" the Congregation raises are so numerous and so diverse that no article of an acceptable length can deal with them coherently and satisfactorily.

2. With regard to "an appropriate theological journal," I do not know what kind of journal the Congregation has in mind. No peer-reviewed journal of scholarly stature (I am thinking of, for example, *Theological Studies, Gregorianum, Louvain Studies, Église et Théologie, Irish Theological Quarterly,* to mention some of the journals in which my articles have appeared) would

accept for publication articles that do not make a significant contribution to the field. Much less would they accept for publication an article written as the result of a disciplinary decision of the Congregation. The article the Congregation demands of me appears to be one that recites the teachings as well as the formulations of Vatican documents such as *Dominus Iesus*. Scholars normally do not write this kind of article.

3. Another important concern I have regards the requirement that the article be submitted to the Congregation, presumably for approval. I suppose that one of the criteria for approval is whether I correct the alleged "serious ambiguities and doctrinal problems." I return to the nineteen observations the Congregation makes on my book. I understand that I am not supposed here to defend myself against and to rebut each and every of these observations. But I must say that *all* of the statements that the Congregation quotes from my book and describes as "confused" and "ambiguous" can be defended as perfectly orthodox on the basis of the teachings of Pope John Paul II, the Federation of Asian Bishops' Conferences, the Pontifical Council for Interreligious Dialogue, and the Pontifical Council for Promoting Christian Unity. Needless to say, I am fully prepared to do so.

Several of the observations are, I regret the bluntness, preposterous. Permit me to cite only two examples. Observation VI.4 states: "The author does not refrain from explicit criticism of the interventions of the Congregation for the Doctrine of the Faith. . . ." Since when is "explicit criticism of the interventions of the Congregation for the Doctrine of the Faith" a theological crime? If there is no criticism (which I have done with great respect), how can the Congregation or any other organization correct teachings and policies that loyal members of the church consider to be ill-advised, poorly handled, or even erroneous? Without criticism how can unjust "interventions" (such as the Congregation's prohibition to reprint my book prior to due process) be corrected? Are all the "interventions" of the Congregation above and beyond the possibility of error and sinfulness?

Observation VI.5 affirms that "there is nonetheless a gnostic tenor running through this book" because "he speaks about a 'new Church,' in which the essential element would be witnessing to the truth about God's love." If this constitutes "a gnostic tenor," then the whole Bible and Tradition would be guilty of it! Has not the ecclesiastical censor of my book confused "New Church"—an expression repeatedly used by the Federation of Asian Bishops' Conferences—with "New Age" when he accuses me of gnosticism?

Clearly, I am not able to comply with the Congregation's second request at this time without a clarification of all of my concerns expressed above.

III. A Fundamental Issue of Justice

There is another issue that I request the Congregation to consider, and that is just and fair remuneration. I am neither a curial official nor a priest engaged in pastoral ministry for which I would be provided with room and board, a salary, a paid vacation, and other benefits. Financially, I am completely and totally on my own. I have to pay for food and clothing, housing and transportation, health and life insurance and retirement benefits, and eventually my own funeral. In addition, I support my family, especially my mother, financially. To meet all these expenditures I have to work more than full-time, teaching, lecturing, and publishing vastly beyond what is normally expected of a professor.

Nor do I belong to a religious order which would permit me to take an unpaid semester off to do research and write the article required by the Congregation. To write such article requires that I set aside time which I have already devoted to other paying tasks. I therefore request that the Congregation pay half of my annual salary (six months, the amount of time that the Congregation originally allotted me to write the article). This is a matter of justice.

Your Eminence, I would be lying if I said that this investigation by the Congregation has not affected me adversely, physically and psychologically. However, the greatest pains will be inflicted not on me but on my loved ones, especially my elderly mother, who have nothing but trust in and love for the church. Their trust and love will be badly shaken if and when they know that an injustice has been done to me by the church.

I am by nature adverse to publicity. I am even embarrassed by this undeserved notoriety, being just a very small fish in the theological pond. While some may revel in celebrity and even try to derive financial gain from it (nothing boosts the sale of a book more than ecclesiastical censure), I have done my very best to keep this investigation secret and informed no one except those who must know, namely, Dr. John J. DeGioia, President of Georgetown University; Dr. Jane McAuliffe, Dean of Georgetown College; Dr. Chester Gillis, Chair of the Department of Theology; and the administrators of Orbis Books. I am afraid that the knowledge, especially by the secular media, of this investigation of me by the Congregation for the

Doctrine of the Faith would further damage the already battered reputation of the American Catholic Church.

I do not think that my book deserves the kind of publicity that a censure by the Congregation will give it. However, because I believe that the observations made by the Congregation on my book are uncalled for, I will be forced to defend my views and my reputation publicly, for my sake and that of my family. This is an argument we need not have, and I humbly urge you to reconsider the entire matter while there is still time to avoid it.

I thank you for your attention and best wishes for your ministry.

Peter C. Phan, S.T.D., Ph.D., D.D.
Ignacio Ellacuría Chair of Catholic Social Thought
Georgetown University

From Most Rev. William E. Lori, Bishop
of Bridgeport, the Committee on Doctrine
to Peter Phan
May 15, 2007

Rev. Peter Phan
Ellacuria Chair of Catholic Social Thought
Georgetown University

Dear Father Phan:

The Congregation for the Doctrine of the Faith has attempted to find a suitable resolution to the problem posed by certain statements in *Being Religious Interreligiously* that do not accord with the teaching of the Catholic Church. The solution it proposed was that you write and publish an article that would clarify and so make unmistakable that the positions that you in fact hold are in conformity with Church teaching. As this proposal has proved unacceptable to you, the Congregation for the Doctrine of the Faith has requested that the Committee on Doctrine examine *Being Religious Interreligiously*. It has done so and feels obliged to publish its own statement indicating the points on which the positions expressed in *Being Religious Interreligiously* diverge from that of Catholic teaching.

Prior to taking such a step, however, the Committee wants to give you an opportunity to respond to its criticisms of your book. Attached you will find a summary of the Committee's concerns with regard to three points: the unique identity of Jesus Christ as the universal savior, the salvific significance of non-Christian religions, and the role of the Church as the universal sacrament of salvation. If you would like an opportunity to present to the Committee written arguments as to how the positions presented in *Being Religious Interreligiously* are in conformity with Church teaching on these points, please send me a written reply by 15 June 2007 stating that you would wish to provide such arguments.

Sincerely yours in Christ,
Most Reverend William E. Lori
Bishop of Bridgeport

Some Problematic Aspects of Being Religious Interreligiously: Asian Perspectives on Interfaith Dialogue, by Rev. Peter C. Phan

Committee on Doctrine
U.S. Conference of Catholic Bishops

1) The Uniqueness of Jesus Christ and the Universality of His Salvific Mission

Being Religious Interreligiously states that "Christ's uniqueness, absolute-ness, and universality are not exclusive, eliminative, and abrogative but, to use Jacques Dupuis's expressions, 'constitutive' and 'relational'" (p. 144). While Christians confess that Jesus is the "fullness of revelation and the definitive savior, there is also a reciprocal relationship between him and other 'saving figures,' since Jesus' uniqueness—should this word still be used—or more appropriately, definitiveness, is not absolute but relational. In this sense Jesus' revelation and salvation are also complemented by God's selfrevelation and redemption manifested in other saving figures" (Ibid.). Thus, "one may question the usefulness of words such as *unique, absolute,* and even *universal* to describe the role of Jesus as savior today" (p. 143).

Such statements make it appear as if the revelation and salvation that God accomplished in Jesus Christ were similar in kind to what he has accomplished through other "saving figures." It has always been the faith of the Catholic Church, however, that Jesus is the eternal Son of God incar-nate as man, in whom a union of humanity and divinity takes place that is by its very nature unique and unrepeatable. The person who is the eternal Son of God is the very same person who is Jesus Christ. Jesus, then, is not simply one among the many founders of religions.

As the Son of God incarnate, he is able to reveal to humanity the fullness of divine truth. Moreover, only Jesus' sacrificial death makes possible the forgive-ness of sins and the reconciliation of sinful humanity with God. In his Resur-rection he conquered death and restored life. As the Risen Lord of heaven and earth he poured out the Holy Spirit at Pentecost. Only by being united to his risen humanity, which is itself united to his divinity, can we share in the divine life through the indwelling of the Holy Spirit and be transformed into adopted sons and daughters of the Father (see Romans 8:14–17). The Father's eternal plan of salvation culminates in Jesus Christ, his only Son.

2)   The Salvific Significance of Non-Christian Religions

While the Church acknowledges that non-Christian religions do possess certain elements of truth—ways of living and teachings that "often reflect a ray of that truth which enlightens all men" (*Nostra Aetate,* no. 2)—she regards these elements of goodness and truth found in other religions as a preparation for the Gospel, not supernatural revelation explicitly revealed by God. Such supernatural revelation is only found within God's intervention in the history of the people of Israel as narrated in the Old Testament and in the salvific work of Jesus Christ as related in the New Testament and the Christian tradition.

Being Religious Interreligiously, however, specifically rejects this view as an insufficient recognition of the salvific significance of non-Christian religions in themselves. The book asserts that "the non-Christian religions possess an autonomous function in the history of salvation, different from that of Christianity," so that "they cannot be reduced to Christianity in terms of preparation and fulfillment" (p. 144). In contrast to Church teaching, the book asserts that non-Christian religions "may be said to be ways of salvation" and that "religious pluralism is part of God's providential plan" (p. xxiii). In this view, not only can Christianity be enriched by insights from non-Christian religions, but these religions can even be a corrective to Christianity (p. 144).

Because of the "autonomous function" of the non-Christian religions, *Being Religious Interreligiously* comes to the conclusion that evangelization of non-Christian persons is no longer appropriate. The book argues that the fact that non-Christian religions are willed by God as part of his providential plan of salvation

> brings with it far-reaching and radical consequences for the practice of Christian mission and raises the thorny questions regarding conversion and baptism as the primary goals of evangelization. Indeed, if religious pluralism belongs to divine providence and is not just the fruit of human sinfulness, then it may not and must not be abolished by converting all the followers of non-Christian religions, at least during our common journey in history. (p. xxiii)

This conclusion, however, is in direct conflict with the Church's commission, given to it by Christ himself, to proclaim the Gospel to all nations (see Mt 28:18–20). It is also inconsistent with Christian belief in who Jesus is and what he does for the salvation of humanity.

3)   The Uniqueness of the Church
as the Universal Instrument of Salvation

While *Being Religious Interreligiously* fails to uphold Jesus' singular and universal significance, it argues that from a historical point of view "the claim of uniqueness and universality of the Christian church" has even less justification (p. 100). History affords reason for skepticism about such a claim, since "a human institution such as the Christian church, with a history of light and darkness, a mixture of good and evil, claims to be the exclusive vessel of divine grace while there is plenty of evidence that other religious institutions, no less than the church, have been instrumental in achieving good (and, of course, evil as well)" (p. 95).

The Church, however, is not merely a human institution. She is of course composed of human beings, but her origins are not merely human. Rather, Jesus, the incarnate Son of God, instituted the Church in accordance with his Father's will through his life, death and resurrection. He sent the Holy Spirit at Pentecost and from that moment the Spirit became the source of the Church's life and holiness. In this deeper sense the Church is a divine institution, the indispensable universal sacrament of salvation, instituted by Christ himself. Because the Church is the universal sacrament of salvation, whatever grace is offered to individuals in whatever various circumstances, including non-Christians, must be seen in relationship to the Church, for she is always united to Jesus Christ, the source of all grace and holiness.

From Peter Phan to Bishop Lori
May 23, 2007

Most Reverend William E. Lori
Bishop of Bridgeport
Committee on Doctrine
Washington, DC 20017

Your Excellency:

Your Excellency's letter dated May 15, 2007 reached me a couple of days ago. Due to the fact that I had to be out of town the past weekend to deliver a commencement address and to receive an honorary doctorate, I can respond to you only now.

With this letter your Excellency requested that I "present to the Committee written arguments as to how the positions presented in *Being Religious Interreligiously* are in conformity with Church teachings" and that I send you a written reply by 15 June 2007 stating whether I "would wish to provide such arguments."

I hereby declare that I am willing to provide such written arguments, as requested.

I would also like to take this opportunity to clarify a statement your Excellency made in your letter. You referred to the solution of the Congregation for the Doctrine of the Faith that I write and publish an article that would clarify and so make unmistakable that the positions that I in fact hold are in conformity with Church teaching. In this connection your Excellency wrote that "this proposal has proved unacceptable" to me.

That the said proposal has proved unacceptable to me is patently false. From my letter to his Eminence William Cardinal Levada, Prefect of the Congregation for the Doctrine of the Faith, a copy of which must be in your possession, it is clear that the request of the Congregation *is* indeed very acceptable to me and that I am most willing to write the article and have it published in a journal. I have also affirmed my willingness to do so to Rev. Thomas Weinandy, of the Committee on Doctrine of the USCCB, on the two occasions when he spoke to me by phone.

As is clear from my letter to his Eminence William Cardinal Levada, I requested that three things be done so that I can write the article. First, I asked that the prohibition to re-print the book be revoked because such prohibition already presumes my "guilt" before I have the opportunity to defend myself. Needless to say, such a procedure is an instance of "shoot first and ask after" and constitutes a grave injustice. I do however acknowledge the right of the Congregation to impose such prohibition but only *after* my explanations are judged unsatisfactory. My second request is for clarifications on the nature and scope of the article that the Congregation envisages. As you well know, no article is acceptable for publication in reputable journals unless it has a clear theme and a coherent focus. My request for such clarifications is an irrefutable proof of my willingness and readiness to write the required article. My third request is also a matter of justice, like the first. Since I do not receive financial support of any kind from the church or a religious order, I requested that the Congregation consider a fair and just remuneration for my work. To this date, I have not received any response from the Congregation to my letter dated April 4, 2006.

From your Excellency's letter it appears that the request of the Congregation for an article to be published in a journal has been revoked. Instead, I am now asked to provide "written arguments." Presumably, these written arguments do not constitute an article, as this is commonly understood among scholars, to be published in a journal. Please confirm whether my understanding on this point is correct.

Furthermore, in your letter several of the nineteen "serious ambiguities and doctrinal problems" which the Congregation finds in my book have been left out and they are now reduced to three topics, namely, "the unique identity of Jesus Christ as the universal savior, the salvific significance of non-Christian religions, and the role of the Church as the universal sacrament of salvation." Obviously, this is an improvement on the July 2005 statement of the Congregation and in a way satisfies my request for clarifications on the nature and scope of the article I was asked to write.

In addition, the fact that I am now given the opportunity to provide written arguments for the orthodoxy of my positions *before* the Committee on Doctrine of the USCCB publishes its observations on my book, presumably in the event that my explanations are judged unsatisfactory, assumes that I am "innocent before proven guilty," a welcome reversal of the Congregation's position.

However, that still leaves two requests of mine unanswered, one regarding the lifting of the prohibition of the reprinting of my book before I have the opportunity to defend myself, and the other regarding a fair remuneration for the work imposed upon me.

I will return to these two requests below. I would like to deal first with the question of the deadline for my written explanations. I do not want to bother your Excellency with a list of all the academic commitments I have already accepted, beside my full-time teaching, until May 2008. Some of these include lectures at the Franciscan Provincial Multicultural Council in June, the Catholic Theological Society of America Annual Convention in June, Payap University, Thailand, in June, John Carroll University in September, Franciscan School of Theology in October, Mount Saint Mary University in October, Austin Presbyterian Seminary in October, the Academy of Religion Annual Convention in November, Catholic Theological Union in November, Church Divinity School of the Pacific in January, Aquinas Institute in February, University of Munich in February, University of San Diego in March, Loyola Marymount University in March, University of Southern California in April, and University of Notre Dame in April. Needless to say, these lectures for a scholarly audience require a huge amount of research and writing. In addition, I have to complete before 2007 a book for John Knox/Westminster (a handbook to Roman Catholic theology) and two books before 2008, one for Cambridge University Press (a companion to the Trinity), and the other for Blackwell (on Asian Christianities). I also serve as general editor for the twenty-five volume series of Theology in Global Perspective for Orbis Books.

This partial listing of my scholarly activities until May 2008 is not a boast of what I do but an argument that my schedule will not permit me to complete the "written arguments" before the end of May 2008. The three topics on which I am requested to produce clarifications are so weighty that a satisfactory (at least to me) exposition of them cannot be done in less than a month of full-time work.

As I mentioned in my letter to Cardinal Levada, I am by nature adverse to publicity nor do I wish to take advantage of it for financial gains. But, having gone through the experiences of being a refugee and having lost everything in the process, I am willing to stand up for what I consider a matter of fairness and justice, no matter the cost, for my family and myself. May I repeat here what I have written to Cardinal Levada, namely that even in my home country, which has a communist government and where religious freedom is sometimes infringed upon, the accused always has the right to due process before being convicted and condemned, even when a trial's outcome has been predetermined. I have the right and duty to expect at least that much from a self-proclaimed champion of human rights such as the church.

While expressing my readiness to comply with your request to provide written arguments for my positions, I ask you to consider my three requests, i.e., the lifting of the prohibition of the reprinting of my book, a just and fair financial remuneration for a month of full-time work to complete the explanations requested, and a May 31, 2008 deadline. I believe that these requests are fair and just. To undertake the "written arguments" without these rights vindicated would be acting in complicity with injustice, and that my faith in our Lord Jesus forbids me to do.

I thank you, your Most Reverend Excellency, for your kind attention, and looking forward to hearing your response to my three requests, I wish you good health and success in your work.

Peter C. Phan, S.T.D., Ph.D., D.D.
Ignacio Ellacuría Chair of Catholic Social Thought
Georgetown University

cc: William Cardinal Levada
Prefect of the Congregation for the Doctrine of the Faith

From Bishop Lori to Peter Phan
June 20, 2007

Reverend Peter C. Phan, S.T.D., Ph.D., D.D.
Ignacio Ellacuria Chair of Catholic Social Thought
Georgetown University

Dear Father Phan,

Thank you for your letter of May 23, 2007 responding to my letter of May 15, 2007 regarding the Committee on Doctrine's concerns that some statements in your book *Being Religious Interreligiously* are not in conformity with the teaching of the Catholic Church.

While you expressed your desire to address the problematic statements, you have also set certain preconditions that must be met prior to your so doing. It must be remembered that most of these preconditions are beyond the competence of the Committee on Doctrine to grant. Moreover, it must also be kept clear that this committee's examination of the content of the book is distinct from your discussions with the Congregation on the Doctrine of the Faith.

The Committee on Doctrine intends to proceed with its review of the content of your book and continues to offer you the opportunity to provide your observations and reflections on its conformity with the teaching of the Church. We propose that you submit any explanations to the Committee by September 1, 2007. If the Committee receives no response, it will move ahead with the publication of a statement that will make clear to the faithful the problems that the Committee found in the book.

With every good wish, I am

Sincerely yours in Christ,
Most Reverend William E. Lori
Bishop of Bridgeport
Chairman

From Peter Phan to Bishop Lori
August 16, 2007

Most Reverend William E. Lori
Bishop of Bridgeport
Chairman, Committee on Doctrine
Washington, DC 20017

Your Excellency:

Upon my return from abroad I received your letter dated June 20, 2007, in which you informed me that the Committee on Doctrine intends "to move ahead with the publication of a statement that will make clear to the faithful the problems that the Committee found in the book" if it receives no response from me by September 1, 2007.

Given my time constraints and my manifold commitments within and without Georgetown University, especially with the start of a new academic year, it is physically impossible for me to meet the stipulated deadline of September 1, 2007.

While I always stand ready to provide a detailed response to the observations of the Committee on Doctrine on my book *prior* to the publication of its statement so as to avoid any untoward publicity, my inability to do so due to circumstances beyond my control will not take away my right to defend myself in public and in detail against any statement the Congregation for the Doctrine of the Faith has made and the Committee on Doctrine will make against my book. I will not be responsible for any adverse publicity that may result for the church, which I have tried to the best of my ability to avert.

I am intrigued by your statement that "this committee's examination of the content of the book is distinct from your [that is, my] discussions with the Congregation on the Doctrine of the Faith." From my two conversations with Rev. Thomas Weinandy I gather that the Committee on Doctrine has been acting on behalf of the Congregation for the Doctrine of the Faith. Otherwise, the Congregation has been seriously remiss in not answering my letter sent to it over a year ago, on April 2, 2006. It is interesting to note that while I am under strict obligation to meet a very short deadline, the Congregation has taken its time even to acknowledge receipt of my letter, let alone answer my requests.

Lastly, with regard to my conditions you referred to in your letter, they are neither arbitrary nor frivolous but are, in my judgment, the elementary demands of justice and fairness, which I must adhere to.

Sincerely yours,
Peter C. Phan, S.T.D., Ph.D., D.D.
The Ignacio Ellacuría Chair of Catholic Social Thought.
c: His Eminence Cardinal William Levada
Prefect of the Congregation for the Doctrine of the Faith

From Bishop Lori to Peter Phan
September 10, 2007

Reverend Peter C. Phan, S.T.D., Ph.D., D.D.
Ignacio Ellacuria Chair of Catholic Social Thought
Georgetown University

Dear Father Phan,

Thank you for your letter of August 16, 2007, which I have shared with the members of the USCCB Committee on Doctrine.

Apparently some further clarification of the distinct roles of the Congregation for the Doctrine of the Faith and the Committee on Doctrine is in order. While I am not privy to all the details of your previous interactions with the Congregation, I am aware that Archbishop Wuerl, as the local ordinary, was asked by the Congregation to ask Fr. Weinandy to contact you on behalf of the Congregation to see if some way forward could be found. Only after these efforts to find a satisfactory resolution to the matter were unsuccessful did the Congregation decide to ask the USCCB Committee on Doctrine to conduct its own investigation. It is our impression that at this point the Congregation is not inclined to issue its own statement if the Committee on Doctrine publishes one, though certainly the Congregation has the authority to take further actions at a later point if it deems this to be necessary.

The Committee on Doctrine investigation of the book is of necessity more limited in its scope than that of the Congregation for the Doctrine of the Faith. It is not a juridical proceeding that could result in canonical sanctions. The concern of the Committee on Doctrine is primarily pastoral, to avoid any confusions or misunderstandings about Church teaching. The aim of the statement that the Committee is currently preparing is simply to clarify particular points in your book that are ambiguous or at variance with the Church's teaching. This is in order to assist bishops in the United States in the exercise of their teaching and pastoral ministries, especially insofar as the book is addressed to catechists and others involved in the pastoral life of the Church.

The Committee on Doctrine is not asking you to produce a publishable article (as the Congregation for the Doctrine of the Faith had), but to respond to questions about certain ambiguous statements in the book, namely those indicated in the materials that I sent to you on May 15, 2007. Given that this task could be accomplished in a few thousand words, you will not be subject to financial hardship. As for the question of the publication of your book, this is a matter that can only be resolved by the Congregation for the Doctrine of the Faith.

The Committee on Doctrine is willing to give you some more time to prepare your response. So that we might have your response in time for consideration at our November meeting, we ask that you submit it to us by October 30, 2007. After this date, if the Committee receives no response, it will move ahead with the publication of a statement.

With the assurance of my prayers, I remain,

Faithfully in Christ,
Most Reverend William E. Lori
Bishop of Bridgeport
Chairman

From Peter Phan to Cardinal Levada
September 18, 2007

William Cardinal Levada
Prefect of the Congregation for the Doctrine of the Faith

Your Eminence:

You might have noticed that last week John Allen of *National Catholic Reporter* had broken the news of my being investigated by the Congregation of the Doctrine of the Faith and the Committee on Doctrine of the USCCB.

In his article he mentioned that *National Catholic Reporter* had obtained copies of the correspondence between me and the CDF and the USCCB.

I would like to attest that I have never given John Allen copies of the said correspondence. Furthermore I have declined numerous requests, here in the US and abroad, for interviews so as to prevent harmful publicity for the church.

Of course, I reserve the right to publish these letters if and when necessary to defend myself against unjust and incorrect accusations.

With best wishes for your ministry,

Peter C. Phan, S.T.D., Ph.D., D.D.
The Ignacio Ellacuría Chair of Catholic Social Thought
c: His Excellency Bishop William E. Lori
Chair, Committee on Doctrine, USCCB

From Peter Phan to Bishop Lori
September 24, 2007

Most Reverend William Lori
Bishop of Bridgeport

September 24, 2007

Your Excellency:

I have received your letter dated September 10, 2007 extending the deadline to October 30, 2007 for my response.

Given the enormous complexity of the theological issues the Congregation of the Doctrine of the Faith and your Committee on Doctrine have raised about my book and the seriousness of the charges against my theological positions, I will try my best to meet the deadline.

Unfortunately, given my current teaching responsibilities, the various lectures I have committed myself to until the end of October, and the publication deadlines for several essays and two books, I cannot promise that I will be able to produce the written explanations as requested.

My eventual failure to do so cannot be attributed to my recalcitrance but only to a physical impossibility even when I regularly put in a twelve-hour workday.

With best wishes for your ministry,

Peter C. Phan, S.T.D., Ph.D., D.D.
The Ignacio Ellacuría Chair of Catholic Social Thought

From Bishop Lori to Peter Phan
November 12, 2007

Reverend Peter C. Phan, S.T.D., Ph.D., D.D.
Ignacio Ellacuria Chair of Catholic Social Thought
Georgetown University

Dear Father Phan,

Six months ago, in May 2007, I wrote to you on behalf of the Committee on Doctrine requesting clarification on three particular points regarding your book *Being Religious Interreligiously.* In response to your request for more time, the deadline was extended to 30 October 2007. As the Committee has not received the requested clarifications, it has moved forward to complete work on a statement concerning problematic aspects of the book. This statement has recently been approved for publication by the USCCB Administrative Committee. You will find a copy enclosed. The Committee on Doctrine plans to publish it in two weeks.

While we feel obligated as pastors to issue a public statement in order to provide clarification on matters raised by the book, if you agree that the book does contain significant ambiguities that need to be addressed in your future publications and public presentations, we are willing to alter the statement to advert to this agreement. In that case, paragraph no. 3 would be modified in the following way:

3. In the light of these concerns, the Congregation for the Doctrine of the Faith asked the United States Conference of Catholic Bishops to conduct an evaluation of *Being Religious Interreligiously.* After examining this book, the Committee on Doctrine *presented its concerns to Fr. Phan, who agreed that the book in its present form contains significant ambiguities on certain points and that he would rectify these ambiguities in his future publications and public presentations.* ~~invited Father Phan to respond regarding statements in his book. Since Father Phan did not provide the needed clarifications, and~~ Since the ambiguities in the book concern matters that are central to the faith, the Committee on Doctrine decided to issue a statement that

would both identify problematic aspects of the book and provide a positive restatement of Catholic teaching on the relevant points.

If you are in agreement with this, please let us know by Tuesday, 20 November 2007.

With the assurance of my prayers, I remain

Faithfully in Christ,
Most Reverend William E. Lori
Bishop of Bridgeport
Chairman
(Enclosed was a draft of "Clarifications Required," which appears below in the published form.)

From Peter Phan to Bishop Lori
November 27, 2007

Most Reverend William E. Lori
Bishop of Bridgeport
Chairman, Committee on Doctrine

Your Excellency:

Your letter dated November 12, 2007, together with the text of the statement by the USCCB Committee on Doctrine on my book *Being Religious Interreligiously*, reached me only yesterday at Georgetown University.

On Monday, November 12 a staff member of the Committee called me and asked whether I would be in my office on the following two days. He said a certified letter from your office would be sent to me and that I would need to sign to acknowledge receipt of it. The letter never came. On Thursday, November 15 I left for San Diego for the annual meeting of the American Academy of Religion which took place on November 16–20. Meanwhile, your letter, I presume, had arrived. The University was closed for Thanksgiving on November 21–25 and class resumed only on Monday, 26 November, when I found your letter.

You gave me the deadline of Tuesday, November 20, 2007 to reply to your letter. The deadline has of course now passed. I was unfortunately prevented from responding by the fact that I was away on academic business and that the letter arrived during the Thanksgiving holiday.

I have always expressed my readiness to supply the clarifications you requested within a feasible time frame. I have asked for the deadline May 31, 2008, which seems quite reasonable in light of a number of activities I had committed myself to doing between September this year and May next year. Given the seriousness of the issues raised, with the best will in the world, I deeply regret that it is impossible, in terms of time, for me to respond to them adequately during the academic year.

With best wishes for your ministry,

Peter C. Phan, S.T.D., Ph.D., D.D.
The Ignacio Ellacuría Chair of Catholic Social Thought

From Bishop Lori to Peter Phan
December 3, 2007

Rev. Peter Phan
Ellacuria Chair of Catholic Social Thought
Georgetown University

Dear Fr. Phan,

Thank you for your letter of November 27, 2007. In this letter, as in all of your previous letters, you state that, while you are more than willing to respond to the concerns expressed by the Bishops' Committee on Doctrine, in the light of all of your numerous activities and responsibilities you are unable to do so in an expeditious fashion. Given the serious nature of the issues involved, issues concerning the truth of the Gospel and the Church's teaching, and the nature of the body raising these concerns, the USCCB's Committee on Doctrine, this matter should not be the last among your priorities. The Committee on Doctrine has given you five months to make some response, and it has most recently extended the deadline. (See my letter of November 26, 2007, which was faxed to you that day.) Moreover, previous to the Committee on Doctrine's study of your work, the Congregation for the Doctrine of the Faith, over an extended period of time, has been asking you to make clarifications on these very same issues.

The Committee on Doctrine, out of pastoral solicitude, will issue its statement. Nonetheless, the Committee very much desires to include the acknowledgement that you have agreed that the book in its present form contains significant ambiguities on certain points and that you will rectify these ambiguities in your future publications and public presentations. (See my letter of November 12, 2007.) I ask you to let me know by noon on Friday, December 7, 2007, whether or not you consent to such an acknowledgement being placed within the text of the statement. Please FAX your response to the following number: 202-541-3088.

Faithfully in Christ,
Most Reverend William E. Lori
Bishop of Bridgeport
Chairman

Clarifications Required by the Book
Being Religious Interreligiously:
Asian Perspectives on Interfaith Dialogue
by Reverend Peter C. Phan

Committee on Doctrine
United States Conference of Catholic Bishops

1. The development of a theology of religious pluralism, that is, a theology that "seeks to investigate, in the light of Christian faith, the significance of the plurality of religious traditions in God's plan for humanity,"[1] is an important task given the exigencies of religious dialogue in our globalized world. The importance of such theological investigation makes it all the more critical that it be carried out in a way that upholds the truth of Catholic doctrine, keeping in proper order a variety of truths that pertain to the Christian faith and to the legitimate integrity of other religions.

2. In his book, *Being Religious Interreligiously: Asian Perspectives on Interfaith Dialogue,*[2] Reverend Peter C. Phan, who currently holds the Ellacuria Chair of Catholic Social Thought in the Department of Theology at Georgetown University, has taken up the task of addressing the cultural concerns and theological questions surrounding the diversity of religions. The way the book addresses some theological issues, however, raises serious concerns.

3. In the light of these concerns, the Congregation for the Doctrine of the Faith asked the United States Conference of Catholic Bishops to conduct an evaluation of *Being Religious Interreligiously.* After examining this book, the Committee on Doctrine invited Father Phan to respond regarding statements in his book. Since Father Phan did not provide the needed clarifications, and since the ambiguities in the book concern matters that are central to the faith, the Committee on Doctrine decided to issue a

---

[1] Congregation for the Doctrine of the Faith, Notification on the Book *Toward a Christian Theology of Religious Pluralism* by Father Jacques Dupuis, S.J. (24 January 2001) (www.vatican.va/roman_curia/congregations/cfaith/documents/rc_con_cfaith_doc_20010124_dupuis_en.html), Preface.

[2] Peter C. Phan, *Being Religious Interreligiously: Asian Perspectives on Dialogue* (Maryknoll, N.Y.: Orbis Press, 2004).

statement that would both identify problematic aspects of the book and provide a positive restatement of Catholic teaching on the relevant points.

4. This statement will address three areas of concern: i) Jesus Christ as the unique and universal Savior of all humankind; ii) the salvific significance of non-Christian religions; iii) the Church as the unique and universal instrument of salvation. Even though this book contains other areas of concern, we concluded that the above mentioned were the most serious and so have focused our attention upon them.

I.   Jesus Christ as the Unique and Universal Savior of All Humankind

5. It is true that the uniqueness of Jesus Christ is affirmed at some points in *Being Religious Interreligiously*. According to the book, Christ can be described as uniquely constitutive of salvation "because the Christ-event belongs to and is the climax of God's plan of salvation. . . . Jesus' 'constitutive uniqueness' means that he and only he 'opens access to God for all people.'"[3] At other points, however, the term "unique" is rejected or else accepted with confusing qualifications.

6. *Being Religious Interreligiously* describes Jesus as "unique" with the qualification that this uniqueness is not only "constitutive" but also "relational."[4] As "relational" (in the sense which the book gives this term) Christ's uniqueness is not exclusive or absolute, since he is not the only revealer and savior in God's plan of salvation. Christ, according [to] the book, has a unique role, but this role is "related" to other figures who also have a place in God's plan. Christ "may be said to be the 'one mediator' and the other savior figures and non-Christian religions participating mediators" since, "insofar as they mediate God's salvation to their followers, [they] do so through the power of the Logos and the Spirit."[5]

7. *Being Religious Interreligiously* specifies that the way that such savior figures and religions participate in the salvation brought about by Christ

---

[3] Phan, *Being Religious Interreligiously*, p. 66; see p. 144. The quotation is from Jacques Dupuis, *Toward a Christian Theology of Religious Pluralism* (Maryknoll, NY: Orbis, 1998), p. 387.

[4] Phan, *Being Religious Interreligiously*, p. 66; see p. 144. The author notes that these expressions are borrowed from Dupuis, *Toward a Christian Theology of Religious Pluralism*, p. 283 (see Phan, *Being Religious Interreligiously*, p. 144 n. 14).

[5] Phan, *Being Religious Interreligiously*, p. 67.

prevents these non-Christian religions from being reduced to Christianity.[6] What they offer is truly different.[7] The book characterizes this difference as one of complementarity:

> In this context it is useful to recall that Jesus did not and could not reveal everything to his disciples and that it is the Holy Spirit who will lead them to 'the complete truth' (Jn 16:12–13). It is quite possible that the Holy Spirit will lead the church to the complete truth by means of a dialogue with other religions in which the Spirit is actively present.[8]

8. While at some points the book affirms the uniqueness of Christ with these qualifications, at another point in the book the use of the term "unique" is entirely rejected. "[O]ne may question the usefulness of words such as *unique, absolute,* and even *universal* to describe the role of Jesus as savior today."[9] Although such terms may have served at one time, "words are unavoidably embedded in socio-political and cultural contexts, and the contexts in which these words were used were, in many parts of the world, often tainted by colonialist imperialism, economic exploitation, political domination, and religious marginalization."[10] From this the book concludes that the terms "unique," "absolute," and "universal" "have outlived their usefulness and should be jettisoned and replaced by other, theologically more adequate equivalents."[11]

9. Since, at the very least, the use in the book of certain terms in an equivocal manner opens the text up to significant ambiguity and since a fair reading of the book could leave readers in considerable confusion as to the proper understanding of the uniqueness of Christ, it is necessary to recall some essential elements of Church teaching. The crux of the issue is that *Being Religious Interreligiously* does not express adequately and accurately the Church's teaching.

10. In its declaration *Dominus Iesus,* the Congregation for the Doctrine of the Faith directly addresses the kind of ambiguities that are found in

---

[6] Phan, *Being Religious Interreligiously*, pp. 66, 144.

[7] Phan, *Being Religious Interreligiously*, p. 65; see also p. 67 n. 20.

[8] Phan, *Being Religious Interreligiously*, p. 144–45; see pp. 65 and 67.

[9] Phan, *Being Religious Interreligiously*, p. 143.

[10] Phan, *Being Religious Interreligiously*, p. 143.

[11] Phan, *Being Religious Interreligiously*, p. 144.

Being Religious Interreligiously. It warns against any misunderstanding of Jesus and of his work of salvation. It states:

> In contemporary theological reflection there often emerges an approach to Jesus of Nazareth that considers him a particular, finite, historical figure, who reveals the divine not in an exclusive way, but in a way complementary with other revelatory and salvific figures. The Infinite, the Absolute, the Ultimate Mystery of God would thus manifest itself to humanity in many ways and in many historical figures: Jesus of Nazareth would be one of these.[12]

Against such a misrepresentation, *Dominus Iesus* declares: "These theses are in profound conflict with the Christian faith. The doctrine of faith must be *firmly believed* which proclaims that Jesus of Nazareth, son of Mary, and he alone, is the Son and the Word of the Father."[13]

11. It has always been the faith of the Church that Jesus is the eternal Son of God incarnate as man. The union of humanity and divinity that takes place in Jesus Christ is by its very nature unique and unrepeatable. The person who is the eternal Son of God is the very same person who is Jesus Christ.[14] Because humanity and divinity are united in the person of the Son of God, he brings together humanity and divinity in a way that can have no parallel in any other figure in history.

12. In the Church's teaching, Jesus is not merely preeminent among many savior figures. As the Son of God incarnate, Jesus reveals to humanity the fullness of divine truth. "And the Word became flesh and made his dwelling among us, and we saw his glory, the glory as of the Father's only Son, full of grace and truth" (Jn 1:14). The Gospel of John also professes: "No one has ever seen God. The only Son, God, who is at the Father's side, has revealed him" (Jn 1:18. See also Mt 11:27; Acts 14:16; Heb 1:1–2). *Dominus Iesus* is very clear on this Gospel truth:

---

[12] Congregation for the Doctrine of the Faith, *Dominus Iesus: Declaration on the Unicity and Salvific Universality of Jesus Christ and the Church* (6 August 2000) (www.vatican.va/roman_curia/congregations/cfaith/documents/rc_con_cfaith_doc_20000806_dominus-iesus_en.html), no. 9.

[13] Congregation for the Doctrine of the Faith, *Dominus Iesus*, no. 10.

[14] See Council of Chalcedon, *Enchiridion Symbolorum Definitionum ed Declarationum de Rebus Fidei et Morum*, ed. H. Denzinger and P. Hünermann, 39th ed. (Freiburg im Breisgau: Herder, 2001), nos. 301–2, and Second Council of Constantinople, *Enchiridion Symbolorum*, no. 424. See also, *The Catechism of the Catholic Church*, nos. 461–69.

[I]t is necessary above all to reassert the definitive and complete character of the revelation of Jesus Christ. In fact, it must be firmly believed that, in the mystery of Jesus Christ, the Incarnate Son of God, who is 'the way, the truth, and the life' (Jn 14:6), the full revelation of divine truth is given.[15]

13. Moreover, Jesus Christ, as the Son of God incarnate, is God the Father's definitive and universal means of salvation. Only Jesus' sacrificial death makes possible the forgiveness of sins and the reconciliation of sinful humanity with God.[16] By his Resurrection he conquered death and restored life. Through him the Holy Spirit was poured out on the Church at Pentecost. Only by being united to Christ's risen humanity, which is itself united to his divinity, can we share in the divine life through the indwelling of the Holy Spirit and be transformed into adopted sons and daughters of the Father (see Rom 8:14–17). The Father's eternal plan of salvation culminates in Jesus Christ, his only Son.

In him we have redemption by his blood, the forgiveness of transgressions, in accord with the riches of his grace that he lavished upon us. In all wisdom and insight, he has made known to us the mystery of his will in accord with his favor that he set forth in him, as a plan for the fullness of times, to sum up all things in Christ, in heaven and on earth (Eph 1:7–10).

14. Because of who Jesus is and what he has done and continues to do as the Risen Lord, the Church, from her earliest days, has proclaimed: "There is no salvation through anyone else, nor is there any other name under heaven given to the human race by which we are to be saved" (Acts 4:12). This does not mean that members of other religions cannot possibly be saved, but it does mean that their salvation is always accomplished in some way through Christ.

---

[15] Congregation for the Doctrine of the Faith, *Dominus Iesus,* no. 5.

[16] See Council of Trent, Decree on Justification (*De justificatione*), *Enchiridion Symbolorum,* no. 1529; Second Vatican Council, Constitution on the Sacred Liturgy (*Sacrosanctum Concilium*), no. 5, and Pastoral Constitution on the Church in the Modern World (*Gaudium et spes*), no. 22; See *Catechism of the Catholic Church,* nos. 613–14.

No one, therefore, can enter into communion with God except through Christ, by the working of the Holy Spirit. Christ's one, universal mediation, far from being an obstacle on the journey toward God, is the way established by God himself, a fact of which Christ is fully aware. Although participated forms of mediation of different kinds and degrees are not excluded, they acquire meaning and value only from Christ's own mediation, and they cannot be understood as parallel or complementary to his.[17]

15. *Dominus Iesus* affirms this singular salvific role of Jesus Christ. "[O]ne can say and must say that Jesus Christ has a significance and a value for the human race and its history, which are unique and singular, proper to him alone, exclusive, universal, and absolute."[18] In the light of this, *Dominus Iesus* concludes that "the theory of the limited, incomplete, or imperfect character of the revelation of Jesus Christ, which would be complementary to that found in other religions, is contrary to the Church's faith."[19] It also asserts that "those solutions that propose a salvific action of God beyond the unique mediation of Christ would be contrary to Christian and Catholic faith."[20] Rather, it must be "*firmly believed* as a truth of Catholic faith that the universal salvific will of the One and Triune God is offered and accomplished once and for all in the mystery of the incarnation, death, and resurrection of the Son of God."[21]

---

[17] Pope John Paul II, Encyclical Letter on the Permanent Validity of the Church's Missionary Mandate (*Redemptoris Missio*) (http://www.vatican.va/edocs/ENG0219/_P3.HTM), no. 5. See also Pontifical Council for Inter-religious Dialogue, *Dialogue and Proclamation* (www.vatican.va/roman_curia/pontifical_councils/interelg/documents/rc_pc_interelg_doc_19051991_dialogue-and-proclamatio_en.html), no. 29: "From this mystery of unity it follows that all men and women who are saved share, though differently, in the same mystery of salvation in Jesus Christ through his Spirit. Christians know this through their faith, while others remain unaware that Jesus Christ is the source of their salvation. The mystery of salvation reaches out to them, in a way known to God, through the invisible action of the Spirit of Christ. Concretely, it will be in the sincere practice of what is good in their own religious traditions and by following the dictates of their conscience that the members of other religions respond positively to God's invitation and receive salvation in Jesus Christ, even while they do not recognize or acknowledge him as their saviour."

[18] Congregation for the Doctrine of the Faith, *Dominus Iesus*, no. 15.

[19] Congregation for the Doctrine of the Faith, *Dominus Iesus*, no. 6.

[20] Congregation for the Doctrine of the Faith, *Dominus Iesus*, no. 14.

[21] Congregation for the Doctrine of the Faith, *Dominus Iesus*, no. 14.

II.   The Salvific Significance of Non-Christian Religions

16. The Church affirms that non-Christian religions do in fact possess certain elements of truth. Every human being possesses an innate desire to know God, who is the common end and origin of the human race.[22] Those searching for God in other religions have established ways of living and formulated teachings that "often reflect a ray of that Truth which enlightens all men."[23] The Church regards these elements of goodness and truth found in other religions as a preparation for the Gospel.[24]

17. *Being Religious Interreligiously*, however, rejects this teaching as an insufficient recognition of the salvific significance of non-Christian religions in themselves: The book defends the view that "the non-Christian religions possess an autonomous function in the history of salvation, different from that of Christianity," and that "they cannot be reduced to Christianity in terms of preparation and fulfillment."[25] The book asserts:

> Religious pluralism . . . is not just a matter of fact but also a matter of principle. That is, non-Christian religions may be seen as part of the plan of divine providence and endowed with a particular role in the history of salvation. They are not merely a "preparation" for, "stepping stones" toward, or "seeds" of Christianity and destined to be "fulfilled" by it. Rather, they have their own autonomy and their proper roles as ways of salvation, at least for their adherents.[26]

---

[22] *Catechism of the Catholic Church,* no. 842.

[23] Second Vatican Council, Declaration on the Relation of the Church to Non-Christian Religions (*Nostra Aetate*) (www.vatican.va/archive/hist_councils/ii_vatican_council/documents/vat-ii_decl_ 19651028_nostra-aetate_en.html), no. 2. See also *Catechism of the Catholic Church*, no. 842.

[24] *Catechism of the Catholic Church* states: "The Catholic Church recognizes in other religions that search, among shadows and images, for the God who is unknown yet near since he gives life and breath to all things and wants all men to be saved. Thus, the Church considers all goodness and truth found in these religions as 'a preparation for the Gospel and given by him who enlightens all men that they may at length have life'" (no. 843). The Catechism is here quoting Second Vatican Council, Dogmatic Constitution on the Church (*Lumen Gentium*), no. 16. It also refers to Second Vatican Council, Declaration on the Relation of the Church to Non-Christian Religions (*Nostra Aetate*), no. 2, and Pope Paul VI, Apostolic Exhortation *Evangelii Nuntiandi* (8 December 1975), no. 53.

[25] Phan, *Being Religious Interreligiously*, p. 144.

[26] Phan, *Being Religious Interreligiously*, pp. 65–66; see p. 143.

The book contrasts what it sees as the Second Vatican Council's deliberate decision to refrain "from affirming that these religions as such function as ways of salvation in a manner analogous, let alone parallel, to Christianity," with the position of certain contemporary theologians, among whom the author includes himself. These theologians believe that it is necessary to go beyond the Council's position and to assert "that these religions may be said to be ways of salvation and that religious pluralism is part of God's providential plan."[27]

18. The book's use of the terms "ways of salvation" and "autonomy" contains serious ambiguities. On the one hand, the autonomy of these ways of salvation is not portrayed as absolute; the salvation of non-Christians remains somehow "related" to Christ. According to the book, the Christ-event is "the definitive realization of God's plan of salvation" and its "definitive point."[28] On the other hand, the nature of this relation remains obscure. The book makes the perplexing claim that "Autonomy and relatedness are not mutually contradictory but grow in direct proportion to each other."[29] This claim is seriously undercut, however, by the fact that the autonomy attributed to non-Christian religions is such as to call into question the very idea of Christian mission to members of such religions.

19. The book affirms in the introduction that the assertion that God has positively willed non-Christian religions as alternative ways of salvation as part of his providential plan of salvation "brings with it far-reaching and radical consequences for the practice of Christian mission and raises the thorny questions regarding conversion and baptism as the primary goals of evangelization."[30] The book reasons that if in fact God has positively willed the existence of the non-Christian religions as ways of salvation, then the very goal itself of universal conversion to Christianity is misguided. "Indeed, if religious pluralism belongs to divine providence and is not just the fruit of human sinfulness, then it may not and must not be abolished by converting all the followers of non-Christian religions, at least during our common journey in history."[31]

20. Since the book as a whole is based on the idea that religious pluralism is indeed a positively-willed part of the divine plan, the reader

---

[27] Phan, *Being Religiously Interreligiously*, p. xxiii; see pp. 139–40.

[28] Phan, *Being Religiously Interreligiously*, p. 144.

[29] Phan, *Being Religiously Interreligiously*, p. 144; see p. 66.

[30] Phan, *Being Religiously Interreligiously*, p. xxiii.

[31] Phan, *Being Religiously Interreligiously*, p. xxiii.

is led to conclude that there is some kind of moral obligation for the Church to refrain from calling people to conversion to Christ and to membership in his Church. According to the book, religious pluralism "may not and must not be abolished" by conversion to Christianity. The implication is that to continue the Christian mission to members of non-Christian religions would be contrary to God's purpose in history. Such a conclusion, instead of being a "theologically more adequate equivalent" of Church teaching, is in fact an alteration that blurs Church teaching. At this point the autonomy of non-Christian religions has eclipsed their relatedness to Jesus Christ.

21. This call for an end to Christian mission is in conflict with the Church's commission, given to her by Christ himself: "Go, therefore, and make disciples of all nations, baptizing them in the name of the Father, and of the Son, and of the Holy Spirit, teaching them to observe all that I have commanded you."[32] Moreover, if one accepts that Jesus Christ is in fact the one affirmed by Christian faith as the eternal Son of God made man, through whom the universe was created and by whose death and resurrection the human race has the possibility of attaining eternal life, then it is incoherent to argue that it would somehow be better if certain people were not told this truth.

22. The Church's evangelizing mission is not an imposition of power but an expression of love for the whole world. The very fact that other religions do not possess the fullness of the Father's truth revealed in Jesus Christ and the fullness of the Father's love that is poured out in the Holy Spirit ought to compel Christians, in their love for all men and women, to share their faith with others. To offer others the gift of Jesus Christ is to offer them the greatest and most valuable of all gifts, for he is the Father's merciful gift to all. Thus there is no necessary conflict between showing respect for other religions and fulfilling Christ's command to proclaim the Gospel to all the nations.[33]

---

[32] Mt 28:18–20. See Second Vatican Council, Dogmatic Constitution on the Church (*Lumen Gentium*), no. 17, and Decree on the Church's Missionary Activity (*Ad Gentes*), no. 1; *Catechism of the Catholic Church*, no. 849; Pope Paul VI, Apostolic Exhortation *Evangelii Nuntiandi*, no. 14.

[33] See Second Vatican Council, Declaration on the Relation of the Church to Non-Christian Religions *(Nostra Aetate)*, no. 2; Pope John Paul II, Encyclical Letter on the Permanent Validity of the Church's Missionary Mandate (*Redemptoris Missio*), no. 55.

23. The fact that *Being Religious Interreligiously* can envisage an end to Christian mission points to a distortion in its methodology as a work of Christian theology, a distortion rooted in its persistent downplaying of the singularity of Jesus Christ as savior of the world. To begin with, the very terms used to describe non-Christian religions as divinely-willed "ways of salvation," that are "autonomous" from Christianity imply a perspective that is somehow beyond that of Christian faith, indeed, that enables one to judge what is of "religious" salvific value in a given religion.

24. Christian theology, however, is founded upon supernatural revelation accepted in faith, not simply upon a natural capacity of the human person to obtain knowledge of God. The Christian theologian, having first embraced the truths of revelation as found within the biblical proclamation and the Church's doctrinal tradition, strives to come to a deeper understanding and appreciation of what God has revealed. For the Christian theologian, the significance and validity of other religious beliefs can only be evaluated from within this faith perspective. Christian revelation demands that the salvific value of any religious truth must be scrutinized and assessed ultimately in the light of the Gospel itself.[34] There is no judge or arbiter that is superior to it.

25. The book distances itself from the claim that all religions can be reduced to a common core of religious experience that could serve as the basis for the construction of a universal theology of religion.[35] Nevertheless, much of the language in the book implies that its basic perspective is not specifically Christian, but a more universal "religious" perspective, one that is somehow higher than that of any particular religion. In addition to the use of the terms "ways of salvation" and "autonomous," another example of this seemingly higher perspective would be the positive portrayal of "multiple religious belonging," which is described as "not only possible but also desirable."[36] *Being Religious Interreligiously* derives its title from this phenomenon.[37]

[34] See Congregation for the Doctrine of the Faith, *Instruction on the Ecclesial Vocation of the Theologian* (24 May 1990) (www.vatican.va/roman_curia/congregations/cfaith/documents/rc_con_cfaith_doc_19900524_theologian-vocation_en.html), no. 10. The Congregation points out that elements taken from any source of knowledge apart from Christian revelation are subject to a discernment for which Christian revelation serves as the final criterion: "The ultimate normative principle for such discernment is revealed doctrine which itself must furnish the criteria for the evaluation of these elements and conceptual tools and not *vice versa.*"

[35] Phan, *Being Religious Interreligiously*, p. 98; see pp. 90–91 and pp. 119–20.

[36] Phan, *Being Religious Interreligiously*, p. 67.

[37] See Phan, *Being Religious Interreligiously*, p. 78.

26. Another example of the tendency toward a universal religious perspective would be the discussion of the ways in which religions "complement" and even "correct" one another. "Not only are the non-Christian religions complemented by Christianity, but Christianity is complemented by the other religions. In other words, the process of complementation, enrichment, and even correction is *two-way* or reciprocal."[38] Although the book claims that this "reciprocal relationship" does not endanger the faith of the Church, at the very least the affirmation of a process of complementation and correction implies the existence of someone above the Christian faith who is able to judge that such a process has in fact occurred.

III. The Church as the Unique and Universal Instrument of Salvation

27. Although *Being Religious Interreligiously* does not adequately uphold Jesus' singular and universal significance, it does maintain that one can and should present the claim for the uniqueness and universality of Jesus Christ in the context of interreligious dialogue, at least in a qualified form.[39] As for the Church, however, it argues that the claim for her uniqueness and universality "should be abandoned altogether."[40] With regard to this claim, the book notes that

> what arouses much skepticism and even outrage is that a human institution such as the Christian church, with a history of light and darkness, a mixture of good and evil, claims to be the exclusive vessel of divine grace while there is plenty of evidence that other religious institutions, no less than the church, have been instrumental in achieving good (and, of course, evil as well).[41]

While it is not clear whether or not this passage represents precisely the position of the author, the reasons that are in fact given for abandonment of the claim for the uniqueness and universality of the Church all concern

---

[38] Phan, *Being Religious Interreligiously*, p. 66; see also p. 144.

[39] Phan, *Being Religious Interreligiously*, p. 91.

[40] Phan, *Being Religious Interreligiously*, p. 100. The book stresses the distinction between Christ and the Church, between Jesus and Christianity (pp. 92–98).

[41] Phan, *Being Religious Interreligiously*, p. 95.

the same issue: the humanness of the Church and her historical entanglement with sin and injustice.[42]

28. The Church, however, is not simply an institution like other institutions. It is true that the Church is composed of human beings and, in this sense, she is a human institution. However, Jesus, the incarnate Son of God, in accordance with his Father's will, instituted the Church through his life, death and resurrection. At Pentecost Jesus sent the Holy Spirit, the promise of his Father, upon the disciples and from that moment the Spirit became the source of the Church's life and holiness.[43] The Church depends upon the presence of the Spirit, who is at work in her. Thus, the Church is also a divine institution.[44]

29. The book is certainly correct when it points out that members of the Church, through the course of history, have sinned and that the credibility of Christian witness to the world has suffered greatly from this. Nevertheless, the holiness of the Church is not simply defined by the holiness (or sinfulness) of her members but by the holiness of her Head, the Lord Jesus Christ. He is supremely holy and the source of the Church's holiness in that he imbues the Church with his Holy Spirit.[45] This Spirit is active in the continual preaching of the Gospel which calls Christian men and women to an ever deeper conversion to holiness. Similarly, it is through the holiness of the sacraments, instituted by Christ, that the members of the Church are cleansed of sin and made holy, especially through the Sacraments of Penance and of the Eucharist.

30. According to the Second Vatican Council, the Church as the messianic people of God is "a lasting and sure seed of unity, hope and salvation for the whole human race. Established by Christ as a communion of life, charity and truth, it is also used by Him as an instrument for the redemption of all, and is sent forth into the whole world as the light of the world and the salt of the earth."[46] The Church is the indispensable "universal sacrament of salvation" that has been instituted by Christ himself and that continues to be sustained by him:

---

[42] Phan, *Being Religious Interreligiously*, p. 100–1.

[43] See Lk 24:49; Second Vatican Council, Dogmatic Constitution on the Church (*Lumen Gentium*), no. 4; *Catechism of the Catholic Church*, nos. 731 & 739.

[44] See the *Catechism of the Catholic Church*, nos. 758–69.

[45] See the *Catechism of the Catholic Church*, nos. 823–29.

[46] Second Vatican Council, Dogmatic Constitution on the Church (*Lumen Gentium*) (www.vatican.va/archive/hist_councils/ii_vatican_council/documents/vat-ii_const_19641121_lumen-gentium_en.html), no. 9.

Christ, having been lifted up from the earth has drawn all to Himself. Rising from the dead He sent His life-giving Spirit upon His disciples and through Him has established His Body which is the Church as the universal sacrament of salvation. Sitting at the right hand of the Father, He is continually active in the world that He might lead men to the Church and through it join them to Himself and that He might make them partakers of His glorious life by nourishing them with His own Body and Blood.[47]

31. Because the Church is the universal sacrament of salvation, whatever grace is offered to individuals in whatever various circumstances, including non-Christians, must be seen in relationship to the Church, for she is always united to Jesus Christ, the source of all grace and holiness.[48] Since all grace flows from our Lord and Savior Jesus Christ through his Church, "it is clear that it would be contrary to the faith to consider the Church as *one way* of salvation alongside those constituted by the other religions, seen as complementary to the Church or substantially equivalent to her."[49]

Conclusion

32. While *Being Religious Interreligiously* addresses a number of issues that are crucial in the life of the contemporary Church, it contains certain pervading ambiguities and equivocations that could easily confuse or mislead the faithful, as well as statements that, unless properly clarified, are not in accord with Catholic teaching. Therefore we bishops as teachers of the faith are obliged to take action that will help ensure that the singularity of Jesus and the Church be perceived in all clarity and the universal salvific significance of what he has accomplished be acknowledged in the fullness of truth.

---

[47] See Second Vatican Council, Dogmatic Constitution on the Church (*Lumen Gentium*), no. 48.

[48] See Second Vatican Council, Dogmatic Constitution on the Church (*Lumen Gentium*), no. 48; Second Vatican Council, Decree on the Missionary Activity of the Church (*Ad Gentes*), no. 2; Pope John Paul II, Encyclical Letter on the Permanent Validity of the Church's Missionary Mandate (*Redemptoris Missio*), no. 10, and Congregation for the Doctrine of the Faith, *Dominus Iesus,* no. 20.

[49] Congregation for the Doctrine of the Faith, *Dominus Iesus*, no. 21.

Most Rev. William E. Lori (Chairman)
Bishop of Bridgeport

Most Rev. Leonard P. Blair
Bishop of Toledo

Most Rev. José H. Gomez
Archbishop of San Antonio

Most Rev. Robert J. McManus
Bishop of Worcester

Most Rev. Arthur J. Serratelli
Bishop of Paterson

Most Rev. Allen H. Vigneron
Bishop of Oakland

Most Rev. Donald W. Wuerl
Archbishop of Washington

From Peter Phan to Bishop Lori
December 7, 2007

Most Reverend William E. Lori
Bishop of Bridgeport
Chairman, Committee on Doctrine

Your Excellency:

I received your faxed letter of December 3, 2007 on the same day. I was at a conference at Catholic Theological Union in Chicago on November 30–December 1 and therefore could not respond to your previous faxed letter dated November 26 which extended the deadline to November 30, 2007.

In response to your comment about time and extensions of deadlines, I assure you that this matter is not "the last" among my priorities. I am very much aware of the elevated ecclesiastical status of the USCCB's Committee on Doctrine. It is in fact for that reason that I do not want to give a rushed or incomplete response to its concerns. However, I have to balance its demands on my time with my primary responsibilities to Georgetown University in whose employment I am and with my other obligations that I had committed myself to prior to receiving your letter dated May 15, 2007.

Given the seriousness and the extensiveness of the observations of both the Congregation for the Doctrine of the Faith and the USCCB's Committee on Doctrine on my book, I believe I should not give a cursory clarification of my positions, "in a few thousand words," as you suggested in your letter of September 10, or in the same length as the statement that the Committee is going to publish. As far as I know, most people whose works have been under investigation had sabbaticals to write their responses, some even in book form, a luxury I do not have, both in terms of time and finance.

Furthermore, in spite of my overloaded schedule, I have tried my best to respond to all the correspondences from church authorities in good time, while I am still waiting for a reply from the Congregation for the Doctrine of the Faith to my letter with its three requests dated April 4, 2006.

Since I have not been able to respond in detail to all the observations of the Committee, it would not be ethically proper for me to affirm, as you suggested, that I have agreed that my book in its present form contains significant ambiguities on certain points and that I will rectify these ambiguities in your future publications and public presentations. I do however take seriously the concerns of the CDF and the USCCB Committee on Doctrine about my book and plan to respond to them in detail as soon as time permits.

With best wishes for your ministry,

Peter C. Phan, S.T.D., Ph.D., D.D.
The Ignacio Ellacuría Chair of Catholic Social Thought

Index

Ad Gentes, 107, 108, 116–17, 118, 120

ad intra/ad extra, church as, 130, 132

Aeterni Patris encyclical, 48

Allen, John, Jr., 204

Amaladoss, Michael, 90–91, 97, 136

Amato, Angelo, 1, 3, 6, 174, 186

Aquinas, Thomas, 37, 48, 54, 57,
    86–87, 161

The Asian Jesus (Amaladoss), 90–91

Asian Synod, 133, 134, 140

auditus fidei, 23, 25–26, 27–28

Augustine of Hippo, 54, 55, 57

Being Religious Interreligiously (BRI)
    background on controversy, *x,*
        16–18
    dialogical ecclesiology, expounded
        in, 145
    Dominus Iesus, not meeting
        standards of, 2, 19, 79, 175,
        179–80, 186
    gnostic tenor, perception of, 184, 188
    as honoring non-Christian believers,
        128
    necessity of mission, accused of
        denying, 155, 217–19
    observations against, 6–11, 13, 51,
        66, 78, 130, 175, 183, 186, 188
    prohibition to reprint, *ix,* 2, 4, 5,
        186–87, 188, 196, 197, 198
    salvific significance of
        non-Christian religions,
        recognizing, 193

See also under Committee on
    Doctrine; Congregation for the
    Doctrine of the Faith

Benedict XVI, Pope, 3, 6, 14, 18, 111,
    166

Bergoglio, Jorge. *See* Francis, Pope

Buddhism, 91, 104, 114
    Christianity and, 60–62, 111, 130
    as complementing the revelation of
        Jesus, 88
    in interfaith studies, 93, 97
    Jesus as bodhisattva, 90
    as non-theistic, 74, 157, 167
    as a primal religion, 117
    as a resource for Asian theologians,
        89
    salvation and, 82, 84–85, 110
    in Thailand, 101–102, 105, 113, 124,
        127, 128

Burke, Raymond, 14

Burrows, William, *xi–xii*

Calvo, Angelo, 76, 77

Carzedda, Salvatore, 77

Catechism of the Catholic Church, 25,
    181, 182

Catholic Bishops' Conference of India,
    127

Chalcedon, Council of, 53

Chinese Rites Controversy, 121

Christifideles, 39, 40, 41

Christology, 51, 88–91, 91–96, 96–98,
    146, 182

church and mission
  Decree on the Church's Missionary
    Activity, 118
  fulfillment of church's mission, 138
  Holy Spirit, aid in building the
    church and realizing its mission,
    139
  in *Joy of the Gospel,* 160–61
  love and service as part of mission,
    142
  missio ad gentes, 146–47, 148, 149,
    153, 155, 156
  missio cum gentibus, 147, 152, 155–57,
    158, 159
  missio inter gentes, 147, 149, 150–57,
    158, 159
  salvific universality of the church,
    80, 105, 116, 129, 155, 180–81,
    194, 220–22
  triple dialogue, employing for
    church's mission, 135–37, 140
  See also conversion; ecclesiology;
    kingdom of God
Committee on Doctrine (CD), U.S.
  Bishops'
  auditus fidei, recommending, 25–26,
    27
  Being Religious Interreligiously
  areas of concern, 15–16, 18–19,
    192–94, 196, 211–22
  clarifications, requesting, 5–10,
    185, 191, 206–207, 209, 210–11
  investigation as distinct from that
    of CDF, 199, 200, 202–203
  National Catholic Reporter leak,
    204
  objections to, 13, 14, 51, 66, 78,
    79, 122, 130
  universal religious perspective,
    charges of, 124–25
  on the church as the unique
    and universal instrument of
    salvation, 105, 220–22
  conflation of magisteria, 46
  creeping infallibility in statements
    of, 33

Elizabeth Johnson, critiques of,
  22–23, 24–25, 30, 66
on non-Christian religions, 100,
  123, 127
on proper theological method, 24–
  25, 28–29, 49, 57, 58, 66–67
theologians, taking for granted, 12
complementarity, 145, 162, 175–76,
  212
Confucianism, 88, 96, 144, 167
  Holy Spirit as present in, 62, 63, 67
  Nostra Aetate, Confucianism not
    mentioned in, 111, 117
  as a resource for Asian theologians,
    49, 89
  salvific universality of Jesus and, 82,
    91
Congregation for the Doctrine of the
  Faith (CDF)
  Being Religious Interreligiously
  background on *BRI* controversy,
    ix–x, 1–5, 5–10
  Committee on Doctrine,
    requesting help in evaluation of
    text, 206, 210
  investigation as distinct from that
    of CD, 199, 200, 202–203
  objections to, 15–16, 51, 66, 122–
    23, 125, 175–84, 190
  request to complete directives,
    173, 186–90, 209
  correspondence of author, not
    responding to, 8, 201, 224
  creeping infallibility of, 33
  financial remuneration requested
    by author, 4, 11–12, 189, 196,
    197, 198
  on Jesus as unique and universal
    Savior, 78, 80, 98
  kingdom-centered ecclesiology,
    warnings on, 143
  on non-Christian religions, 114,
    127
  Pope Francis and, *xi,* 161
  on proper theological method, 49,
    145

scrutiny of controversial material,
13–14, 17–18, 90
See also Dominus Iesus
Constantinople, First Council of, 54,
58, 71–72
Constitution on the Church. *See*
Lumen Gentium
conversion
of Asians, 140, 149, 150, 168
fourfold conversion of Christian
theologians, 29
of Jews, 181–82
lessened emphasis on, 154, 155, 166,
177, 193
in *missio ad gentes* theology, 153–54,
156, 157
Pope Francis on, 160
proselytism method, 146
religious pluralism and, 217–19
cosmotheandric mystery, 116
Curran, Charles, 17
Cyprian of Carthage, Saint, 41–42

D'Ambra, Sebastiano, 77–78
Daniélou, Jean, 116
Daoism, 49, 62–63, 67, 74, 96, 111,
117, 167
Declaration on the Relation of the
Church to Non-Christian
Religions. *See Nostra Aetate*
Decree on the Missionary Activity of
the Church. *See Ad Gentes*
DeGioia, John, 5, 189
Di Noia, Joseph, 3
Dialogue and Proclamation document, 126
Divine Spirit
Asia, presence in, 57–59, 59–64, 68
in the church, 65–66
as the foundation stone of Christian
beliefs, 51
God as Spirit, 52–54, 55, 67
theology of, 69–74
See also Holy Spirit
dogma, 32, 33, 48
Dogmatic Constitution on the
Church. *See Lumen Gentium*

Dominus Iesus (DI)
BRI, not meeting standards of, 2, 19,
79, 175, 179–80, 186
church of Christ in the Catholic
Church, teaching on, 181
ex opere operato concept expressed
in, 163
on exclusiveness of Christ, 178, 213,
215
on historical Christianity as grasping
the truth about God, 86–88
interreligious dialogue, not
encouraging, 44–45
on kingdom of God, church
orientation towards, 131–32
kingdom-centered ecclesiology,
condemning, 144, 145
misrepresentations of Jesus,
addressing, 212–14
missiology and, 146, 147
on non-Christian religions, 44, 79,
105, 112–15, 117, 118, 123,
127, 176
supersession concept and, 120
teaching of contempt, 121
on unicity and salvific universality
of Christ, 79–80, 97, 104, 129,
143
Vatican II influence on, 106, 188
Dupuis, Jacques, 13, 18, 79, 106–107,
167, 177, 184, 192

East Asian Pastoral Institute, 75, 76
Ecclesia in Asia (EA), 134, 138, 139,
140, 145
ecclesiology
cosmic ecclesiology, 146
dialogical ecclesiology, 143, 145
kingdom-centered ecclesiology,
131–35, 135–37, 143
local church, FABC on
characteristics of, 137–43
pneumatological ecclesiology, 65
of Pope Francis, 160
as popular post Vatican II subject, 130
as sign and instrument of salvation, 51

Eckhart, Meister, 169–70
Ellsberg, Robert, *xii*
Estepa, Pio, 151
Eugenius IV, Pope, 111
Evangelii Gaudium. See Joy of the
    Gospel
ex cathedra, pope teaching as, 32
ex opere operato concept, 36, 112–13,
    163
exclusivism, 115–16, 168–69

Federation of Asian Bishops' Conferences
    (FABC)
    on harmony, 145–46
    on the Holy Spirit, activities of, 86
    kingdom of God, focus on, 133
    on local churches, recognized
        characteristics of, 137–43
    New Church as common
        expression used by, 188
    option for the poor, advocating for,
        151–52
    Pope Francis, giving voice to ideas
        espoused by, 160, 161–62
    on receptive pluralism as cultivated
        in Asian pneumatology, 68
    Seventh Plenary Assembly, 137,
        140–43, 144
    SWAT, issued by, 57–58, 66, 91, 96
    theological method, 46–49, 67
    triple dialogue of Christian mission
        in Asia, 17, 137
Filioque, 72
Florence, General Council of, 99, 100,
    111
Fox, Thomas C., 133
Francis, Pope, *x–xi,* 106
    exhortation to live like the poor, 43
    interreligious prayer, promoting, 167
    Joy of the Gospel, 132–33, 146,
        159–64
    joy under pontificate, 165
    Raymond Burke, demoting, 14
Fredericks, James, 117

Gaudium et Spes, 30, 130

Gillis, Chester, 5, 189
Grahmann, Charles, 1–2, 173, 174,
    185, 186
Greene, Colin, 94–95

Haight, Roger, 14, 97
hierarchical magisterium. *See* episcopal
    magisterium *under* magisteria
Hinduism, 93, 103, 104, 156, 167
    Christianity, encounter with, 130,
        144
    Hindu analogies for Christian
        concept of Spirit, 95
    Indian Christians identified as non-
        Hindu, 110
    interfaith Christology, Hindus
        pioneering, 96
    Nostra Aetate on, 111, 117
    as a resource for Asian theologians,
        49, 89
    in *SWAT,* 60
Holy Spirit
    in anonymous Christianity, 116
    Asian pneumatology, 65, 67–68,
        68–69
    complete truth, leading church to,
        212
    gifts of, 33, 139
    in the Gospel of John, 171
    John Paul II on, 122–23
    mutual dependence with the Son,
        69–74
    in non-Christian religions, 73, 126–
        27, 162, 163, 179–80
    as operating beyond the person of
        Christ, 182
    at Pentecost, 192, 194, 214, 221
    in religio-cultural traditions of Asia,
        59–64, 67
    salvific universality of, 85–86
    sensus fidei/fidelium aroused and
        sustained by, 40
    in the Trinity, 54–57, 58, 67, 95
    two-hands analogy, 55–56, 69, 70,
        73, 83, 86, 98, 122, 124, 135
    at work in the Church, 221

inclusivism, 115–16

inculturation, 17, 89–90, 137, 142

intellectus fidei, 23, 28, 39

interreligious dialogue
  as an urgent necessity, 18, 117
  Asian churches, as an essential task
    of, 137
  BRI, on dialogue with Asian
    religions, 17
  Christology and, 92
  DI, not an instrument for
    interreligious dialogue, 79
  Douglas Venn, experience of,
    163–64
  Jewish-Christian dialogue, 119
  John Paul II, contributing to, 122
  non-interest in, 44
  Pope Francis on, 161, 162
  promotion of, 115
  reasons for dialogue, 166
  Spirit at work in, 66, 73
  theological differences, discussing,
    166
  uniqueness and universality of
    Christ, maintaining in dialogue,
    220

Irenaeus, St., 55–56, 70, 83, 120, 122,
  124

Isaac, Jules, 120

Islam, 93, 104, 114
  devotional practices, 102
  Doug Venn, experience with, 98,
    163–64
  interfaith Christology and, 92
  Muslims as others, 165
  Muslims of the Philippines, 76–78
  Nostra Aetate, mentioned in, 117
  post Vatican II doctrine on, 99–100
  as a resource for Asian theologians,
    49
  restrictions on Christian mission
    in Muslim-majority countries,
    157
  salvation of Muslims, 107
  SWAT on the presence of the Spirit
    in Islam, 64

Jainism, 74, 111, 117

Jesus Christ
  in anonymous Christianity theory,
    116
  as *auto-basileia,* 135
  Christology, 51, 88–91, 91–96,
    96–98, 146, 182
  Divine Spirit at work in Christ, 65
  Dominus Iesus on, 79–80, 97, 104,
    129, 212–15
  FABC portrait of, 143
  kenosis and, 115, 118–19
  kingdom of God as focus of, 134,
    156–57
  Logos and Holy Spirit, relationship
    with, 123, 125, 179
  missionary practice of, 150, 153
  Religious Other in relation to, 170
  as source of salvation, 100, 126, 214,
    219
  in supersessionism concept, 120
  Trinity, role in, 53–54, 55–57, 69–74
  as unique and universal Savior
    alternative understanding of, 122
    CD concerns with author's
      understanding of, 6, 10, 51, 78,
      191, 211–15
    as a matter of faith, 93
    salvific universality of Jesus, 81,
      82–88, 89, 91, 177–78, 192
    unicity of Christ, 80–81, 84, 89,
      91
  work of, as complementary to that
    of Holy Spirit, 59

John of the Cross, 87, 134

John Paul II, Pope, 58, 126, 188
  Day of Prayer for World Peace,
    convoking, 166
  Ecclesia in Asia exhortation, 134,
    145
  Ex Corde Ecclesia mandatum,
    requiring, 38
  forgiveness for the church's
    behavior, requesting, 124
  on the Holy Spirit, 122–23, 125,
    136

John Paul II, Pope *(continued)*
   Jewish-Christian dialogue,
       contributing to, 119
   on non-Christian religions, 106
   Redemptoris Missio encyclical,
       Dominus Iesus following,
       131–32
   theological method deemed as
       proper by CD, 23, 24
John XXII, Pope, 169
John XXIII, Pope, *xi*
Johnson, Elizabeth, 22–23, 24, 25, 30,
   66
Joseph, Milam, 173
Joy of the Gospel, 132–33, 146, 159–64
Judaism
   conversion of Jews, not seeking,
       181–82
   Dominus Iesus, not including
       Judaism in evaluation of
       non-Christian religions, 79
   interfaith Christology and, 92
   Jewish-Christian dialogue, 119–22,
       162
   Jews as other, 165
   Nostra Aetate, Judaism mentioned
       in, 117
   place in order of relationship to the
       church, 107, 111
   Vatican II, changing attitudes
       towards, 99–100, 175

kenosis, 115, 118–19, 130–31, 132–33
kingdom of God
   church, not identical with, 132,
       134–35, 157
   dialogue as a method of
       implementing, 135–37
   as the endeavor of all religions, 169
   as goal of mission, 156, 159
   kingdom-centered ecclesiology,
       133–34, 137–43, 144, 145
   non-Christian religions,
       contributing to, 114, 140
   Spirit, drawing people to, 65
Knitter, Paul, 115, 116, 130

Krishna, 96, 103
Kwan Yin, 102, 105

Leo XIII, Pope, 48
Levada, William
   financial remuneration, author
       requesting, 11–12
   leak to *National Catholic Reporter,*
       informing of, 204
   mentioned in letters, 195–96,
       197–98
   preconditions of author, making
       known to, 4, 5
   as prefect of the CDF, 3–4, 6
   request by author to reconsider
       investigation, *ix–x*
   response from author to CDF
       concerns, 186–90
Lonergan, Bernard, 29
Lori, William
   BRI, requesting clarifications from
       author, 6, 9–10, 206–207, 209
   canonical sanctions on author,
       advising of possibility, 8–9
   distinct roles of *CD* and CDF in
       BRI investigation, clarifying,
       202–203
   letters from author, 195–98, 200–
       201, 205, 208, 224–25
   notice to author of *CD* involvement
       in investigation, 191
   preconditions of author, rejecting,
       7, 199
Lubac, Henri de, 116
Lumen Gentium, 32, 40, 100, 107–108,
       130, 131, 177, 181

magisterium
   conflation of different magisteria, 46
   episcopal magisterium
       auditus fidei and, 27
       authority of, per CDF, 183
       dialogue with theological and lay
           magisterium, 42
       divergent views and perspectives,
           as composed of, 26

Divine Spirit, understanding through, 57

fidelity of theologians to teachings of, 38–39

four types of teaching, 32–33

fundamentalistic position of, 28

infallibility derived from *sensus fidei,* 41

neo-scholastic theology, giving precedence to, 48

SWAT, not beginning with teaching of, 58

teachings of the church not identical with, 31

theological education of bishops, 34–37

theological stagnation, danger of, 81

failure to respond to magisterium as a mortal sin, 11

lay magisterium, 28, 31, 39–42, 45

magisterial documents of Asia and focus on mission, 132

magisterium as starting point of theology, 24–25, 26, 29, 30, 67

non-Christian believers, magisterium of, 28, 44–45

the poor, magisterium of, 28, 42–44

teaching mission of magisterium, 158

theological magisterium, 28, 31, 37–39, 41, 42, 45

universal magisterium, Elizabeth Johnson charged as misrepresenting teachings of, 22, 24–25

Marcion, 56, 70

McAuliffe, Jane, 5, 189

McVey, Chrys, 152

missiology, 15, 16, 134, 147. *See also* church and mission

Müller, Gerhard, *xi*

multiple religious belonging, 18, 168, 219

National Catholic Reporter, 204

Niceno-Constantinopolitan Creed, 72

Noah, 83, 120

non-Christian religions
analogies for Christian concept of Spirit, 95–96

Dominus Iesus on, 44, 79, 105, 112–15, 117, 118, 123, 127, 176

function of, in history of salvation, 15

Holy Spirit in, 59, 126–27, 162, 163, 179–80

as lacking in faith, 118, 123, 163

as mutually complementary to Christianity, 124, 176

non-Christian as a patronizing term, 99, 112, 117

Nostra Aetate, teachings on, 109–12, 148–49

as part of a new Christology, 92

salvation of non-Christians, 107–109, 125–27, 177

salvific significance of, 6, 10, 104, 123, 175–77, 191, 193–94, 216–20

scriptures of, Spirit active in, 65

Vatican II, revision of views on, 106

Nostra Aetate (NA), 107, 108, 109–12, 115–18, 118–19, 120, 148–49, 193

obsequium as a religious response, 32, 33

Office of Theological Concerns (OTC), 47–49, 57–58, 145. *See also* Federation of Asian Bishops' Conferences

ordinary process, 3

orthodoxy and orthopraxis, connection between, 43–44

pagans, 168, 184
Christians, learning from, 104

as *gentes,* 146, 148

holiness of, 105, 113, 128, 172

in the kingdom of God, 159

pagans *(continued)*
  magisterium of, 45
  as the Other, 165
  use of term, ceasing, 99
Panikkar, Raimon, 97, 116
Paul, Saint, 10, 41, 82, 121, 150
Peddicord, Richard, 14
perichoresis, 70, 71, 143
Philippines, 64, 75–78
Photios, Patriarch, 72
Pieris, Aloysius, 43, 97, 150
Pius XII, Pope, 37, 180
pneumatology. *See* Holy Spirit
Pontifical Biblical Commission (PBC), 182
Pontifical Council for Interreligious Dialogue, 126, 188
postmodernity as a challenge to Christian faith, 18, 19
pre-evangelization, 159–60
proof-texting, 25–26

Quest for the Living God (Johnson), 22–23, 24, 66

Rahner, Karl, 16, 56, 93, 116
Ratzinger, Joseph. *See* Benedict XVI, Pope
Religious Other, 166, 167, 170, 171
Rhodes, Alexandre de, 17, 153

salvific universality
  of the church, 80, 105, 116, 129, 155, 180–81, 194, 220–22
  Dominus Iesus, addressing salvific universality of Christ, 79, 80, 97, 104, 143
  Holy Spirit and, 85–86
  in the Indian context, 127
  of Jesus, 81, 82–88, 89, 91, 177–78, 192
  in kenotic theology of religion, 130
sensus fidelium, xi, 40, 41, 42
signs of the Spirit, 60, 67
signs of the times, 30, 46, 67
Sikhism, 93, 102–103, 111, 117

Silsilah Dialogue Movement, 77
Sobrino, Jon, 3, 14, 43
Special Assembly of the Synod of Bishops for Asia. *See* Asian Synod
The Spirit at Work in Asia Today (SWAT)
  on Asian pneumatology, 68
  Buddhism, possibility of encounter with Christianity, 60–61
  on Confucianism and Daoism, 62–63
  on Divine Spirit, 73–74
  Islam, affirming work of Divine Spirit in, 64
  OTC, issued by, 57–58
  on pneumatological ecclesiology, 65–66
  resonance between non-Christian beliefs and Christian theology, 59–60, 67, 91, 96
supersessionism, 120, 182

Taoism. *See* Daoism
teaching of contempt, 119, 120, 121
Thailand, author's experiences in Chiang Mai, 101–103, 105
theologoumenon, 126, 177
theology
  CD, taking theologians for granted, 12
  CD on proper theological method, 23, 24–25, 28–29, 49, 57, 58, 66–67
  CDF on proper theological method, 49, 145
  Christian theology, resonance with non-Christian beliefs, 59–60, 67, 91, 96
  of Divine Spirit, 69–74
  FABC on theological method, 46–49, 67
  fulfillment theology of religion, 111, 115, 116–17, 118, 120
  of harmony, 145–46
  International Theological

Commission, statement on
Christianity and the World
Religions, 126–27
kenotic theology of religion, 130
liberation theology, 18, 43
magisterium as starting point of,
24–25, 26, 29, 30, 67
non-Christian religions as resources
for Asian theologians, 49, 89
Office of Theological Concerns,
47–49, 57–58, 145
theological education of bishops,
34–37
theological magisterium, 28, 31,
37–39, 41, 42, 45
theological stagnation, danger of, 81
Toledo, Third Council of, 72
Townsend, Tim, 14
Trinity
economic and immanent Trinity,
56–57, 69, 71
God as three divine persons, 53
Holy Spirit, role in, 54–57, 58, 67,
95
koinonia within, 138
mission of the Trinitarian God, 159
perichoresis of the Trinitarian God,
143
triadic structure of, preserving, 72
unity in relationship of love *vs.*
unity of substance, 182

unicity
of the Buddha, 85
complementarity *vs.,* 145
Dominus Iesus, use of term, 79–80,
97, 104, 129, 143
Holy Spirit and, 86
of Jesus Christ, 80–81, 84, 89, 91
in kenotic theology of religion, 130

kingdom of God and unicity with
the Church, 132
renunciation of, 118, 155
United States Conference of Catholic
Bishops (USCCB). *See*
Committee on Doctrine

Vatican I, 41, 130, 144
Vatican II
on church as seed, 135, 221–22
Church of Christ *vs.* Catholic
Church, 180–81
Dei Verbum on understanding of
God's revelation, 31
ecclesiology in the hierarchy of
truths, 133
equality among all Christians,
affirming, 138
on grace as offered to all, 167
John Paul II, going beyond
teachings of, 122
Lumen Gentium text and lay
magisterium, 40
on non-Christians and
non-Christian religions, 63,
100, 106, 123, 126, 175, 217
Nostra Aetate teachings, 107, 108,
109–12, 115–18, 118–19, 120,
148–49
pagan, ceasing use of term, 99
Pastoral Constitution on the
Church in the Modern World,
30, 130
See also Dominus Iesus
Venn, Douglas, 98, 163–64

Weinandy, Thomas, 5, 6–7, 195, 200,
202
Wuerl, Donald, 5, 6, 7, 8, 202